EUROPE: A Cosmic Picture

Frontispiece. *The Cosmic Virgin* (The Glorification of the Virgin).
By Geertgen tot St. Jans. Leiden ? c. 1460/65 – Haarlem c. 1490/95.

By courtesy of the Museum Boymans-van Beunigen, Rotterdam.

EUROPE
A Cosmic Picture

MARIA SCHINDLER
author of 'Goethe's Theory of Colour Applied'

Foreword by GLADYS MAYER
Edited by John Fletcher
Translated by Peter Gorge

RUDOLF STEINER PRESS

Rudolf Steiner Press
Hillside House, The Square
Forest Row, East Sussex RH18 5ES

www.rudolfsteinerpress.com

Reprinted by Rudolf Steiner Press 2019
First published in English translation by New Knowledge Books 1975

Originally published in German under the title *Europa und sein Sternenmythos: Völkerbegabungen und unsere individuelle Verantwortung* by Die Kommenden 1967

A catalogue record for this book is available from the British Library

ISBN 978 1 85584 569 5

Cover by Andrew Morgan Design incorporating image © Monika Huňáčková
Printed and bound by 4Edge Ltd., Essex

Contents

PART III *Historic Responsibility*

List of illustrations

List of illustrations in text

8

Acknowledgements

To: Catherine de Bruyne for her valuable revision of the text; Mary Brett for reading the text and for her suggestions; Dr. Karl König for his suggestions; the late Dr. Alex Leroi who helped with Portugal; Andreas Grunelius for his suggestions; Willi Sucher for his help and for supplying and correcting some of the diagrams.

While believing no copyright has been impinged, the editor offers apology for the few cases where the maker or the owner of a picture has not been traced and recorded.

Translator's Note

EUROPE—A NEW PICTURE. That was the title chosen by Maria Schindler for the first version of the present book. In 1943, when she had for various reasons decided to write under the pseudonym Joanna Scott, any book on Europe might well have seemed an obituary. And what of the obituarist? . . . though indeed she was a confirmed anti-obituarist.

By birth and from choice Maria Schindler was closely linked with Europe's fate. A central European, a refugee of her own free will, she had decided that rather than enjoy an affluent existence under the Nazi *régime* or in Switzerland, she would help those anthroposophists less fortunate than herself. Quite inevitably, anyone who lived through some of those years in Germany, and who, by race, became an outcast, will judge people by the stand they made at that time. Maria Schindler, I think, need not fear to be judged by this measure.

Before coming to England in 1938, Maria Schindler had written a number of books in German, among them a biography of Richard Wagner and a study of St. Columba, whose story had always been of particular interest to her. From 1943 onwards she devoted herself to Goethe's Theory of Colour and its application in art. Her book, *Pure Colour*, written in collaboration with Eleanor C. Merry, represented until then one of the very few attempts at an interpretation of Goethe's work in English.

Again with Eleanor C. Merry, she founded the New School of Painting, an enterprise run with great enthusiasm and no prospect of financial success—not surprisingly perhaps, since both principals sometimes also paid for their students' paints.

The German version of the Europe book appeared, much enlarged, in 1962. Its publication, as the impact of Britain's entry into Europe becomes increasingly difficult, is now timely.

To have known her was an intense experience, to have lived closely with her book—scarcely less so. Of all she possessed she has given freely, to causes and to friends.

Maria Schindler died in 1968.

PETER GORGE

Foreword

THIS REMARKABLE BOOK which, behind an apparently rather simple presentation, conceals profound erudition, has already been published successfully in Germany and is now, in particularly appropriate circumstances, translated for English readers.

The point of view from which it is written is extraordinarily new, yet related to the oldest science in the world, that science which built the Great Pyramid, the great Druid monument of Stonehenge, and all the colossal monuments of ancient Mystery Centres, whose secrets are still a mystery to modern physical science. It is a point of view which links the mysterious movements and order of the Universe of Stars with the progress of mankind upon the Earth.

Astronomy and astrology formed one great science in Egypt and Babylon and it was that science—the only one—from which the ancient monuments were built and the affairs of mighty peoples were guided. Today a discredited science, astrology has fallen into the decadent form of newspaper horoscopes and other forms of fortune-telling whilst astronomy, aided by the physical sciences, attempts to climb to the stars in a merely physical way, and a new astrophysics attempts to investigate and comprehend the world of stars through the physical laws of our own planet. That these laws, e.g. of gravitation and crystalline formation, are already shewn to be different even in our nearest neighbour, the Moon, suggests the idea that the other more distant planets may also each have their distinct individuality and that in each, the interrelationship with the planet Earth creates much ground for further study.

Recent research has found, for example, in the great Egyptian Pyramid that ' its orientation shows that in all Mystery Centres there was a deep knowledge of the differentiation in the cosmos '. So says Dr. Wachsmuth in his book, *The Evolution of Mankind.**

Again, in *Stonehenge Decoded*** by Gerald Hawkins, it is told that Stonehenge shows similar features:

> Each significant stone aligns with at least one other to point to some extreme position of the Sun or Moon. All the evidence indicated that Stonehenge was a sophisticated and brilliantly conceived astronomical observatory.

These are only two examples from the ancient world, where astrology and astronomy combined as an exact science, not materialistically one-sided as it is now, but where the supersensible and the physical went hand in hand.

Today when the laws of space as we know them are being to some extent replaced, even in our air travel, by the laws of time, it seems evident that space-covering techniques which can

---

* Published in German by Philosophisch-Anthroposophischer Verlag, Dornach, Switzerland. Available in translation.
** Souvenir Press, London.

land us on our own satellite, the Moon, are quite inadequate in a Time sense, to reach any but the nearest planets, unless we should borrow techniques from ancient Eastern sources greatly to prolong human life. Likewise it would seem that if we are bound by laws of space, we are too small ever to be able to cover the astronomical distances involved for travel even in our own universe, not to mention the manifold universes beyond.

Sir James Jeans in his book, *The Mysterious Universe**, concludes that:

> The stream of knowledge is heading towards a non-mechanical reality: the universe begins to look more like a great thought than a great machine. So thought must have been involved in its creation.

In his thought-provoking book, *The Drama of the Universe*, Willi Sucher presents an unarguable case for further research.

> The Cosmos is the stage of all factual and potential existence of which we can think. Man cannot escape the fact that he is a part of it, however small. The part must be at least to a certain extent, dependent on the whole. Therefore man's existence cannot be satisfactorily accomplished unless he knows the nature, purpose and workings of the universe. Otherwise man may in his ignorance, act against the meaning and laws of cosmic life—it could mean the elimination of human life.

Willi Sucher, who writes and lectures on a new spiritual scientific cosmology, is the author of *Isis Sophia, Man and the Stars* and *The Drama of the Universe*** already mentioned. These important books describe actual happenings on Earth, disasters brought about by natural forces such as earthquakes, tornadoes and floods: 'Acts of God', as they are termed legally in England, also man-made disasters affecting aircraft, railways etc. are brought into connection with this new star-wisdom, aptly named 'Astro-Sophia' or Astrosophy, which combines modern astronomy with the ancient knowledge of the stars.

The drama of the universe and all its several parts then appears as something like a drama played out on a space stage—our Earth and Universe so far as we can know it—but motivated in Time in almost immeasurably vast periods, revealing cosmic laws, predictably exact, but not invariable.

Thus, for example, the shifting of land-masses, known only rather recently to geographers in relation to spiral movements of the Earth's axis, leads one in thought from geo-physical to astro-physical science.

Rudolf Steiner at the beginning of this century introduced a new cosmological and spiritual science of man and the universe, from which almost all other sciences, e.g. cosmology, medicine, education, natural philosophy, botany, ecology, agriculture, etc. have been fructified and renewed. In the sphere of cosmology, Willi Sucher is one of his very brilliant pupils.

The author of this book as a geographer and experienced traveller, with an intimate knowledge of European languages and folk-lore, has brought this into connection with the star-knowledge of Willi Sucher, the immense historical knowledge of Dr. Walter Johannes Stein, the scientific work of Dr. Eugen Kolisko, with all of whom she was closely associated, and who

---

* Sir James Jeans, *The Mysterious Universe*, 1930.
** Out of print. Available from the Rudolf Steiner Library, 35 Park Road, London NW1.

all, brilliant in their own professions, were inspired further by Rudolf Steiner and his Anthroposophy. From this background she has developed her own work, as an astrosophical view of Europe.

Were this book written only for leisured entertainment, with erudite, imaginative and fascinating themes to beguile our thought, it could serve that purpose effectively. But in fact it has a much more serious purpose. Over twenty years' work has brought the book into existence as a serious contribution to a more esoteric understanding of Europe, at a time when a closer relationship with this whole continent is our destiny.

It has obvious significance for all Europeans. Europe is still the centre of Western civilization, culture and history, and so in fact the world-centre of present day thought. It has a world-wide impact on older systems of thought, through modern science which shakes these more ancient forms of civilization down to their foundations and brings about world-conflicts on a scale beyond all previous imaginings. What we think as Europeans—what we comprehend of our universe, however slight or poor our comprehension, must have a bearing on the evolution of the whole of mankind. No one can belittle the responsibility laid upon us by such a situation.

Then what is this new science called Astrosophy? A science of cosmos, earth and man—geo-centric as it was originally in the Ptolemaic system, where the Sun appears to revolve round the Earth; helio-centric as it has become through Copernican astronomy where the Sun is seen as the centre of the orbital revolutions of all the planets in the universe including our Earth. The geo-centric view seems to hold us on Earth within the limits of space—while the helio-centric view introduces us to a universe where spatial considerations are transformed into pictures in time. It expands thinking beyond our comfort and maybe beyond man's intelligence—who knows? Fred Hoyle, our noted British astronomer, some years ago finished a long course of lectures on the BBC concerning the marvels of the heavenly bodies, with this frank and revealing remark: ' And now how I wish that someone would come and tell me what it is all about '.

From her long-developed background of this new form of star-wisdom, Maria Schindler has woven a pictorial tapestry of her view of Europe's life-history in all its cosmic, earthly and human content. It is her life's work, a product of both manifest devotion and prodigious learning, woven with artistry and technical skill. It may seem too great a picture for our normal mundane thinking, but as we move out from space to time in our thought, so picture-thinking will replace the strictures of mundane mathematics, and the answers to essential problems of what is the nature of man, of whence we come and whither we are going, will reveal themselves not alone to poets and artists and other visionaries, but in imaginative pictures to the thinking life of our times.

GLADYS MAYER

Introduction

EUROPE'S MISSION has been described in many ways and from many different aspects. In the following pages an attempt has been made to show the links between ancient temple wisdom and modern knowledge, not seeking to bring proofs, but to suggest a possible path to wider understanding.

A reader finding some of the content strange at first may regard it as a kind of travel book, and as with any guide to countries yet unknown, offer a certain readiness to follow the author in thought.

Descriptions of unfamiliar territory begin by marking out the chief characteristics and elaborating them in some striking details. Here in a similar way attention is drawn to outstanding relationships of nations and the cosmos, and to the conduct of leading personalities where it is symptomatic of the nature of a certain people.

In the descriptions of the stars and of Europe as a whole, images from ancient mythology have been used. These come from an age when men could still knowingly experience the stars and link them with spiritual beings. In their language the title of this book might perhaps have been: ' Divine Guidance and Human Fulfilment '. For its aim is to trace such spiritual guidance with modern consciousness.

This work would not have been possible without research into the work of Rudolf Steiner. The first indications of the link between the peoples of Europe and the twelve parts of the Zodiac were given by Eugen Kolisko. Willi O. Sucher helped in working out the cosmic rhythms and their manifestation in European history, as well as in the study of the qualitative aspects of the Zodiac and the planets. To all three the author would like to record her gratitude.

Her external acquaintance with the peoples of Europe, except for the Balkans, Russia and Poland, is the result of travels and prolonged visits. The work was continued through twenty-four years, and a large number of English, German, French and Italian books were consulted so that the working of cosmic forces in their cultural and historic manifestations on earth could be investigated. Original writings and early reports were used where possible, since these often mention significant detail omitted by later commentators.

Far-reaching explanations would be needed to support convincingly the logic of much that is put forward. Not only every chapter but almost every paragraph, and particularly every important manifestation of cosmic links—here only mentioned in passing—would demand elaboration. In a general picture this is not possible. But despite this inevitable limitation the reader may find that many questions are answered in the course of his study of the book. Those who, moved by their own historic conscience, try to penetrate the spiritual background of history unite themselves thereby with Europe's healing mission. Its fulfilment, from the middle of the twentieth century onwards, is a matter of life and death for the whole of mankind.

The Present Age and the Myth of Europe

EUROPE today has become a clearly defined geographical territory explored in every corner; but to the seers of ancient Greece, Europe was a soul being, recognized in realms of spirit, and the Greek myth of Europa speaks of Europe's soul. Events taking place in supersensible worlds have been recorded for the human race in the form of mythology, and from the later tales of demi-gods and heroes, who by deed and sacrifice led men's development, prophetic elements can be seen emerging.

As attention turned more and more to the sense world, the guarded knowledge of inspiring beings was left behind, and interest grew in written history and travellers' tales. Cosmic powers, once clothed by Egyptian art in animal forms, yielded place to the fabulous animals of early natural history. Yet through saga and legend, recognition was kept alive. Wolfram von Eschenbach in his Parsifal epic, writing of the Holy Grail as the force that makes renewal possible, connects it with the Phoenix, the sacred Bird of the Sun that underwent its fiery death and resurrection in the Egyptian city of Heliopolis. Wolfram says of the nature of the Grail:

> By its might the Phoenix
> burned till he to ashes grew
> and out of the flames rose once more anew.

As the Phoenix knew the hour to sacrifice existence and pass through the ashes, so for European man renewal will depend on the ability to burn what is no longer true on the altar of the Spirit of the Sun.

Before the beginning of history, Europe's soul dwelt in supersensible worlds. The transition from divine remoteness to the earthly task of leading the culture of a new continent, was of far-reaching importance. In the myth, Zeus in the shape of a gentle white bull approached Europa as she was playing on the seashore at Tyre with her companions, and carried her westward on his back to the island of Crete. Poseidon smoothed the waves. Triton, and Nereids led by Aphrodite, accompanied them. Europa bore Zeus three sons, of whom one was the demi-god Minos. After Zeus left her she was married to Asterius, the reigning king of Crete, a being linked with the stars, who is shown on the earliest Cretan coins with star and rays. In Lebadeia, south-east of Delphi, Europa was identified with Demeter as the spiritual figure behind Greece.

Of King Minos who followed Asterius it is told that he deceived Poseidon over the sacrifice of a sacred bull, and Poseidon in revenge caused the queen to bring forth a monster with a human

17

body and a bull's head—the Minotaur, so savage that he had to be imprisoned in a cave in a labyrinth where he required the sacrifice of youths and maidens for his food.

The Minotaur destroyed the youthful forces of mankind. None of his victims could find their way out of the labyrinth to the light of day, but were doomed to be lost in its winding passages. Here the story obviously anticipates the path mankind was to go. The Minotaur with the bull's head is the activity of thinking divorced from the divine and imprisoned in the hollow of the head, the distorted image of divine wisdom. And the dark passages of the labyrinth are the convolutions of the human brain, where it dwells.

This brain-bound thinking with its inventions and conclusions brings about the most powerful achievements of modern humanity, which is now captured—and captivated—by its tyranny. Young people are delivered into its spell. Today even small children are exposed to the influence of wireless, television and the cinema; illusion is presented as reality. All too often the aim of education is to make the child strive for money and success; for ' there is only one life ' and that is ' what you make it '—that is to say, as comfortable as possible. Young people growing up are told they are descended from apes and that soul and spirit are mere attributes of the body. They have learned in school that they are the product of heredity and that death is the end. The memory of their own life in the cosmos before birth is wiped out by the picture modern astronomy presents of the oppressive vastness of the sky. Little scope remains in all this mechanized monotony for the development of any truly responsible individual.

The idea that history repeats itself and that historical events can be attributed entirely to heredity, instinct, and the struggle for survival, springs from the same dark labyrinth of the brain. It is true, these do accompany the development of the human race; but if doubts of the meaning of human existence prevail, all life becomes a prison. The destructive Minotaur forces will attack increasingly the whole of Earth existence if they are not recognized and tamed, from another direction.

Modern thinking produces loneliness. Deep within, the soul can often sense unconsciously during life on Earth that it has been placed in a world to which it can never fully belong, and where everything is only half-truth. Most revolutionary unrest and other disturbances in social life are in the last resort based on this feeling of frustration. In former times man had the protection of his family, the state and the Church, and was thus guarded against loneliness and god-forsakenness in the modern sense. But through scientific thinking, inherited tradition has declined, and all our thinking today faces the onslaughts of materialism.

So if man is to use new concepts to enlighten him concerning the feeling he may still carry in his heart about the aims of human existence, he must decide on his own to do so, without any outward support. He is called to perform deeds of freedom—to think differently from public opinion, to care for other things than outward success, to seek his aims in worlds other than those recognized by the limited, earth-bound intellect.

Souls who will to live on Earth in the next hundred years have a special longing to experience such decisions. While in the world of the stars, they know that the immediate future can be of decisive importance to them and to the whole of mankind. They approach the Earth with love, knowing that man needs the resistance of matter to learn to use his freedom. They would like to kindle awareness of responsibility in men on Earth, who are in danger of losing their love for their own planet. They would fain free those who have fallen prey to the Minotaur; but if they are not to lose their own path in the labyrinth, they will need the thread of Ariadne.

According to the myth, Theseus, about to be sacrificed with other youths and maidens, planned to overcome the monster and escape from the labyrinth with the help of Ariadne, who gave him a thread that would lead him back. Ariadne was a daughter of Minos and Pasiphaë, whose father was Helios, the visible Sun. Her thread is the logical, crystal-clear thinking which can lead out of the prison of the brain. One who can uncompromisingly follow his experiences and observations to their conclusions will, out of his sense of truth, reject the image of himself as a higher animal or machine, and will not consider birth a beginning or death an end. A determination to hold this thread can lead to a remembrance of one's own life among the stars before birth and to the knowledge of a future journey through spiritual worlds towards a new, responsible Earth existence. Perspectives of time and space expand. This light-permeated will to think can overcome the Minotaur.

When Theseus had left the labyrinth behind he wanted to marry Ariadne, who loved him. But Diodorus* tells that the great Dionysos appeared to him in a dream, demanding her as his wife, and Ariadne had to resign herself to her fate. According to early stories her bridal wreath, made by Hephaestos in the form of roses, was set by Dionysos among the stars.

The constellation of the Crown, Corona Borealis, still shines from the heavens as a sign of the light-filled thinking that must be affirmed with sacrifices. It stands next to the mighty, visionary figure of Heracles—Hercules—on whose other side is the Lyre. Hercules kneels, one foot resting on the head of the dragon** while above him is the serpent—the two great adversaries who threaten man's progress on his spiritual path.

Modern astronomy discovered that our entire solar system is moving towards Hercules and the Lyre. Sun and planets are flying towards them. This is the direction of the divinely ordained future which Europe's soul longs to serve. Outward conditions on Earth change, and what seems firmly established today will take other forms tomorrow. In this lies Europe's hope.

---

* Diodorus Siculus, V.
** For the connection between the dragon and the Fourth Labour of Hercules, see *Isis Sophia*, Part I, by W. O. Sucher, 1952.

The Seal of Europe

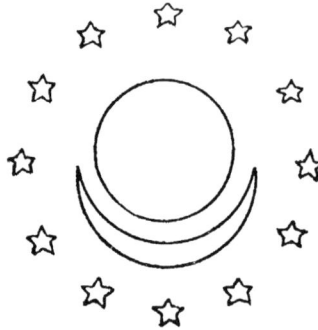

To STUDY THE development of the European nations one after the other is like observing the building of a house. Stone is being added to stone, rafter to rafter. Seeing them fitted together we begin to recognize the architectural plans that made the construction possible.

It is difficult for modern man to visualize simultaneously both the fundamental structure of history and the single facts, and to acknowledge them as integral parts of the same process. The scattered events are so often studied separately and not in their relation to the whole. Secondary facts in their thousandfold variety are regarded as important, while others of greater importance are overlooked. Moreover the assumptions that history is ruled by chance and that causes and effects are limited within small periods of time prevent recognition of the living forces underlying it.

We are faced with the difficulty of discriminating between the building-stones of evolution, and the sand and dust cast off in the chiselling of the blocks. Sand and dust are carried by the wind and lie in heaps all round the building under construction and modern attention is directed to the investigation of these as if they were of main value. Men's eyes, looking downwards, do not see the pillars gradually rising and shimmering in the light of Sun, Moon and Stars, and openly revealing the creative wisdom that set them up.

A clear-cut sense of values is needed for the study of history. If what is unimportant can be set aside the details of leading historical events make a general survey possible. Then one is able to enter the building and reach the very centre whence the light, that shimmers on the pillars, is streaming forth.

Here the inner eye beholds the Seal of Europe: the chalice of the Moon, with the Sun, and the Stars shining from twelve directions. It is only a sign; but one which is the imaginative expression of living spirit, of deeds of love and deeds of will, impressed into the history of man in the course of time—an expression of the active forces which, with their creative power of cosmic thought, have contributed to the building of our human past.

All those events which have brought about the quiet and orderly evolution of nations remind us of lunar influences. The coming into existence of the various dynasties and their generations are like the regular movement of the ebb and flow of tides. Moreover, the tendency to establish

20

definite frontiers, to sequestrate each nation, resembles the creating of a vessel wherein each cultural development could be made individually secure. This finds its symbol in the crescent cup of the Moon, a chalice ready to hold what it is destined to contain.

In the calmness of these lunar forces the rhythms of number are revealed.* Present in all history, they represent a starry geometry around which the destiny of mankind is woven. And from the same powers there streams also all that is expressed in culture through the predominating qualities of the single senses.

These formative currents of the world have been permeated by powers flowing from the veiled mysteries of the Sun. They are concealed in the great legends of the Palladium, the Golden Fleece and the Holy Grail.

It was the Sun that guided the footsteps of the great saints who in the first thousand years of our era sowed the seeds of Christianity in the soil of one nucleus after another of the evolving nations. Sun-powers kindled in the heart of the Maid of Orleans the strong will to accomplish her mission, and ripened the fruit of her deeds to build the form of modern Europe. Sun-powers stirred the tempestuous waves that sundered the peoples, creating from these separations the nuclei of others. Light of the spiritual Sun shone in the genius of the great spirits who animated the cultural life of nations—consuming the old in the fire of their footsteps and lighting the flame of the new by the force of their courage.

The spiritual power of the Sun lives in everything that moves onward into the future and rouses it into action, whether it springs with quickening power out of depths that are veiled and inscrutable or whether it surges in storm and tumult, with volcanic and overwhelming force.

It is also the guidance of the Sun which brings humanity the inspiring formative powers of the Moon that shape the nations. It is the Sun that is mirrored in the moonlight, and shows us there the image of its cosmic working.

---

* *Encyclopaedia of Numbers: Their Essence and Meaning*, by A. E. Abbot, Emerson Press.

PART I

The Stars

Plate 1. *The Extern Stones.* Near Detmold, West Germany, the east side.

Photograph by John Fletcher.

Plate 2. *The Extern Stones.* The west side.

Photograph by John Fletcher.

Plate 3. *The Extern Stones.* Sun Temple rock on the right. View from the east.

Plate 4. *The Extern Stones*. The Deposition Rock Relief.

Photograph by John Fletcher.

Plate 5. *The Deposition Rock Relief restored.*

Shaded drawing by Alan Fenn.

Plate 6a. *The Irminsul.* Sacred symbol of the ancient Saxons.

Shaded drawing by Alan Fenn.

Plate 6b. *The Irminsul.* As depicted in the Rock Relief on Extern Stones.

Shaded drawing by Alan Fenn.

The Holy Grail

THE POINT at which the peoples of Europe became an expression of the cosmic order, inadequate at first, yet nevertheless distinct, appears to lie in the ninth century.

Modern Europe has largely been shaped by the events of that time: Scandinavia, the Netherlands, Spain, Great Britain, France, Italy, Germany, Russia, Bulgaria, Poland, Austria, Switzerland and Finland all received impulses reflected in their later development.

In 872 King Harald I was ruling over Norway; Denmark was unified under a single ruler. The region which later became Holland had at its centre Utrecht, whose bishop, Radbert, had been educated with Charles the Bald, the grandson of Charlemagne, at the Carolingian court. In Spain, a number of small Christian successor states were formed after the Arabs had been pressed back by the Carolingians. Alfred I, an Anglo-Saxon, gave England her significance. Through the division of the Carolingian Empire, France became independent in 843. Italy, united with Burgundy, received a ruler of her own. Germany as a result of the division was for the first time free to develop her own impulses. Rurik, the Swedish Norman, became the first prince of Novgorod and founder of Russia. He arrived in Russia in 862. Bulgaria's first tsar was born in 890. Poland's princes can also be traced back to this period. With this general crystallization of the peoples of Europe into their separate identities, the different language impulses began to assume form. The first written document composed in German as well as Latin dates from 842. In the Strasbourg oaths, sworn by the grandsons of Charlemagne, one of them promised ' *In Godes minna ind thas christliche forches* '—' For the love of God and the Christian people '—and ' *Pro Deo amor et pro Christiano publico* ', the other. In England Alfred translated Latin works into Early English, thus spreading the vernacular and making its study possible. In the East, Cyril and Methodius worked in a similar direction by translating the liturgy into the Slav tongue. All this was the expression of ordering, Divine thoughts.

Twelve groups of peoples evolved. Though their national frontiers might to some extent be the result of group egotism whose traces extend even to cultural achievements, the specific quality of each national destiny is unthinkable without the guidance of exalted beings who endowed the diversity with twelve characteristic moods. The seeds of new historical development can only germinate when there are men whose souls are filled with hope for the future. For such a future, dedicated activity radiated, in the ninth century, from the centre of the Holy Grail.

The Holy Grail was the heart of Europe's development. Just as we cannot see the heart of someone standing before us though it is the mainspring of his life, the reality of the Holy Grail, working from hidden depths, is the source of all the later development of the peoples of Europe in their striving for cosmic harmony.

The name of the Grail's castle is unknown. Similarly all other knowledge of the nature of the Grail's Order was kept secret for nearly four hundred years and was passed on only through oral tradition. But between 1130 and 1250, and until the beginning of the fourteenth century, manuscripts containing reference in prose and verse to the Grail impulse appeared in different countries.

In France Chrestien de Troyes probably began his *Perceval* or *Le Conte du Graal* between 1188 and 1190. He claimed that the theme of his poem was taken from a small book given to him by his patron, Count Philip of Flanders. Chrestien died before he had finished his work, which was completed by another hand. Walter Mapp wrote his *La Queste del St. Graal** between 1180 and 1210. The author of a further French *Perceval* manuscript—before 1220—is unknown. The detailed description of a Grail temple in the *Jüngere Titurel* is frequently attributed to Albrecht von Scharfenberg. Wolfram von Eschenbach wrote his great *Parzival* epic before 1220. He describes Kyot of Provence as his teacher and tells of him that he, in turn, had first heard of the Parsifal legend in Moorish Spain. Though this gives the tradition Spanish origin, the mention of Kyot points to the south of France. The French scholar Fauriel found allusions to events only mentioned in Wolfram von Eschenbach's *Parzival* amongst several Provençal troubadours. The language of Provence is also said to be the only one containing the word ' grail ', literally a vessel. The name Perce-val, however, can only be explained out of the idiom of northern France. The French Parsifal poems interpret it as ' passing through valleys '. Wolfram makes Sigune say: ' Truly thou art called Parzival. The name means: right through '.

Unmistakable Parsifal traces also appear in Wales, where heroic legends speak of Peredur, whose adventures resemble Parsifal's experiences. Stories of the Grail seem to have been written down around 1200 at Glastonbury Abbey. Independent traces of ancient memories of Grail mysteries also appear in the *Mabinogion* and in the metric romance of *Sir Perceval de Galles*. It may be that the carefully guarded tradition was preserved for centuries in the British Isles as, through his consort, King Alfred was closely linked with the Grail impulse. Simrock speaks of the stories of the *Meistersingers*, where we are told that Wolfram von Eschenbach was first told of the Grail in Scotland by his master, Friedebrand von Siegebrunnen. None of the surviving reports throw very much light on the tradition which tells of a great treasure, the Holy Grail, kept in a carefully hidden place in Europe and protected by mighty forests. But all indications point to a place where the presence of the Risen One was experienced as the central event.

As religious communities nursed a common image, such as the Queen of Heaven or the Divine Sophia, the Knights of the Grail had before them the picture of the Grail vessel, formed like the waning Moon and shining forth a quickening light that was the concentration of all the radiance of the cosmos.

The active presence of the Christ lived in the Grail and in the Grail temple, where the Risen One is surrounded by angel and archangel choirs led by His great herald, St. Michael, who bears His features and faces mankind. Where the Grail impulse is active, there is Michael, radiating star wisdom.

---

* Actually the work of several authors.

In preparation for the Grail events powerful impulses were active at a very early stage of human development. They flowed out from the region of the Teutoburg forest, and made possible Europe's individuality in a much later time.

Hovering above the earth over the ancient sanctuary was a serene centre of inspiration where exalted spiritual beings were active. Their divine thoughts, embracing past and future, were experienced through the cosmic forces of sound, and in images invisible to physical organs. In pure sun-like inspirations they could behold the future of humanity. Here ancient priests experienced the link of the Earth with the Christ spirit who still lived in cosmic heights. Word and tone surrounded them on the peaks of the towering rocks and in the caves, and radiated into distance. In this sacred centre of cosmic forces, initiations were performed. (Plates 1–3.)

Dr. Alfred Heidenreich in a magazine article describes these stones and their possible significance.*

> . . . These Extern Stones in the Teutoburg forest, not very far from Paderborn, are all the more remarkable, as they combine reminiscences of the ancient Nordic cult and of early Christian worship. . . . Time-worn steps lead to a dark cave at the bottom of one of the rocks. We may climb up stairs hewn into the stone to the top of the middle one of the rocks. On the height we suddenly find ourselves entering into a small sanctum. There is a circular window, looking precisely to the point where the sun rises on Midsummer's Day, and another similar window facing precisely to the point where the sun sets on Midsummer Day. And there is an altar, different from Christian altars. Here we stand at a place of worship of long forgotten times (high above the great beech forest). Deep down in the first rock is a second chapel. It seems that originally it was entirely closed in, like a cave. In it recently the rune of the winter-sun has been discovered. In these chapels in all probability the Midsummer and Midwinter rites were celebrated. The orientation of the windows gives some indication as to the age (for the points of sunrise gradually change through thousands of years). From this evidence it is assumed that the place is about 4,000 years old. Other constellations of stars seem to have guided also the whole planning of the ancient paths leading up to the rocks. . . . And the very name 'Externsteine' is suggestive. It is probably contracted from 'Sternensteine an der Egge', which means 'Star-Stones on the (river) Egge'. Beneath the cave of winter worship is an empty tomb. It is covered with runes which later times tried to erase. . . . There is no doubt that it is a place where the ancient form of Initiation was carried out. . . . There is also increasing belief that the Extern Stones are also the place where the 'Irminsul' stood,** . . . and the expeditions of Charlemagne who admittedly went out to destroy it, point to this district. . . . On the massive rock next to the lake a beautiful piece of early Christian sculpture can be seen. . . . The scene is dominated by a large cross from which the Christ is being taken down. Sun and moon witness the scene. . . . It is significant that we are not shown Christ on the cross. The cross is empty. Above the left arm of the cross, near to the royal head of the sun, is a second picture of Christ:

---

* The Externsteine, Christian Community Journal, June, 1935.
** Irminsul—World Pillar.

The Risen One. Is it a symbolic representation of how the old Saxons felt? Or may we take it as a prophecy for our own time? . . . (Plates 4, 5.)

Emil Bock in an article* describes and ponders in some detail this same sculpture. 'The carving is one of the finest monuments of cosmic Culdee Christianity. The stream of cosmic powers has been discreetly intimated in a manifold way in the depiction of the carving'. It shows the removal of Christ's body from the Cross by Joseph of Arimathea. Nicodemus forms part of the group.

> The body of Christ forms an outright circular sphere. And the figure of Nicodemus rounds itself like another concentric sphere outside it. It is as if the spherical discs of the heaven, which reveal their countenance in sun and moon (shown just above and on the right and left of the Cross) were rounding themselves before us. In Christ the sphere of the sun, in Nicodemus the sphere of the moon. Nicodemus stands on a strangely powerfully-shaped throne which resembles a downward-turned pillar with two wings.

F. Seitz in his book, *The Irminsul in the Rock Relief of the Extern Stones*,** deals in some detail with the rock carving of the removal of Christ's body from the Cross and its connection with the 'Irminsul'. He says:

> This downward-bent form is considered by many writers to be the Irminsul, the most sacred symbol of the pagan Saxons. With it the triumph of Christianity over paganism had been here expressed and thus the downward-trodden pagan symbol under the feet of Nicodemus had found also its psychological expression in a Christian work of art. (Plates 6a, 6b.)

Emil Bock continues his description and interpretation:

> The figure of Joseph of Arimathea has the strangest form. He resembles a giant from mythology with his forcefully-bent body. We understand the grandiose power of his figure: his body is nothing else but the repetition of the pillar-throne on the other side of the Cross. But how can a man be so powerfully formed into a throne by the trivial weight of the consumed body of Jesus? Joseph of Arimathea carries no mean weight. Here is more than the outer appearance. The sphere of the whole universe rests upon him. Joseph of Arimathea is the Christian giant Atlas carrying the heaven on his back. The cosmic power and greatness that breathes in the relief stirs a divining of cosmic piety and the divine experience of nature which are slumbering in a rightly appreciated Christianity.

Long before European centres of initiation existed, however, the spiritual power who was later to become the folk soul of the Scandinavian people was given the task of carrying the the earliest impulses of this centre to the north and of guarding them there for thousands of years. Out of light-permeated wisdom he transformed the knowledge of world past and future into the images of the Edda. Other spirit beings were later to become folk souls. The people of Europe shared these experiences. When the time came for the Grail mystery to enter its active stage, the northern Archangel passed on to this centre all that he had guarded. Europe,

---

* In *Die Christengemeinschaft*, Stuttgart, 1931.
** Pähl, 1953.

ordered according to cosmic laws, could now be guided towards her fulfilment. She was to become the image of stages of human consciousness.

The Grail temple was the temple of the divine Sophia, the world-embracing cosmic star wisdom. In the ninth century, Scotus Erigena, himself probably a knight of the Holy Grail, wrote of this temple:

> If to celestial heights
> Thou dost thyself uplift,
> With shining eyes thou wilt behold
> The Temple of Sophia.

In the development of the peoples of Europe whose identity begins to take form from this time onwards, we can see the working of a wisdom that towers above all human wisdom. Twelve groups of different peoples could arise, because the preservation and continuance of the working of heavenly forces was made possible through the experiencing of the Risen One at carefully-guarded centres.

In these pages the peoples of Europe and the Signs of the Zodiac appear in the following relationship.

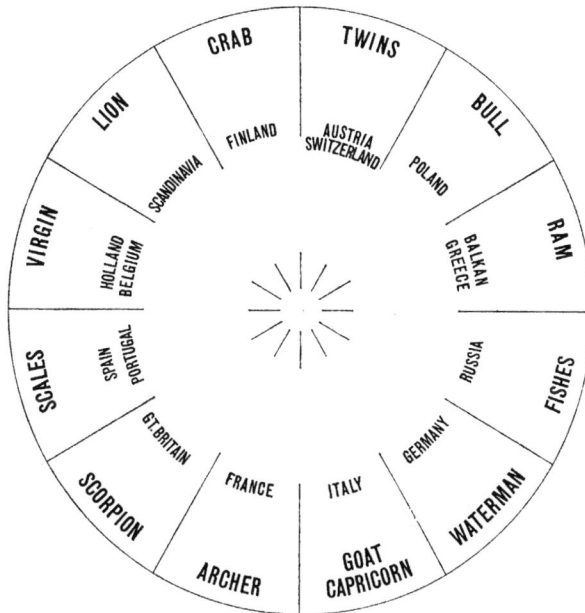

The Knighthood of the Grail is historically authenticated. Charibert of Laon is connected with it. After him his grandson, Charles the Great, owed to it his honour and dignity. Even very much later when the origin of its dignity was already forgotten, the stream of its posterity did not lose importance. Nearly all the royal families which for a thousand years have worn

the crowns of European countries had some link with the Carolingian dynasty. To be related
to Charlemagne laid a secret seal upon the spiritual rightness of the Crowns of Europe.

The above diagram gives the names of those through whom the royal families and thus the
different peoples of Europe became connected with the Carolingian stream. The dates indicate
the year of marriage.

It was one of the intentions of the Knighthood of the Grail to create select royal houses through which the esoteric Christian current could flow for the guidance of Europe's future. Nevertheless, as early as the ninth century, this plan was frustrated.

It is a spiritual law that wherever positive intentions are active, the forces of opposition enter in great strength. In the Grail legend the decline of the early Carolingian house merged into the figure of the wounded Amfortas.* Louis the Debonair, and after him Charles the Bald, married wives in whom anti-Grail projects were at work. These opposing forces arrayed themselves against Louis through Judith the Guelph and Bernard of Barcelona; Charles the Bald came under their influence through Richilda, of the Boso family. By these insidious penetrations into the Grail dynasty the Carolingians came to speedy ruin. But so great had been the spiritual impulse of their beginning that in spite of the tragic end of the Carolingian house, for centuries all the kingdoms of Europe felt that they owed much of their dignity to it. There are no written documents nor pronouncements from accepted authorities for this cosmic attribution. The confirmation lies in the events themselves: the simultaneity of cosmic events—the writing of the gods—and specific occurrences will appear convincing on closer investigation. From a heliocentric point of view it is also clear that the personalities to whom particular attention is drawn experienced, at the time of their birth or even nine months earlier, the constellation or the Sign** of specific importance to their people. We thus find these links confirmed by the cosmos itself.

---

* The origin of the legend of the Grail is given by Rudolf Steiner in *The Mysteries of the East and of Christianity*. Rudolf Steiner Press, London, 1972. And by W. J. Stein in *World History in the Light of the Holy Grail*. (Typescript, Rudolf Steiner, Library.)

** Regarding the distinction between Constellations and Signs, Willi O. Sucher gives the following guidance.

To understand the concept ' Sign ' one may look at the ' apparent ' orbit of the Sun in the course of one year. This is *relatively* close to the Earth and all the planets move with mostly small aberrations on the plane, the Ecliptic, which is indicated by the Sun-orbit. We divide this Sun-circle into twelve parts of equal 30° angles, starting from the point where the Sun appears to stand at the Spring Equinox, 20/21 March of each year. This entity or space-division may be taken as an expression of etheric (substances and) forces combining with Earth activity.

Apart from this Sun-circle, we see deep in cosmic space the actual twelve Zodiac configurations (Constellations) made or depicted by the fixed stars. They appear also to stand at the outer fringe of the plane made by the yearly Sun-orbit. They may be seen as an expression of the cosmic-astral forces working, for instance, into Earth existence.

At present the two circles do not coincide. Today we see, beyond 0° of the Sign of Aries (Ram) where the Sun appears to stand on 20/21 March, the fixed stars belonging to the Constellation Pisces (Fishes). And in future the two, Ecliptic Signs and fixed star Constellations will come more and more apart. This is caused by the so-called Precession of the Vernal Equinox; that is, with regard to the position on 20/21 March, the Sun falls back every year by *circa* 50 minutes of the arc in its relationship to the fixed star Zodiac.

At the time of Christ the two circles corresponded exactly. One would have seen behind 0° of the Sign Aries (Ram), where the Sun is at the Spring Equinox, the first fixed stars of the Constellation Aries. This offers an additional illumination of the significance of the Christ Event. Once within a Platonic Year, Signs and Constellations coincided, meaning that the Cosmic–Astral Zodiac could impress itself upon the Etheric-Sign Zodiac, and sent the latter on its journey during the following 26,000 years.

Thus the word Sign (when used in these pages with initial capital) points to the etheric as background, and the Constellation to the cosmic astral origin of the characteristics in question.

Cosmic Worlds and the Spiritual Guidance of Mankind

THE CREATIVE FORCES of the cosmos are hidden by the blue of the sky by day and by the starry heavens at night. There is as yet no proof in the accepted sense that spiritual beings dwell in the cosmos and it is unlikely that such proof will be forthcoming in the foreseeable future. The purely mathematical and astronomical edifice, based on vast numbers which cannot be grasped by the imagination, much less understood, now seems to encourage even more abstract concepts than before.

In attempting to trace the links between cosmic and earthly trends, the greatest care has been taken to keep to scientific data established by modern astronomy. But only a spiritual astronomy can reveal the more intimate aspects of relationship between the stars and man if these are to become as manifest as solutions of mathematical or algebraic problems. Just as these cannot be described in brief to give the untrained listener a comprehensive picture, access to spiritual history will not be gained without some effort.

The stars are rich worlds that do not yield their secrets too readily. We can see them in the sky as isolated sources of light. In the Middle Ages and even earlier they were seen as constellations. By studying these in closer detail we can to some extent discover their significance. Here the pictorial language of the Zodiac used in old star calendars, which still bear the direct imprint of an ancient wisdom, will prove particularly helpful. In ancient times the leaders of the temple schools all over the earth knew that spiritual forces radiate from the cosmos from the direction of the constellations through which (as seen from the earth) the sun and planets pass. Clairvoyantly and in dreams those initiates could see in the constellations powerful beings to whom they gave different names. Those accepted in the European tradition are: the Ram, the Bull, the Twins, the Crab, the Lion, the Virgin, the Scales, the Scorpion, the Archer, the Goat, the Waterman and the Fishes. Astronomers still use these names and often substitute for them their ancient signs.

The stars of the Zodiac as they shine from the heavens are gateways to higher spiritual realms that contain the seeds of all earthly existence and of all divine memory.

It is difficult to speak of cosmic worlds. No ordinary concepts can do them justice. It is a realm without matter or tangible substance. We can to some extent form a picture of the world of the stars if we imagine sense impressions without their physical sources. Nothing remains but constantly changing floods of flowing colours, cosmic light, streaming odour, music of the spheres—and yet these comparisons only remotely describe what in earthly life we call colour, light, the experience of smell and sound. The impulse of the constellations can be likened to an orchestra of twelve instruments resounding throughout time, although the basic theme is almost forgotten. The echo of the memories of creation cannot reach us directly from the heights. Intermediate stages are needed as a bridge from the serenity of the world without matter to conditions on earth. This transition finds expression in the planets, which modify in greater or lesser rhythms the influences upon earth of the constellations through which they are passing. Our system of time is ordered by the Sun. In the cosmos time is ordered by the planets. What is one year to us can be twelve, thirty, sixty, hundreds or even thousands of years there. Time in the ordinary sense does not become any less important because something experienced and fought out here in a single hour as the result of deep inner struggle can live on in the cosmos for thousands of years.

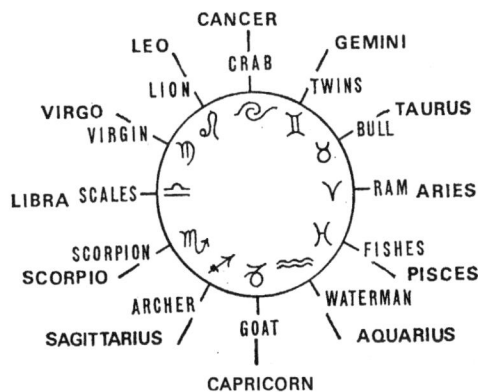

```
                        CANCER
              LEO         |
                \       CRAB      GEMINI
                 LION           / TWINS
        VIRGO   \                      TAURUS
          VIRGIN                     BULL

  LIBRA SCALES                       RAM ARIES

        SCORPION                    FISHES
      SCORPIO                          PISCES
           ARCHER              WATERMAN
                      GOAT
      SAGITTARIUS            AQUARIUS
                     CAPRICORN
```

The ideas of a cosmic nature emanating from the planets were in former times called gods. Where the author speaks of gods in this work the term indicates exalted beings of such an order. After the appearance of the Christ these beings were experienced as angel choirs in His service, and this knowledge lived on in the beliefs of the first centuries of Christianity until it was lost in modern times.

When St. Paul was teaching in Athens, there were men living to whom the spiritual hierarchies were a valid reality. Paul's pupil, Dionysius the Areopagite, called them Angels, Archangels, Principalities, Powers, Mights, Dominions, Thrones, Cherubim and Seraphim.

The nations are guided by the different archangels; their realm is indicated by the course described by the planet Venus. In ancient times Venus, as understood by modern astronomy, was called Mercury. Venus has mercurial character in an occult or esoteric sense, and the task of the beings whose symbol she is consists in uniting and healing.

The relationship between the cosmos, the folk souls and man evoked certain moods which gave European culture its characteristic trends among the different peoples. To the guides of mankind these moods were like spiritual sense organs that could serve them to shape the destiny of each nation.

33

Each of the twelve groups belongs to the realm of a certain sense organ which in turn is governed by one of the twelve directions of the Zodiac. Rudolf Steiner drew attention to this relationship.*

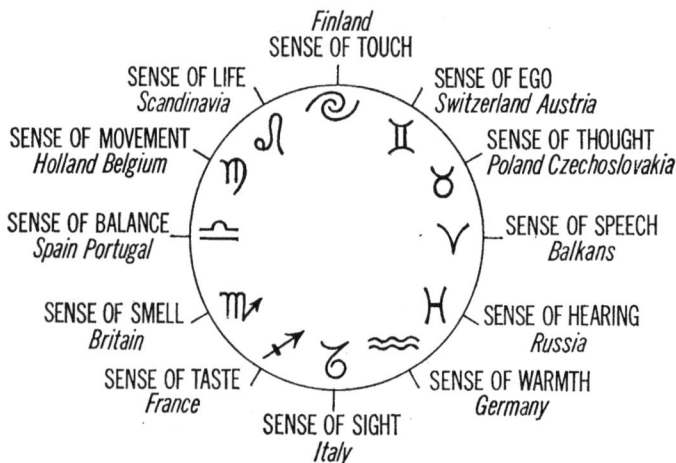

The senses are modified versions of the forces of the Zodiac. To obtain a comprehensive view of the world of the senses, everything may be called 'sense' which gives the human being information concerning the outer world. This 'outer world' includes different realms: first of all, the whole of nature; then man's own bodily organism; finally the speech and even thought of other human beings. The whole of this awareness is made possible by means of senses.

The Sense of Touch is spread over the skin of the whole body. One feels the contact with outer objects as pressure. Whether it be a sharp blow or the gentlest touching we become aware, through this sense, of external matter. With the sensation of warmth the case is different. This does not underlie the Sense of Touch as is usually supposed. It is not merely the impression of external heat or cold that is perceived; the inner organism also experiences them. The perception of warmth is a continual equalizing of the heat of the body with the surrounding temperature of nature. The faculty of being aware of this comparison represents a special sense, the Sense of Warmth.

Then there is another special sense which constantly interprets to us the life-conditions within our organism. We feel whether it is healthy or unhealthy. Even slight disturbances are perceived. The sense which imparts this to us is spread over the surface of all our inner organs. It is the Sense of Life. Its main organ of perception is the heart.

Further, we have the faculty of being aware of the movements of our body. For that purpose we require neither seeing nor touching nor any of the other senses to feel quite directly the

---

* *The Twelve Senses and the Seven Life Processes in Man.* A lecture given in Dornach, Switzerland, 12 August, 1916. *The Golden Blade,* 1975.

position assumed by our arm or our foot, or whether we are standing or walking. The Sense of Movement tells us. It is distributed through all the muscles.

In the ear, protected by the hardest bone in the body, we have three little hollow rings which are connected with our feeling of balance. They are in fact the organs of the Sense of Balance, situated in the head. In the central section of the human body there are also organs of balance, the arms, of which we always make use to maintain an upright position if we are in danger of falling. In the lower part of the body the hips keep the balance. Thus the Sense of Balance is distributed over the whole body.

The senses of Hearing, Sight, Taste and Smell—familiar to all—are located in the head.

All these senses are also present in the animals and often strongly developed. The Life-sense provides the animals with their sure instinct for food. The Sense of Movement gives birds their certainty in flying. The Sense of Balance in animals enables them to climb and accounts for their agility even on the edge of precipices. The animals develop particular senses as characteristic of their species, and to the utmost perfection. In Hearing we recognize different tones, whether of music, sounds or merely noise. But the understanding of speech—of words—requires a different activity from the mere hearing of sounds. Man understands speech through the Sense of Speech. In tone we become aware to some extent of the inner nature of the outside world, but this awareness is lifted to a more intimate experience when the tone or sound is filled with meaning, as in words. The Sense of Speech which communicates to us the meaning of spoken sounds is a purely spiritual instrument. The silent tension which lives in attentive listening is the means by which this sense can be educated.

A similar process, but even more intimate, occurs when we comprehend someone else's thought. Just as we understand speech because we ourselves can speak, but are silent, so we perceive another person's thought because we ourselves are thinking beings, able to silence our own thought, and thereby capable of living in the thoughts which others think. We thus develop the Sense of Thought.

Besides these senses there is one that is still higher. When we are suddenly confronted by someone not met before, we know without any doubt that that person is a human being. We feel this with the same certainty as that with which we are aware of warmth or pressure. But in order to be able to perceive the individuality of the person we must develop a special sense-organ—a gate—through which we come into direct contact with the other being. This gate is the Sense of the Ego. Its activity is allied to the fact that we ourselves are individuals. By the force of our own individuality we recognize at first sight that we are meeting another individual whose destiny is as important as our own. We plunge with our inner being into his being and thus become aware of it. Our own Ego is the instrument which forms the foundation of the Ego-sense.

A complete study of the senses increases their number from five to twelve. The human senses can be educated and developed. We can strengthen our seeing by looking with interest at everything in the world around us; and our hearing by concentrated listening. The higher senses in particular—Speech, Thought and the Ego-sense—depend on self-education. It is our inner attentiveness which decides whether we are really aware of all that sounds through the speech of others, or whether we absorb another's thought as completely as if it were our own, or whether we take the personality of another as seriously as we take ourselves. An aptitude for these faculties is latent in everyone. That they become effective depends on our own efforts. But if the effort is to be successful we must first realize that these latent faculties really exist. Man will only be fully aware of himself and of the world when he has developed all twelve senses in balance and harmony.

To receive the numerous external impressions in purity and truth it is profoundly necessary that sense-activity should become ever more consciously controlled; and this refining of the sense-apparatus is the task of the white races. The ability to make use of the senses began in primeval ages and became the possession of all mankind. But the harmonious establishment of all twelve senses still lies in the future. He who can grasp the importance of this evolution will find it less difficult to see the working out of distinct sense-tendencies distributed singly among the different nations.

Each of twelve main European groups of peoples which have evolved in the course of history has developed for itself a special connection with one or other of the senses and these relationships can be studied in the external facts of their past. Investigation should include artistic, scientific and religious achievements of the different peoples.

In the following pages which deal with history from the point of view of the folk-souls and the special tasks of the nations, these aspects connected with the senses will be included. Twenty-four of the most important European nations are studied: Finland, Sweden, Denmark, Norway, Holland, Belgium, Spain, Portugal, Great Britain, France, Italy, Germany, Russia, Turkey, Greece, Romania, Bulgaria, Yugoslavia, Albania, Poland, Czechoslavakia, Austria, Hungary, Switzerland.

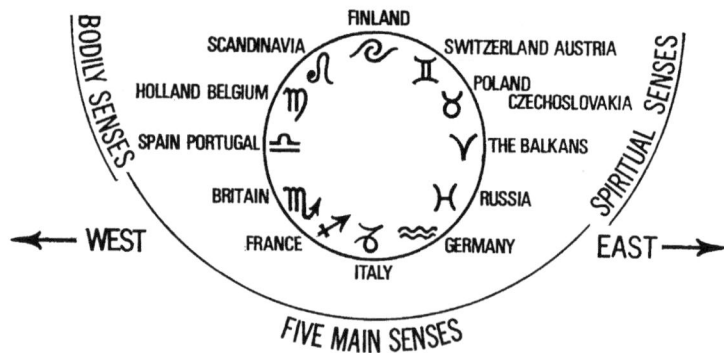

FIVE MAIN SENSES

Study of these connections shows that the development of the bodily senses predominated mainly among the smaller nations living on the Atlantic coasts of Europe; the spiritual senses eastwards and in the centre. The five great nations, Britain, France, Italy, Russia and Germany have a special relation to the main senses of Smell, Taste, Sight, Hearing and to the Sense of Warmth.

36

Single individuals develop all twelve senses, no matter to what country they themselves belong. Everyone can be free and universal, uniting the possible streams of development within himself as a synthesis. If men are studied as individuals they will show all kinds of universal characteristics; but from the standpoint of the whole nation they may be found to be faithful servants of a specific invisible plan. In individual life men could be aware of striving towards all-embracing interests—and this has been the case for centuries—but in a more general sense a man's connection with his particular folk-soul is only now beginning to become fully conscious.

The folk spirit weaves through everything that surrounds the people of its particular sphere. Its manifestations extend to the landscape and the life of nature. It is complemented by another living reality of the spirit, the folk-soul. The folk-soul pulsates with the emotional experiences of a people, its activity or lethargy, its genius or its dullness.

The working of folk spirit and folk-soul is not necessarily limited by national frontiers. If different political organisms are governed by the same folk spirit, this has its reasons. Higher beings, like man, have an articulated inner organism which allows their guidance to take different forms. Thus it may happen that one archangel may permeate his domain more with his feeling, another with his will and so forth.

The life of the individual human being, whose membership of a certain people is decided while he still dwells among the stars, is placed within this manifold activity. In life before birth, each constellation was to the soul a moral force to which it felt drawn in greater or less degree. Carried in its descent to Earth by the planets, it had an experience akin to the serene sound of bells each time one of the planets passed through the constellation with which it knew itself particularly connected. The ringing of the bell indicates that the hour has come when another step can be taken towards the Earth. In these experiences the soul, guided by divine wisdom, accumulates the spiritual substances congenial to its nature.

While the soul passes through these preliminary stages, the race and nation where it is to be active are decided. For those born outside Europe other factors may be decisive, although their tasks for the whole of humanity will be no less important or less cosmic in origin. In searching for an incarnation in a European people, a soul might feel attracted by the being that governs the constellation of the Lion. If spiritual guidance now decides that it is suited to develop further the inherent tendencies of this constellation, it will be placed in a country —say Scandinavia—whose basic tendencies are derived from the same impulse. Here it will find parents who can make possible its intended physical development.

But to man about to incarnate, the mission of his people is never the main reason for his coming journey on Earth. The national task is merely one of the many garbs he will wear. In the course of his life he will colour and perhaps remodel these garments with his own personality. At death, these robes of nationality will be discarded, but the consequences of his deeds will impress themselves on the character of his people.

The folk spirit leads a people only for a limited period. It turns to other tasks when a national impulse has been exhausted. But archangels constantly work towards change and advance. When a human being tries to overcome his own retarding forces, he is taken into the healing rhythm of the archangels so that he can serve in the building of truly social impulses wherever he may be.

The guiding spirits of the peoples live together at peace in the cosmos. They all look upon the centre of evolution, the Christ, whom they serve by guiding the peoples according to cosmic laws. They are active in realms of peace even when the peoples on earth are at war. They do not merely bring them memories of past worlds but also spiritual impulses directly connected with the Earth's mission. They aim to permeate man with the being of the Christ so that he can achieve an inner state of harmony that would not have been possible without the union of the Christ spirit with the Earth.

To the angel choirs the working of a Divine being among the human race was of the utmost importance. The whole cosmos shared in this event, and what happened on Earth was written indelibly into the stars. The archangels who are active in the realm of Venus experienced from there the Christ event in Palestine. Those happenings are reflected in the cosmic rhythms of Venus, related to the Sun. However, to those who can understand the working of the folk spirit, the planet itself is like a piece of chalk that records important cosmic and earthly links although it cannot produce them.

In circling the Sun that is passing through the Zodiac, Venus comes at rhythmic intervals into 'conjunction' with the Sun, that is, into direct line with Sun and Earth. Its position, seen from the Earth, may lie either between Earth and Sun—which is called 'inferior conjunction'—or behind the Sun ('superior conjunction'). Seen from the Earth, inferior and superior conjunctions take place alternatively.

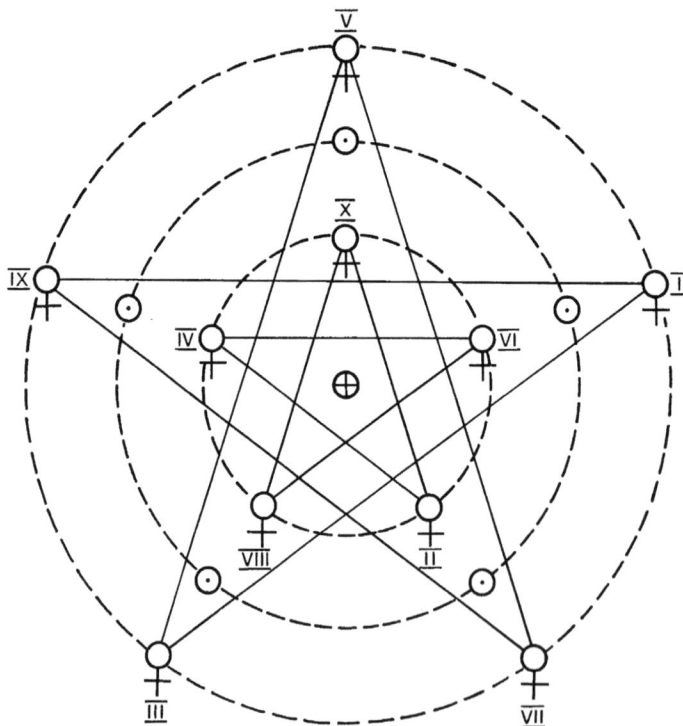

Conjunctions of Venus with the Sun.

Inner circle: Inferior conjunctions.
Middle circle: Path of the Sun.
Outer circle: Superior conjunctions.
Numbers refer to conjunctions in sequence, in the course of eight years.
Between two conjunctions, from inferior to superior or *vice versa*, elapse c. 290 days.

W.O.S.

If the positions of Venus in the Zodiac at the times of conjunction are observed and recorded, it can be realized how, by interacting rhythms, particular patterns are constantly created in the cosmos in the course of time.

One such pattern is of vital significance for our Earth evolution. We find it if we imagine (or draw) a path, not following the orbit, but in straight lines, between the points where meetings of a similar kind occur—namely the points of five inferior, and five superior conjunctions. This path traces five diagonals across the Zodiac, inscribing there over a period of eight years an almost but not quite exact, five-pointed star—a pentagram.* The difference between the position of one conjunction and the following one eight years later is very small but very important. The first point of the new pentagram cycle, after eight years, is a few degrees distant from the first. And in this way the pentagram-star as a *whole* makes a continued cyclic journey round the Zodiac—as if rotating upon the Sun at its centre. To follow one single revolution of this pentagram round the whole Zodiac, we may join the points in an enclosing figure—a pentagon. Twelve hundred years must pass before the pentagon

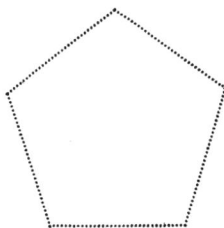

performs one complete rotation through the Zodiac. The meetings between Venus and Earth continue for about a century in each constellation but the period varies according to the direction of the Zodiac in which they are taking place.

The combined pentagon-pentagram figure may recall a five-petalled rose about to open.

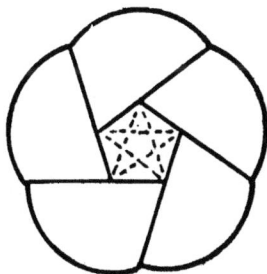

This beautiful figure is a spiritual reality. As its rhythms evolve the patterns in time, they reveal the harmonious relations and proportions recognized on Earth in many spatial and

---

* In the eight-year cycle, as Mr. Sucher's diagram shows, there are ten conjunctions of Venus, five superior and five inferior, in alternation. So two pentagrams arise within the cycle. The time between two superior or two inferior conjunctions is c. 584 days (nineteen and a half months) and the completion of one pentagram star takes 2,920 days, or eight years.

organic forms as those of the Golden Mean. In old days, this invisible star of Venus was more important than the visible planet in its orbit.

The movement of the pentagram can be calculated into the distant past. The last years of the life of Christ gave truly outstanding significance to the movements of Earth and Venus. This most important phase of the life of the Earth is impressed into seemingly unimportant and frequently recurring events. Venus shares in the great cosmic memory of the Christ event.

Experience has shown that the five angles of the Venus pentagon are related to different dynamic experiences of the soul:

1. The meeting with the adverse powers of evolution.
2. The overcoming of outlived traditions which impede progress.
3. The search for the sources of spiritual and cultural advance.
4. The assimilation of the great apocalyptic perspectives of the future development of mankind.
5. The awareness of the Godhead in man and the realization of its working as a social impulse.

Throughout history man has been faced again and again with this fivefold experience, as the Venus pentagon moves from Sign to Sign, casting the radiance of the five experiences from the life of Christ over the whole of humanity.

Because the thought impulses of archangels do not work on the surface but are hidden in the depths of human consciousness, they were given no attention by contemporary chroniclers or later historians. Yet the workings of these inner events are reflected in human experience; their emanations gave the peoples of Europe an inner unity despite their differences, for the Christ-events, with which the sphere of Venus is connected, contain the secret of all lasting community.

But every development is faced by hostile powers who aim to prevent mankind from achieving its earthly mission, love and freedom. These powers are also of a purely spiritual nature. Some of their points of attack in the cosmos, whence they try to gain control of the evolution of the world, can be found wherever a constellation indicates that divine thoughts are trying to gain access to the Earth. The forces of temptation surround these bridges between heights and depths in order to distort divine impulses. If we want to trace the spiritual guidance of mankind, we must give up all wishful dreams of the realm of the heavens as a tranquil paradise. In reality the planets are a battlefield, where the forces of divine progress, struggling to realize their impulses, are subjected to constant attack by the powers of evil.

The archangels and other divine spirits devoted to the Christ always work towards freedom. As folk-souls they never exert compulsion over man, who is to achieve freedom and inner strength. Human wisdom and piety help towards this end.

The adverse powers aim to conquer man and to tie him to himself through dullness and ambition. The Christ-memories of the Venus pentagon can therefore often appear in the course of history as their opposites:

1. Men may fall prey to the adverse powers.
2. They may become rigid and set in tradition, seeking to preserve it under all circumstances, or they may rush towards the future, completely without inner support.

40

3. They deny the spirit as the true source of all culture and progress.
4. They drift in the realm of culture, either losing themselves in an empty aestheticism or striving towards a national expansion that often proves highly destructive to the forces of the ego.
5. Instead of perceiving the Godhead in man and in the formation of human communities, they deny the Divine and fall victim to agnosticism.

The folk-souls, themselves living in the light, had to lead European humanity through the valley of darkness where inner freedom must be acquired through error and pain.

Even in the past, European evolution presented difficulties so great that the folk-souls alone could not offer sufficient protection against final disaster. The original groups of peoples had united on the basis of natural protection or blood relationship and had developed out of an instinctive awareness of their identity. Had this tendency remained unbroken until modern times, humanity would have been swamped by dullness and egotism, for it is through national instinct and selfishness that the powers of darkness can gain hold of man.

To prevent this the folk-souls are helped by still more exalted forces whose planetary access is through Pluto, moving through the constellations. The continued guidance of a people, linked through its folk-soul to a particular constellation, gives opportunity for further development in accordance with divine impulses. Pluto's influence brought revitalizing but often disquieting inspiration, coming like a cosmic fire to prevent man from becoming rigid and withered.

Pluto does not possess the characteristics of the other planets, which have been known since earliest times. It was only discovered in 1930, through calculations later confirmed by astronomical observation. Since then, its markedly elliptical course has been worked out; its passage through the Zodiac lasts approximately 246–247 years. Many astronomers believe it may have been a comet, penetrating into the solar system from distant worlds and trapped in it. Comets are purifiers of the solar system. Pluto pushes aside the compulsive and instinctive elements in the life of peoples and creates space for impulses of the spirit. It clears the space between cosmos and Earth, so that the peoples can become star-organs.

To this end, men had to transform the flames they had to face at such times into individual initiative. In the Christian era, when freedom can become a reality, any new impact takes the form of an opportunity. Every European country has brought forth personalities who could use the opportunities created by Pluto's opening of the world to the wisdom of truly cosmic impulses. The active striving of individuals created a mood in which the need of the age could find fulfilment. The Normans who ventured on the seas, the Dutch who created the very land they live on, the Spaniards and Portuguese who discovered and colonized new continents for the first time, the English who founded modern science, the French who strove for progress, the Italians who brought about the Renaissance, the German philosophers and the Austrian saints—they all made possible through human and individual effort the realization of the gifts that form the destinies of the peoples. The Pluto rhythm affected some of them in the early part of their lives, some in the middle and some late.

All creations and characteristics of national cultures were divine thoughts, accepted, permeated and transformed by the human heart. They were like the different-coloured light produced by the meeting of cosmic light and the darkness of the Earth. Such twelvefold colour accompanies Pluto's travels through the Zodiac.

The divine thoughts indicated by Pluto's position during these travels are subject to attack by forces hostile to evolution—thus whether a people will touch heights or depths of development depends on living personalities. In Russia, during the two and a half centuries representing Pluto's full course, the appeal from the gods was answered from both directions: Ivan the Terrible, possessed, allowed his own passions to intrude and brought disaster; St. Seraphim through inner training helped on the spiritualization of mankind. The cosmos gives the opportunities for human salvation. The responsibility to decide between these and the forces of darkness lies with the individual man.

Until the end of the nineteenth century the consequences of aberration from this path were still softened for the different peoples by the protecting impulses of the folk spirits. But as a result of modern materialistic science and the related lapse in healthy and normal living conditions where creative realities could still survive, the guidance of human destinies will depend increasingly on man's own insight. No other path to real progress any longer exists.

The planet Pluto, invisible to the physical eye, was discovered when a fanatical nationalism based on ancient group instincts began to assume its most menacing form. Seen superficially this may appear pure coincidence, because Pluto was discovered by applying the law of gravitation to the cosmos. But the simultaneous study of history and cosmic rhythms proves that this discovery was a deep necessity.

In assessing cosmic-earthly events, not only visible star-constellations must be considered but also the Signs of the ecliptic—that is, its division into twelve equal lengths with the Vernal point, 0°, beginning the Sign of the Ram. At the time of Christ a Sign and the visible constellation of the same name almost completely coincided; but owing to the movement of the Vernal point, they separate and only meet again in cycles of about 26,000 years. But since all the beings of the Zodiac, and those active in the ecliptic, experienced the Christ-event as the turning point of time, the quality of the images and the Signs remains similar. The working of the Signs of the ecliptic is more intimate, more related to man; the character of the fixed stars is more serene. In the case of Pluto, with a course far beyond the Sun and the planets, it is the constellations that are of more importance. Venus is closer to Earth and here the Signs have significance. Her movements are visible to the eye; sometimes she appears as morning, sometimes as evening star.

In connection with this work, the author has traced the course of Pluto through the single constellations since the ninth century. This rhythm has been taken into consideration in describing the gifts of the different peoples. Most of the personalities and historical events described were touched by it, but the scope of this volume does not allow of greater detail. The passage of each of the five points of the Venus pentagram through the Signs of the ecliptic has also been worked out and is mentioned from time to time.

Ten planets have so far been discovered and all, including Venus and Pluto, are of great significance to the student of history. Venus points to the folk spirits; Pluto to will impulses that penetrate to the Sun cosmos from outside. The Moon, Mercury, the Earth, Mars, Jupiter, Saturn, Uranus and Neptune follow no less important rhythms. Their movements in relation to one another and to the Sun, and between their Nodes—the points where a planet's orbit cuts the ecliptic—often span long periods of time. These cosmic events are witnesses of the spiritual guidance of mankind and also an outward expression of the struggles fought against divine powers. Everything that occurs in the cosmos casts its reflection into the Earth.

Although the reader will find the stars frequently mentioned, this work has little in common with orthodox astrology. Heavenly events were not interpreted according to old and unfathomable rules. By the use of a discipline of scientific research comparable to the attitude demanded in laboratory work, they have been shown to be the expression of the guiding forces working in the cosmos.* If these descriptions seem strange at first, they may be approached like a work of mythology. Gradually the mythos can become less strange. And if a reader is not frightened by apparent obscurities or aspects still unknown, he may come to see its relevance to the destinies of the Earth. It is as if healing forces could flow into mankind through the particular gifts of each people. From our own experience and by observing the events of our own time, many of us may well feel that Europe today is seeking to discover her own specific tasks and is anxious to nurture the seeds for the well-being of the whole of humanity.

The reader may indeed rightly object if statements are offered again and again without their supporting arguments. This shortcoming lies partly in the inevitably limited scope of the work, and partly in its very nature. Mythology is something we can try to fathom, but not to prove. But often, what is seemingly far-fetched will become obvious to the careful and unbiased observer.

---

* Willi C. Sucher. *The Drama of the Universe*, Larkfield, 1958; *Isis-Sophia*, 1950.
  These works are out of print but are obtainable through the Rudolf Steiner Library, 35 Park Road, London, NW1.

Europe's Star Mythos

WHEN WE LOOK at the peoples of Europe we generally think of their geographical relationship. Their geographical setting appears the most important factor. Indeed it can so dominate our approach that any other aspect is apt to appear subordinate.

Yet this volume does not deal with the different peoples from the point of view of their geographical proximity. It begins with Scandinavia, the Netherlands and Spain. These are followed by Britain, France, Italy and Germany. Afterwards come Russia, the Balkan countries, Poland, Austria, Switzerland and Finland.

The geographical setting reflects purely earth-bound concepts of locality that did not develop until post-Grecian times, while the division attempted in these pages corresponds to an inner dynamism. It indicates Europe's star mythos, a cosmic world order that is mirrored —although at times but faintly—in the character of the peoples. To understand it we must think in terms of historical development rather than of geography. In earliest times, when creation had advanced sufficiently for the Earth to consolidate and for the continents to assume their shapes from the still clouded and watery air, it was the succession of events in time rather than the setting in space that was decisive in the guidance of mankind. 'Time' in its cosmic sense means an increasingly awakening consciousness. The metamorphoses we survey today as 'the course of evolution' embrace mankind as it was in the past, capable of sharing in the experience of gods, though in a dreamlike way; as it is in our time, in the gradual progress to human independence; and in its return to the Divine, on a higher level, in a very distant future. Evolution can be seen indeed as the experience of gods made manifest in time. The peoples of Europe, developing their gifts, reflect the twelve-fold nature of the Zodiac; but the spiritual background of what we today see as the Zodiac is the experience and memory of divine worlds.

As the peoples of Europe are an image of the cosmos, so is the individual. Before birth, he receives out of the heights the forces for the formation of his physical body, so that he can afterwards experience his body as part of himself. Europe in her destinies is like an individual evolving in time rather than space. The groups of peoples, with the stamp of the Zodiac, are the image of man's development from Atlantis where he could still dream clairvoyantly, to a more aware state whence he could rise to new forms of consciousness.* Whereas the group of peoples may reflect the divinely thought human form, the Greek myth of Europa tells of dangers and temptations that come to threaten the soul.

---

* Rudolf Steiner. *Cosmic Memory.* (*Atlantis and Lemuria.*) Rudolf Steiner Publications, New York.

The beginnings of this mythos are found in Scandinavia. The songs of the *Edda*, which speak of Asgard and Nifelheim—Nebelheim, the land of fogs—describe an Atlantean past. The mood that was dominant there found its echo later in the close relationship of the Scandinavian peoples with the living forces of nature. They could take in the now invisible aura around them. This process resembled the experience of a distant past. The mood of the constellation of the Lion could become reality.

The next stage of these early developments is shown in the very much later legends of Sigurd or Siegfried. This phase of evolution brought the awakening of human self-awareness. Man began to separate himself from the universal mother element and in consequence the gold of ancient wisdom was cast into the Rhine. This points to the constellation of Virgo, the Virgin, giving conditions which were to evolve very much later in the Netherlands. The Rhine in question is not the river we know today, but another which, when Britain was still linked with the continent, flowed into the sea from Scotland. At that time an increasingly opaque veil was being placed between the cosmic Virgo secrets and the gradually-awakening consciousness.

A further step towards increased awareness became possible when the fogs above the continents lifted and Sun, land and seas became visible. The conditions for the making of tools were being prepared; the same impulse was later responsible for the magnificent cave paintings of south-western Europe. As the starry heavens lit up, man attempted navigation for the first time. This is mirrored in the history of Spain and Portugal, countries belonging to the constellation of the Scales. The voyages of discovery, which had their source there, were to establish a state of balance in Europe between Western and Eastern spirituality.

The earliest population of the British Isles was connected with the Iberians and Basques; in this fact, we can see the transition from Spain to England in the mythos of Europe. The next stage of development was reached in Britain. Like eagles, men directed their senses towards outer nature. It therefore became a necessity to them to make the secrets of the stars manifest, as for example at Stonehenge, Glastonbury* and other Mystery centres. King Arthur also experienced the cosmos mirrored in the physical world and revealed to the senses. He felt himself as the representative of the Sun, and the twelve knights of his Round Table as the personification of the twelve forces of the Zodiac. (See diagram overleaf.)

The Eagle of the heights later became the Scorpion of the depths.

The original inhabitants of France were the Gauls, as the Romans called them. ' Gaul ' means ' fighter '. Here we already find the background to Sagittarius, the Archer. This element has been preserved in the highly sanguine French temperament. The archer is the centaur, half man and half horse. The whole development of France is like a constant struggle for balance between the animal and the human element.

Europe's star mythos, originating in the distant past, now unfolds entirely in the world of the senses where historical facts speak with the utmost clarity. The world of the senses, to which man is to devote himself completely in the course of time, contains a hardening tendency that can also be characteristic of Capricorn, the Goat. This came to merge with Roman

---

* *Glastonbury's Temple of the Stars.* K. E. Maltwood. *The View of Atlantis.* John Michel.

civilization, where practical considerations were paramount. Vast networks of roads were built, the rights of the Roman citizen were laid down, alien peoples were governed according to their own laws. To the course of evolution the Roman manner of life was like a crystallization into purely outward form. But the Romans also encountered other peoples, whose Mysteries they could not disregard. Through this very hardening, Italy, the centre of Roman civilization, could become the source whence the spirituality of the East, the Mysteries of Isis, of Mithras, and later also Christianity were to spread throughout the world. Roman organization served as a vessel to preserve the seeds for the future. Later the impulse to a Christian transformation of the senses also had its origin in Italy.

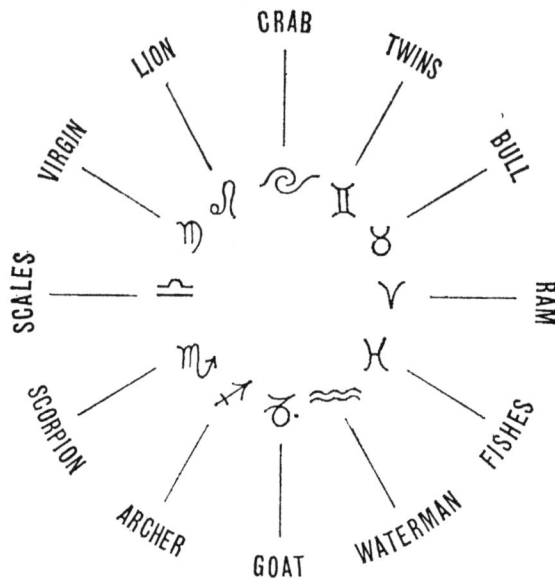

There is one aspect of the Zodiac particularly related to the Moon. One half is connected with the descendant, *Nidsigend*, the other with the ascendant, *Obsigend*.

Here, Capricorn is the turning point from descending to ascending constellations. This is strikingly illustrated by the events of the Roman era. At that time Jesus Christ was born as the Son of God who dwells within man. He opened the door anew to the Divine. Man had been given the possibility of ascending. In the future course of history the Germanic peoples counteracted the hardening process. Their Aquarius—Waterman—tendency was like a bridge between Italian trends and the characteristics of the west and north-west.

The development of this healing faculty is the basic condition for the progress of the Slavonic peoples whose greatest representative is Russia, through the constellation of the Fishes. What has happened so far through the greatest of her children is merely an indication of the potentialities of Slavonic culture. All Slavonic peoples belong to the future.

The cradle of a European culture of the future will be the Balkans. In the background of this future evolution stands ancient Greece where all European history began. This points to the Ram, the leader of the Zodiac, which is reflected in the destinies of all Balkan peoples.

The future development of humanity is threatened by a danger the Poles are trying to counter through their connection with the Bull. Through the Bull impulse the soul can sink back into an entirely passive absorption into the divine mother element. Should this happen, the course of the Slav mission would be diverted. The Polish path was a trial towards preservation of the personality, which will remain even after a higher degree of spirituality has been achieved.

When the Slav peoples fulfil their mission the metamorphosis of Finland will also appear in its full significance. The spirituality of the realm of Cancer, the Crab, and therefore also of Finland, points to the transition from a completed world cycle to a new beginning. This concerns all humanity; for just as the Sun, seen from the Earth, passes through the Zodiac and in the course of its journey enters Cancer, so the inner Sun of every human being passes through a kind of Zodiac within the soul in the course of life on earth. At a certain stage, whether now or in the past or the future, everyone is faced with an inner Cancer constellation. That is when he must find or build the bridge from impulses of the past to new spiritual perspectives. He must bridge his own inner abyss.

In Europe's star mythos there is no direct transition from the Slav peoples to Finland. Another important element enters. The mythos turns once more towards Central Europe, to the Twin peoples of Austria and Switzerland. This indicates that the essence of what is striven for in Central Europe must be transformed so that the change towards the future can come about in the right way. Germany has also a specific task here. The Slavonic future-element— the Fishes, the Ram and the Bull—is supported on the one hand by the German Waterman nature and on the other by the Austrian–Swiss Twins character. German idealism and the great classic German authors, whose work carries the seed of the future, belong to this flowing Waterman element. The Austrian and Swiss character, formed in the land of the Alps, will later give strength and integrity to the Slavonic soul. What has been thought, striven for and actually attempted in these countries is an indication of all that will be needed on the future path as bread and wine.

There is another, also ancient, concept of the dynamism of the Zodiac. Here the upper portion is experienced as bright, the lower as dark. This aspect belongs to the Europe of today. On the dark side stand the great powers, Britain, France, Italy, Germany and Russia.

47

Their peoples carry the largest share of the burden which must be transformed for the vessel of Earth existence to be filled with light. Theirs is today the chief responsibility for the course of outer history.

With the passage of time, all the peoples have adapted themselves in greater or less degree to present conditions. Every individual, to whatever people he may belong, is in his own way a synthesis of all the European peoples. He has possibilities of insight into the final goal of the greater humanity which all folk spirits aim to serve. He gives Europe, and all history, its true meaning.

Through an understanding of the star destinies of the European peoples, certain laws governing space become apparent. The circle carries a cross within it. Britain, France and the

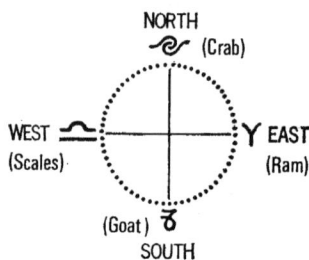

NORTH
♋ (Crab)

WEST ♎ (Scales)

EAST ♈ Y (Ram)

(Goat) ♑
SOUTH

Spanish Peninsula represent the West, Italy the South, Russia and the Balkans the East, Finland and Scandinavia the North. The time dynamism of the star mythos becomes a division in space.

Written into Europe, this cross represents the confluence of universal forces of growth. Many epochs and many countries throughout the world have prepared what should be continued in Europe for the salvation of mankind.

PART II

National Gifts

Scandinavia

The scandinavian folk spirit connected with the destinies of Sweden, Norway and Denmark transmits to their people from the region of the Lion of the Zodiac a gift of devotion to life and heart forces. Life on Earth is bound up with the forces of nature, while cosmic life is one with light and wisdom. Wisdom that can permeate retrospection and vision illumines both the past and the future. It was this light-filled wisdom that brought forth the songs of the great Scandinavian epic, the *Edda*. Vala, the visionary, speaks of the creation of the world, of the ancient gods and their decline. In pictures, overwhelming in splendour and horror, she describes the sorrows and tribulations the world must pass through, but also a future where spiritual life can flourish afresh. Then the silent Widar will begin to speak and the shining Baldur will return.

The epic reached Iceland in about 874 with the Norwegians. Iceland, surrounded by the Atlantic whose winds are the bearers of ancient memories, also belongs to the realm of the Scandinavian folk spirit. Icelandic soil forms a thin, dark crust over volcanic flames that heat the springs to boiling point. As a rainbow may often stand out there for long periods against a retreating storm, so the pictures of the *Edda* live on with all the force of their rich colour in the souls of the Icelandic people.

In Scandinavia men were able to unite spiritual vision with the experience of nature, for inner experience was in harmony with the rhythm of the seasons. An old Norwegian folk song* tells how on Christmas Eve Olaf Åsteson fell into a dream from which he did not awaken ' till the thirteenth day '—January the sixth. He could then describe how he had passed through regions of the dead and the landscape of the Moon, and came at length to the Gjaller Bridge where he encountered three wild animals. These were the unpurified forces of his own soul, with which he had to come to terms. He saw other souls, also passing through this state, who had to account for the consequences of their deeds before the spiritual world. In the light of those nights the world after death became a reality for him; he had shared in the life of higher worlds.

Midwinter is of particular significance in the course of the year. Christmas and the Holy Nights mark the gap between the lunar year of 354 days and the Earth–Sun year, the 365 days needed for the Sun to rise again in the same fixed-star position.** In the 354 days the Moon completes twelve cycles from full Moon to full Moon, and so a difference of between eleven and

---

* *The Dream Song of Olaf Åsteson*, translated and illustrated by Eleanor Merry. New Knowledge Books, 1961.
** Fractions of days are omitted.

twelve days arises in the two rhythms. Outwardly this is the darkest time of the year, inwardly the brightest. A world normally invisible to the soul is illumined by the Sun of the spirits.

The exalted Beings whose activities originate in the region of the Lion are bearers of knowledge of the sources of life. As the Sun is the heart in the life of the planets, the Lion is like a sun and heart in the Zodiac.

Orthodox astronomy still represents the Sun as a gaseous ball, producing warmth and light in a course of combustion and explosion. But this description may well fall short of reality since from another aspect the Sun is a centre of give and take, a cosmic vacuum without physical substance, drawing its strength from the surrounding stars. On this basis we can imagine the Sun as the source of processes of life-giving transformation that result in the warmth and light that nourish our Earth; in this conception the Sun lives in attraction and dispersal, a life-rhythm of systole and diastole.

The astronomical sign for the Lion points to this inner dynamism. It consists of a small circle at the base of a loop winding round a larger, open circle, and it illustrates a centre drawing life from the periphery whence it radiates it again.

The Lion, the heart of the Zodiac, and the Sun, the heart of the planetary system, are reflected in man in the heart and circulation of the blood. Systole is the contraction and diastole the expansion of the heart; contraction and expansion are the pulsation of life.

This connection between the Lion, the life forces and the heart is expressed in old Scandinavian coats-of-arms whose designs are still inspired by the folk soul. In an old Danish coat-of-arms, the shield, surrounded by foliage, displays three lions among thirteen hearts. The fourteenth-century coat-of-arms of Erik Magnus of Sweden is also surrounded by foliage, and the lion, amid twenty-four hearts, has a tail branching out like a tree. Above its leaves rise a pair of bull's horns and twelve banners. In a Norwegian coat-of-arms thought to date from c. 1460, life ripples through the leaves from which a stag's head rises. The stag's collar suggests that the emblem illustrates, not untamed life forces, but rather an awareness of them in human consciousness. All these coats-of-arms speak of cosmic forces brought to bear on the mood of the Scandinavian peoples by their folk spirit; they portray rhythms of heart and life that underlie historical events. (Plates 7–9.)

Some Norwegian church paintings of even earlier date show the relationship to the forces that permeate all life. In the Historical Museum at Oslo a late thirteenth-century painted chancel from the demolished Stave church of Ål shows the dying Christ spreading His arms in blessing

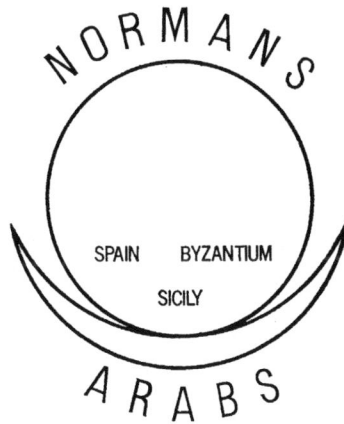

above a world of formative forces. Formative elements normally invisible have been drawn into His aura. (Plates 10–13.)

The secrets of the Holy Grail were open to the powerful Archangel who guided the peoples of Scandinavia. Between the ninth and eleventh centuries the path of the Norman voyages enclosed like a circle the European countries where the Grail impulse was active. To the folk soul this was an important diastole, taking in those who belonged to Europe. The men of Scandinavia, called Vikings and later, Normans, came forth from the lands of the North— where in summer the day never dies and the Arctic nights glow with the coloured splendour of the Aurora—to sail in their small ships round all the shores of the continent. Some of the Normans sailed first eastward and then south; others went westward and then east.

Wherever those men of the North-lands went, a stimulating element of life accompanied them. Pleasant guests they were not, and many regions were plunged into bitterest terror. Even so, their presence evoked life forces as they went from one people to another who had to rouse themselves to meet and come to terms with the unwanted visitors. The Swedes travelled round the North Cape, penetrating Russia along the lakes and rivers. Rurik, the real founder of Russia was a Norman. Those Swedish Normans were called *Wareager*. Following the rivers, they travelled ever farther east, and southwards to the Black Sea and Constantinople. There, in the eleventh century, they were called *Varanger*, and formed the bodyguard of the Byzantine Emperor.

The Norwegians on the other hand went to the Faroe Islands, Shetland, Orkney and the Hebrides at the end of the eighth century, and formed settlements along the coasts of Scotland. Others reached Ireland where they remained for some centuries.

In the ninth century, the Danes landed in Friesland and in Flanders. During the reign of Charlemagne they appeared on the coasts of France. Next they pushed their way up the Seine, the Loire and the Garonne into the interior, until finally Rollo received Normandy from the king of the Franks and himself contrived to hold the other Normans in check. From France, they entered Spain, about the middle of the ninth century. England was invaded in 1066 and kings of Norman descent continued to reign. In Italy, the Normans arrived in 1017 and Sicily was taken from the Arabs in 1071. Roger II was crowned king in Palermo by the Pope in 1130. From Southern Italy they crossed to Greece in 1147.

While one group of Norsemen, crossing Russia, reached Constantinople, the voyages of others also led them there, as if they were drawn by some secret power of attraction. Thus the directions of their wanderings formed a clearly marked circle, enclosing the lands of evolving Europe.

The southern part of the continent had been in the hands of the Arabs. They too, in their movements, traced a cosmic design but in this case no full circle was drawn. Their expeditions enclosed the southern part of Europe in the shape of a crescent moon. These people were dark-skinned and dark-haired, clever and passionate. In the same period when central Europe knew the influence of the Knights of the Holy Grail, the blue-eyed Normans with their fair skin and red-gold hair were laying the Sun-circle of their path into the dark chalice holding captive the southern shores.

Norway, Denmark and Sweden, though belonging to the same folk spirit, are nevertheless clearly differentiated. Vast forests still cover a great part of Sweden; its southern plains are windswept and fertile, bathed in a sun-filled, perfumed atmosphere. Stockholm is often called the Venice of the North. Its magnificent art collections are reminiscent of Italy. The University of Uppsala was founded as early as 1477 and that of Lund in 1668. The country's great libraries contain the wisdom of all ages. The bodies of the Swedes are strong, their souls sensitive and passionate. They embrace life with a full-hearted enjoyment like the Italians; but beneath the surface there slumbers a mood of earnestness and of strong self-possession.

In the Danish character there is much that resembles the French, though transformed in the northerner to something more calm and collected. The whole country of Denmark is cultivated; magnificent bridges lead from island to island, and the capital, Copenhagen, is a most beautiful city. The welfare of the people is carefully fostered.

Majestic is the rocky and precipitous land of Norway. The sea flows up the deep indentations made by the wild and sombre fiords, on whose steep lichen-covered crags a few solitary birches grow. The Norwegian has to battle for his living against the elements. Fishing and commerce have driven him out on to the waters. His determined spirit of enterprise is similar to that of the British; he is austere, fearless and resolute. But his soul, deeply rooted in the Northern folk soul, has wings that can bear him to the heights of spiritual vision.

Three times in the mysterious ebb and flow of history the three peoples were guided by one king. In very ancient pre-Christian centuries King Svidagerus is said to have ruled over Sweden, Denmark and Norway. At the beginning of our era Froho III of Denmark, 'Pacificus', 'the Peaceful', united them. He died in 15 A.D., eighteen years before the death of Christ. The union of the three countries occurred for the third time in the fourteenth and fifteenth centuries, when seven Danish kings wore the triple crown.

A study of various ancient chronicles worked out by the Viennese historian Johann Huebner shows that at the time of this last union Norway had its thirty-third king; Denmark had had ninety-nine—three times thirty-three, Olav V being the hundredth—and Sweden had had four times thirty-three, beginning with Torillo and Totila, Kings of the Goths, and ending with Erik Magnus II, who was the one hundred and thirty-second. To appreciate the destinies of the European nations—and any historical event—attention has to be paid to the explicit numerical rhythms which may be found in world history.

Numbers have become shadowy things today. To be able to feel their significance we must try for a moment to forget everything connected with modern reckoning. Pythagoras could recognize forces in numbers in which secrets of the divine world were hidden. In history they are the signs of a spiritual geometry pointing to the foundations of human existence. Some basic numbers are twelve, seven, eighteen, thirty-three, three.*

Twelve, as already seen, is the number of the zodiacal constellations of fixed stars through which run the orbits of Sun and planets. The twelve Knights of the Round Table of King Arthur, who had to accomplish heroic deeds, reflected these celestial powers. The Greek hero, Heracles, experienced them in his twelve great labours. Christ Himself had twelve apostles. When the Irish monks went to the continent to preach Christianity they left their island in groups of twelve. Charlemagne as late as the ninth century had his twelve paladins. They too represented the forces of the Zodiac which are the prototypes of the Twelve.

Seven is the number of the planets as men of old saw them. This number reappears in the seven days of the week, the seven colours of the rainbow and the seven notes of the scale.** The stages of development of every human being are regulated in accordance with this same rhythm. The child changes his teeth at the age of seven years, reaches puberty at fourteen and finishes his growth at twenty-one, when he is recognized as an independent personality in the social order. In studying biographies it can be seen that even after this age, throughout the whole of life, periods are completed every seven years.

The rhythm of eighteen years and seven months is familiar to students of astronomy and is known as a Moon-cycle. It can be shown, moreover, by reference to the biographies of important people that this cycle plays a prominent part in the lives of individuals. The ages from eighteen to nineteen years, thirty-six to thirty-seven, and fifty-four years, usually represent high points of psychological development, giving rise to a series of crises and finding expression in intensified spiritual productivity, as well as in sharp conflicts with far-reaching effects on individual destiny. A kindling and vitalizing even of dream-life takes place at these critical times. Psychological phenomena are connected with the number eighteen. We breathe on an average eighteen times a minute, while to every respiration the heart beats four times. Seventy-two pulse beats is the average number per minute. We can normally think of a human being's life as lasting about seventy-two years and this we can conceive as a single prolonged respiration —inbreathing at birth and outbreathing at death. Thus the four included cycles of eighteen years and seven months appear as four heart-beats which bring about the four climaxes of inner experience.

Economists and statisticians are familiar with the cycle of thirty-three. It is clearly seen in economic life and in the growth of populations. It has been established that the higher birth-rates following wars are repeated like an after-wave in thirty-three years, and then after

---

* ' The Secrets of Numbers ' by Lionel Stebbing, New Knowledge Books.

** ' The Number Seven ' by A. E. Abbot, Emerson Press.

another thirty-three years, a third correlated wave arrives. Thirty-three years are taken as the length of a generation; they indicate the point of time at which a man stands at the zenith of his strength, living contemporaneously with the preceding and the succeeding generation—with his father and with his children.

But though this cycle appears in individual life, its significance is still more marked in history. Its operation explains why great inventors seldom see the success of their own work. New ideas do not as a rule permeate cultural life before thirty-three years have passed. Thus one generation hands over its innovations to the next, to bear fruit. The consequences of our own deeds today, whether progressive or destructive, will come to maturity in thirty-three years. The duration of the life of Jesus Christ was thirty-three years; thus the cycle finds its prototype.

The number three is manifested not only in historical events but is fundamental in nature. The significance of threes should be obvious to those who live in the British Isles where, during long centuries, the Bards composed their Triads. They experienced the Three in all existence. The divine Trinity expresses itself throughout the Creation.

The Union of the three Northern nations, at Kalmar, was brought about through the personal destiny of the Danish princess, Margareta. In 1375 her father, the King of Denmark, died and her five-year-old son Olaf was crowned. Her husband, the King of Norway, also died and her son succeeded to the throne in 1380. Seven years later Olaf himself died, before he was quite eighteen. These three deaths laid in Margareta's hand the rulership of two countries, and in 1397 she was asked to accept the throne of Sweden as well.

In Sweden the union had been instinctively felt many decades earlier. During the reign of Erik Magnus who had been crowned at the age of three, in 1319, coins were minted on which three crowns were stamped. They represented the triple nature of the Northern folk spirit. After the Union, Erik's successors incorporated this triple sign in the Swedish coat-of-arms.

Another, more complicated numerical rhythm occurred in the kingly family of Norway, before the Union. From the time of the first king of all Norway until 1397, there were thirty-two kings; the thirty-third was crowned at the Union of Kalmar as king of all three realms. On two occasions three brothers had been elected at the same time to rule over a shared Norway. What they did during their reigns is of less importance than their simultaneous election. There were twelve kings before the first three brothers; after them, two kings and another election of three brothers. Then again came twelve kings; and the series closes with the crowning at Kalmar of Margareta's chosen successor, Eric of Pomerania. These numbers arising geometrically may be taken to symbolize in this event a significance beyond the ordinary human sphere.

On another plane, for the folk souls, this must have been a tremendous moment. The spiritual reality of the one great northern folk soul was physically demonstrated when the three peoples, who had already developed different outer characteristics, belonged for a last brief period, even externally, to one and the same guiding force, to one king.

The Archangel of Scandinavia developed in his peoples a devotion to all living things. An intimate relationship arose with the plant world, where life and its manifestations are at their purest and least disturbed. The very events of history encouraged this tendency. When the monastic orders were dissolved in the sixteenth century, the gardens that had hitherto supplied medicinal plants to wide circles fell into secular hands. Two Danes, Christen Peterson and Henrik Smith, now enthusiastically taught their compatriots the use and cultivation of plants. Within a very short time men and women began to compete in the art of gardening. The Scandinavians, hitherto almost entirely dependent on meat for their food, came to include vegetables in their diet. Many varieties were grown in kitchen gardens, tons of cucumbers, and marrows weighing up to 30 lbs. were produced on the tiniest plots. In 1541, not only parsnips, cabbage, onions, green peas and parsley, but also large quantities of thyme, sage and other herbs, were served daily at the table of King Christian III. In the royal gardens at Rosenhof, lavender, peonies and carnations were grown and seeds and seedlings exchanged. The queen took part in these activities. In 1551, she asked Brigitte Goye to send her marjoram, basil, carnations, cypresses, yellow pansies and other plants. Flowers were not merely used as decoration; methods of distilling them were soon found so their scent could be enjoyed indoors.

Many northern gardens were famous, among them those of Cornelius Hamsfort at Odense, of Peter Oxe near Gisselfeld and of Tycho Brahe at Hven. These were the first botanical gardens and the inspiration of many others throughout the world.

In Norway, where little growth could flourish, the love of flowers also developed rapidly. Even the poorest fisherman's hut displayed flower pots at its windows. More than elsewhere, graves were covered with flowers, renewed each Saturday; no grave was left bare as long as anything blossomed at all.

Karl Linné, the great botanist, grew up in one of Sweden's finest gardens: his father, the pastor of Stenbrohult, had laid it out and planted rare trees and flowers. These flowers became the boy's playmates; when he was naughty, a flower put into his hand would calm him. Linnaeus looked back to the hour of his birth with joy: 'At one o'clock, at the best time in spring, when the cuckoo called the summer and the leaves and flowers opened.' At the outskirts of the farm where he was born stood a lime tree held sacred by the villagers. In honour of this tree Linnaeus's ancestors, on being ordained, had adopted its name. When the famous botanist was honoured in 1761, he too called himself after the linden tree—de Linné, Linnaeus.

Linnaeus created an arbitrary system of classification, chiefly according to pollen and stamens. But very soon he came to see his own scheme as no more than a necessary evil. He felt increasingly that the pulsating life that fascinated him in the plant kingdom defied his method. In 1737, he wrote in the *Genera Plantarum*: 'This artificial system merely serves for identification.' And he added that he had never meant to deny the affinity of related species, for 'we are the servants of nature, not her masters.' Indeed, it seemed as if he had been the enemy of his own artificial divisions: quietly he planned to re-arrange his system, of which he said, ' I cannot complete it, even if it were to take my entire life.'

He longed for a comprehensive view of the plant world and rejoiced when the East India Company gave him the right of a free return journey each year to other continents. He sent his 'apostles' to Canada, Egypt, India, Malabar, Southern Europe and Spitzbergen. Some of them died on the journey and with sorrow in his heart he wrote to a friend: ' The death of many whom I encouraged to travel has turned my hair grey. And what have I gained? A few dried flowers, and much anxiety, unrest and sorrow.'

In 1749 he went to the island of Hven where the great Scandinavian astronomer Tycho Brahe had lived. To Linnaeus this visit was a pious pilgrimage. He wanted to pay tribute at the Uranienburg whence Tycho Brahe had observed the world of stars, the very source of life, and in the subterranean laboratory at Stelleberg where he had tried to fathom the secrets of the kingdoms of nature on Earth. A hundred and fifty years had passed since Tycho, bitterly hurt and misunderstood, had left the island. Linnaeus found a scene of complete desolation. ' Neither rat nor snake can be found on the island,' he observed, ' it has become a very primitive place indeed.' When he afterwards came to Helsingborg, he carefully copied the epitaph placed there by Tycho's daughter.

Through his researches into the movements of the planets, Tycho had come to feel the need for a new system of the universe which, he hoped, would halt the spread of Copernican teachings. He knew that the Ptolemaic system was outmoded. But his century was not ready for a new picture of the universe in harmony with the cosmic life impulse; he himself could not find it. His proposals were ignored and swept aside by the rise of materialism.

Linnaeus, likewise, realized a need of new concepts in the living realms of botany and zoology; but he surrendered to the tendency of an age more concerned with collecting and classifying than with living metamorphosis. German, French, English, Italian, Dutch and American universities heaped honours upon him. His theories dominated botanical research. Among the tributes paid after his death was a letter from Goethe, who wrote: ' Next to Shakespeare and Spinoza, Linnaeus has been the most important influence in my life.'

Goethe himself was not content to stop at the achievements of Linnaeus. In patient observation and contemplation he found the key to an understanding of the metamorphosis of the plant. Whereas Linnaeus had established a nomenclature for seven thousand plants known at that time, Goethe looked for the conditions of life itself and for the underlying law that produces the plant. He found in the principle of expansion and contraction the living impulse behind nature. In Sweden the name of Linnaeus was the terror of schoolchildren, who had to compile a a herbarium with Latin names as their annual summer-holiday task. With anxious eyes father and and mother had to scan the hedgerows for plants the children might have forgotten. In both parents and children, a deep sensibility for the growing forces of nature rebelled against this method.

The Scandinavian peoples have developed the Sense of Life. Their devotion to the life forces directed their consciousness towards everything likely to further physical well-being: this resulted in an intimate insight into the importance of everyday life, with the daily and annual rhythms that govern even the humblest tasks. The rhythmic coming and going of growth and decay, of day and night, of spring, summer, autumn and winter, of birth and death, has been called by the Scandinavian historian, Troels Lund, 'the hidden springs of history'. He wrote:

> Everyday life is at once the most significant and the least observed aspect of any people . . . And the intimate relationships that have for generations expressed the attitude to nature, the course of the day or the year, or to marriage, birth and death, harbour the sources of all culture, poetry and piety throughout the centuries. These hidden springs of history—we can call them everyday life in its infinite reflections—may flow less noisily than the rivers of outer history, but they carry a far more precious burden. The laws of this silent world are not those of the whirlpool above and outside . . . and the names that count there are not those that matter among the mighty of the Earth. Here, earlier than elsewhere, men have learned to live together harmoniously; the name of the smallest master whose invention has brought blessing to mankind has greater value in these circles than the name of the most powerful prince.

Out of this love for the hidden sources of history and out of a profound experience of life, the spirituality of the North could inspire a system of adult education seeking harmony between heart and head, man and nature.

Kesten Mikkelsen Kold, a farmer from Jutland, founded one of the first of these schools. As a young man applying for a teaching post, he was interviewed by Dean Reehof in Apenrade who asked what he wanted to teach the children. He answered: 'I will tell them about Danish history and read them Ingermann's novels'. 'Impossible', said Dean Reehof, 'we have no Danish folk spirit here.' 'That we certainly have,' said Kold, 'but in any case there is a Danish heart and if we appeal to that, all else will come.' Such teaching was not acceptable. Kold was in despair and thought of going overseas, perhaps to the American forests, never to return. Eventually he went to Smyrna as a valet. In 1847 he returned to Denmark, planning to emigrate from there to America. But in the end he decided to stay. He read Grundtvig's historical works and made up his mind to teach young folk. In Smyrna, he had earned 500 *Reichstaler*; the folk high school at Roeding had cost 48,000 *Reichstaler*. He went to ask Bishop Grundtvig's advice and the historian was encouraging: 'It will come. Go home and write an appeal. Then bring it to me and I shall be the first to sign.' Kold's longing materialized.* His impulse corresponded so completely to the people's need that he could later, without any help from the state, build a school costing 25,000 *Reichstaler*, where grown-up peasant lads were taught in winter, peasant girls in summer, and schoolmasters in autumn.

Four years before his death, Kold was asked by Grundtvig to tell what had led him to his work, and what he thought about it. Absorbed in his great scheme, he had never written anything. Kold then described how an inspector had once asked him what his system was. 'We have no system'. 'Yes, but what is the school for?' 'When I was eighteen I learned to love God and my neighbour. This gave me such joy that I decided to give my time and strength to teach it to others. That is the aim of the school: to love God, one's neighbour and

---

* Kold set up his first 'free school' in 1851 with a capital of 1,100 *Rigsdaler* (£125), about half of which represented his own savings: the rest was subscribed by Grundtvig and friends. *Education for Life*, N. Davies, 1931.

one's country'. 'A worthy aim', agreed the inspector. Kold said later in his report; 'I am not as good at explanations as at bringing life to people. I arouse life first, and then comes the explanation . . . Enlivening is what we most need and is therefore as much the task of my school as enlightment.'

This educationalist who had himself had 'no proper education' believed that the better one knew the Danes, the more one would realize they must feel life in the truest sense before instruction was possible, or at least the two must go together.

The idea of a folk high school had been conceived first by Bishop Nicolaus Fredrik Severin Grundtvig, a representative of the star impulse of the Northern folk spirit, and a contemporary of Goethe. He aimed at something entirely new: 'A centre where people can gradually gain true self-awareness, and where teachers and pupils will learn from one another.' After many vain attempts towards his goal in Denmark, he appealed to the Norwegians: 'Whether we study the " mighty dreams " of the Divine in pagan times, or their manifestation in deed, song and verse, before Roman influence and the Latin language made them wither, we find again and again that there is no greater joy than to see human life unfold in the fulness of its relationship to the whole cosmos . . .' He believed a demand must soon come for centres for adult education with a 'universal' character. He wanted schools that would strive for a free humanity, and he wrote: 'Let us understand what we really need. It is freedom that serves us best; though not like that of fire and water, hunger and pestilence, like wolves and bears. Let freedom be our motto in the North, freedom for Locke and freedom for Thor—freedom for all that is of the spirit. Only the beast shall remain bound!'

> O'er the earth black midnight hovers.
> Terror-filled, the thunder crashes.
> Wildly rage the wind-driven tempests.
> Wildly seethe the storm-tossed waters.
>
> Woe that storm and flood and thunder
> Howl unheard, since men lie sleeping.
> Over eyelids slumber-weighted
> Trolls breathe fogs with poison laden;
> Trolls, dread-haunting darkling pastures,
> Mutter spells of dire enchantment.
>
> O my people, sunk in slumber,
> In the fog's distorting mirrors
> False the dreams that would decoy you!
>
> Ye, Light of the Earth,
> Flame, O Flame! Stream forth your radiance!
> Fogs dispel with towering torches!
> Stand fast, warriors! Battle bravely!
>
> Sleep you still? . . . Can you be sleeping?

He appealed to all those responsible for the spiritual development of his people. Today his words are more alive than ever.

The great people's university of the North did not materialize, but local evening schools and centres for further education sprang up everywhere.

Grundtvig's pupils founded schools throughout Scandinavia. They had the greatest reverence for the manifestations of the spirit in even the humblest aspects of everyday life; and they respected the work of the individual. Christopher Brunn, a founder in the North, said ' These schools are based on a revolutionary principle. They are an assertion of the individual against everything associated with official institutions. They have nothing to do with guarantees demanded by the state. Their only guarantee is the personality of the teacher.'

In the course of time, Denmark alone had 2,500 schools for further education, including sixty universities. Each was owned by the farmers of the region, who formed co-operatives to support them. At least a third of the population attended classes. The state had no hand in their development, nor did it interfere.

The Scandinavian peoples did not produce social and political theories. They respected the health of the land, and even with the complete electrification of the countryside did not lose their feeling of human dependence on the natural fertility of the plant and animal kingdoms. By adapting themselves to life and observing ways of increasing physical well-being, they made the most of conditions as they found them. From this realistic attitude, based on sense experience, all kinds of activities were organized along healthy and fruitful lines.

Most of the peasantry combined in one vast co-operative which became the heart of the country's economy. A small country like Denmark was thus able to supply a third of the world's butter. In the middle of our century the Federation of Danish Co-operatives included five thousand smaller organisations whose activities, apart from production, embraced distribution, credit and the safeguarding of the interests of consumers. These societies represent a sense of true brotherhood in the economic life, as the popular high schools stand for freedom in the life of the spirit.

The working of the cosmic Lion through the Scandinavian people is also evident in the gifts of individuals. In Norway Bjornsen appeared, like the blood-stream that pulsates through the body. He was gay and talkative, and always spoke of himself as ' we '; he felt himself as part of a greater whole. Ibsen, also a Norwegian, experienced the world altogether differently. He was like the dark chamber of the heart. Problems flowed towards him and aroused questions that would not be solved. While Bjornsen's soul strove outwards, Ibsen went into the depths.

Bjornsen preached morals and understanding. Ibsen had no desire to instruct. He stood amid the problems of his age, asked questions and made others think. Yet he longed for a less sombre life. His whole existence was dedicated to art and at the end he made the hero of his last play speak the words: 'Is it not infinitely more valuable, to live a life of sunshine and of beauty than to struggle one's whole life in a cold and damp cave with lumps of clay and blocks of stone?'

Henrik Ibsen who, until his old age, had never loved wholeheartedly, felt himself condemned by his folk soul. New life can only flourish in an atmosphere of love. The joint love of the parents is essential to the health of the children. The mother's love helps the soul to unfold, while the father's gives protection towards the world. Spiritual science teaches that even where the father has died before the birth of his child, he follows its destiny spiritually. The Scandinavian folk soul enable its peoples to seek a love that permeates life with happiness and particular warmth.

Through science, everything within man's reach as a natural gift is open to arbitrary interference. This danger is all the more acute where life is experienced at its most direct. Sweden was the first European country where the loveless, mechanically controlled dragging of souls into bodies became legalized. This was a rushing to the future without any inner life-supporting force. Where a soul striving towards the Earth does not meet the love of two people, a fundamental law of life is violated. Such failure undermines true humanity and stands in direct contrast to the Scandinavian mission. The further natural science advances, the more important it will become to feel with those souls who are seeking healthy conditions to begin their life on Earth. To understand the seriousness of the whole problem, it will become increasingly necessary to see the connections between birth, the pre-natal existence of the soul, and the balancing wave-beat of cosmic life. This is the only way of guarding against the aberrations which already threaten human life before birth. It is not only the growing human life, moreover, that needs protection and compassion; but also the spirits of nature, who behind the veil of history have carried mankind in endless devotion. They are part of all growth: there are legions of them at their different tasks. The gnomes dwell in the hard earth, the undines in water. Air is the home of the sylphs and flames give dwelling to the fire spirits.* These nature spirits, who sacrificed their powers to man, can only be brought back to their cosmic origin by him; but modern man in his overbearing conceit mocks at the very thought of them and interferes in their realms without any understanding.

The result is a chaos, its real source disguised by scientific terms. Behind floods, droughts, new diseases, behind increasingly active earthquakes and hurricanes, stands the despair of the nature spirits and their determination to rouse man from his lethargy. The Scandinavian peoples are called upon to pay attention and thought to these outcries. They must come to feel the anguish of the elemental beings. Only then can freedom turn into healing power.

The living need for such compassion was implanted in children's hearts by Hans Christian Andersen. In telling his stories he took the children with him into a world where compassion counts for more than riches or honours, and where help is found in hours of danger through deeds freely given. Andersen was the son of a poor cobbler in Odense and from earliest youth he was determined to become an author, even a dramatist. But it was not the will of the guiding forces of the world, and his early efforts met with no success. Yet when he was with children his soul overflowed with fairy tales, and he could go on telling stories indefinitely. To him it was all a matter of course and he would never have thought of putting his tales to paper had it not been suggested to him. He hoped that when they were published, parents would learn them by heart, so that they could re-tell them in their own way to their children.

Fairy tales exist in every European country and indeed throughout the whole world. But usually they are memories of an ancient clairvoyance through which men could at one time

---

* R. Steiner, *Man as Symphony of the Creative Word*. Rudolf Steiner Press, London.

experience the working of the spiritual world in nature. Hans Christian Andersen created his from the overflowing riches of his own heart, fired by the impulse of the Scandinavian folk soul. In his stories the mainsprings of history rise, tentatively, to the surface.

He looked on all created things as children. Animals were children who are always asleep and dreaming; they may at times be stupid, but never wild. The children he described were never wicked. Again as a matter of course, he spoke of trolls, mermaids and daughters of the air, of dryads and of the leaf that fell into the forest from heaven, and grew into a miraculous plant whose flowers sang, as if they harboured a wealth of melodies that even thousands of years would not exhaust. His imagination gave life even to inanimate objects.

To children of every country, his tales gave health-bringing forces to sustain them in their later years and even in old age. Some could later experience the nature spirits as true companions of mankind on earth, because they had lived with them in their childhood through the atmosphere of the Scandinavian fairy tales.

Nature philosophers and sages sometimes spoke of elemental beings, but men did not take them seriously. Andersen, who describes their kind deeds with great warmth, kindles love for them. He travelled a great deal. In outline, his journeys at the different periods of his life appear to follow almost exactly the travels of the Normans. He visited the Faroe Isles, Scotland, England, France, Portugal, Spain, Southern Italy, Greece and Turkey. It seemed as if, through him, the folk soul was once more embracing all Europe with a sunlike circle. He was mourned by the whole of Denmark at his death.

An even greater representative of Northern spirituality was Selma Lagerlof. She was the forerunner of all that the Scandinavian folk soul will seek to achieve in the future through human development. Andersen's fairy tales, compassionate and imaginative, were products of the moment. In Selma Lagerlof there is none of this playful element. She could see with unclouded judgment the forces that play into our lives from another world. What was magic enchantment in Andersen appeared to her as emanations of evil and utterly real forces who also belong to the spirituality of nature, and whose influence on individual destinies can be disastrous. Sinister elemental beings often try to cross the human path. They only yield to free deeds of compassion whose motive force is rooted in other worlds.

Selma Lagerlof described for children the story of little Nils Holgersson and the wild geese. Here the world of the fairy tale merges with the Swedish landscape and permeates and enlivens its creatures. The outer reality, described in considerable detail, rests upon a background of creative and feeling spirit beings. All life is endowed with soul and meaning; compassion and boldness are the driving forces.

When men's hearts embrace both the distress of the nature-beings and of human suffering, they resemble the Sun that holds the planetary system together. Such people will realize within themselves the life impulses of the Lion of the Zodiac. This heart impulse that recognizes and tames the forces of darkness in man and in nature spirits lives in the work of Selma Lagerlof. In the Christ legends she leads to the source of this Sun radiance. She was the servant of the light-filled Widar, of whom the *Edda* speaks.

The ancient Scandinavians experienced the *Edda* as cosmic thought. Bishop Grundtvig, who spoke of their profound natural awareness of the connection between earth and heaven, implored his contemporaries to go to the dreams of their pagan forefathers, to their deeds, tales and songs. The *Edda* contains a key to the significance of the twentieth century. It describes the same happenings as the *Revelation of St. John*. Both are prophecies of powerful changes that can be understood today in a new light.

An unbiased observer of recent history may feel that the battle of Ragnarok of which the *Edda* tells is already raging behind the curtain of outer events. The *Edda* describes events among the gods. But the future of man is closely interwoven with this experience of divine beings and the battle of the gods on a higher plane is man's historical destiny.

The *Edda* tells of the Fenris Wolf who kills the god, Odin. The Fenris Wolf is the spirit of lies, undermining all life and seeking to destroy the link between the Earth and the divine world. But the silent Widar, Odin's youngest son, fights and overcomes the Fenris Wolf. The Light-filled victor is the lord of life and the lord of the spirits of nature.

It can be sensed how desperately the Scandinavian folk soul longs for his people to unite with him in the struggle for progress.

> Ye, Light of the Earth,
> Flame, O Flame! Stream forth your radiance!
> Fogs dispel with towering torches!
> Stand fast, warriors! Battle bravely!
> Sleep you still? . . . Can you be sleeping? . . .

Europe and the world need the light forces of the North.

The Netherlands

As THE stars of the Virgin move across the spring sky, their gentle glow is hiding powerful deeds of creation, for this constellation points to a divine wisdom in which the priests of Saïs, in ancient Egypt, recognized Isis. Isis guards the mysteries of growth and decay, of conception and life, and the chemical laws of organic metamorphosis; but the star majesty of these secrets is hidden by three dense veils.

The Netherlands folk spirit links the destinies of its people with the Virgin mysteries. Isis impulses have sought expression there in many different ways. Spinoza, that powerful thinker, believed the starting-point for a true world-picture was to be found in that which could rest completely within itself. He called it 'substance', and to him it was God. Two attributes of this spirit substance could be recognized by man; the physical world and the thinking within his soul. Thinking without imagery Spinoza touched the hem of the garment of divine wisdom, and the inner certainty which could thus fill him affected his whole attitude to life. He was persecuted by fanatics; voluntarily he gave up his fortune and lived as an artisan. His soul, knowing itself part of the world soul, remained undisturbed. He and Erasmus of Rotterdam, who with ceaseless energy acquired a truly universal knowledge, were both of reserved disposition.

Many scientists who sought the divine wisdom that works in man and nature were born in the Netherlands. Though their striving turned into abstract science in more recent times, hidden in their souls remained the wish to penetrate the cosmic Mysteries of Isis. With all the burning urge to find the secrets of life through the investigation of the world around, they remained at heart contemplative.

The mysterious regions whence the Virgin stars send down their light harbour the creative origin of movement. Transformed and reflected in many different ways, this impulse was carried into the general mood of the Netherlands people by their Archangel. They could thus play an active part in the life of their very earth. They faced an enormous task, since the working of the constantly-moving forces of the Virgin extended even to the landscape. The land had to be wrested from the waves and once gained, carefully preserved: it was a ceaseless struggle against ever-recurring loss.

In early times the Netherlands formed a raised plateau which later disappeared under the sea. Swamps and moors existed along the coast until comparatively recently. Pliny, a few years after the Christ event, wrote of the northern part, Friesland, that it consisted largely of mud and clay, mixed with brackish salt water. To protect their villages against flooding the inhabitants of Friesland built clay hillocks. The old Friesian law said: 'We defend our country with three weapons: spade, pitch fork and hand cart.' A strong people arose, determined to protect themselves and their soil through the work of their hands. The people of

Friesland still sensed their relationship to the cosmic Virgin. She was *EWA*, the source of the eternal law from which all human initiative flows. ' Ewa dwells in you, she teaches you what is right and wrong '.

The Netherlands were a cold grey region and men needed warmth to preserve life against the threat from the sea. They burned the turf forming the soil under their feet and the earth of their country thus flickered and glowed in their hearths and ovens. For centuries, generations kept warm by burning their very land. Gradually water filled the excavated pits, but the need for warmth remained. The surface of cloud-covered lakes which consequently came to extend all over Holland was often below sea level. The remaining soil fell prey to the rivers that carried Europe's flood water into the muddy plain. Water, storm and the need of warmth undermined the ground whose main foundation was sand. For thousands of years, the subsoil of other European countries has been rock. The Netherlands had only a narrow strip of solid ground given them by nature: the rest was no more than a tiny foothold against the waves.

Like a dream image forgotten during the day, the cosmic Virgin watched as the land was gradually won back from the sea. The folk spirit itself was like an alchemist, able to transform water into earth, flooded lands into meadows, swamps into fields, and sand banks below sea level into flourishing towns.

The struggle was hard indeed. About 1100 or 1200 the sea flooded Friesland, then still a peninsula. Much of the country was devoured and the mainland was left with a jagged coastline where the water could gnaw incessantly. The islands thus formed remained in danger. In Zeeland, the construction of protective walls had begun as early as the tenth century. At first they were built at a distance from the sea and were of sand and sea grass, and later of clay and straw. After the twelfth century they became very numerous. They were built further and further out towards the sea and finally in the water itself. Rivers were also dammed. The land so gained was dried out with windmills, drained with a system of canals, and divided into strips. The Netherlands became a mother-country guarding many new-born children. The watery element went on fighting for old regions and for new; but the Zuider Zee remained arable land surrounded by a fresh-water lake until, in the thirteenth century, the advancing North Sea destroyed the whole area. Amsterdam was then a small fishing village. In the south, in 1270, ' Polder Holland ' was dried out by the damming of the river Meuse and much land was gained. A hundred and fifty years later, the work collapsed. The sea broke in from Dordrecht and only sixty miles of solid ground were left between Rotterdam and Amsterdam. 270 villages disappeared; 10,000 people were drowned; and ships sailed over the former countryside, ' *het verdronken land van Zuid-Beveland* '—the drowned land of South-Beveland— that rested below.

United, the Dutch went on fighting. Well aware that the earth they had created could be taken from them again, they were willing to work without rest to preserve it. More and more walls rose against sea and rivers. To build, lose and rebuild was their national destiny.

In the sixteenth century, when they had to contend not only against the sea but against foreign oppressors, the land was in the greatest danger. Thirty-six miles of moor and lake were saved at that time but the whole area, which was to become the country's centre, was still in hazard for centuries, for the large salt lake extending as far as Amsterdam was a veritable sea-wolf that howled anew with each storm.

It was found that the bottom of Dutch lakes consisted of fertile clay. Much new territory was gained, and islands, partly below sea level, were wrested from the floods through dams. The coastline was a particularly exposed zone. In 1840 it was still 1100 miles long. In many places three walls were built between the dunes, 'the watchman and the sleeper and dreamer'. When the first broke, the second would take the assault and if that failed the third must serve. Broken sea walls were common. There was also constant danger from subsidence and other disturbances.

The most important protection, the dunes—piled up by storm and sea—were also under threat. Without dunes there would be no Holland. But sand is volatile; and against the ever-active sand the Dutch set their own activity. They planted the dunes with a grass to reduce the speed of wind along the ground. The roots secure the soil and the stalks accumulate the flying sand around the plants. In spring, the dunes are now clothed in a protective green mantle that glitters in places with the small flowers of the sweetly scented dune roses as if it were covered with stars.

Not only Holland's earth owes its existence to human activity; the Dutch state too is the outcome of heroic deed. In the sixteenth century the Netherlands formed part of the Hapsburg Spanish Empire, and with their sober and industrious population they were one of its most flourishing regions. The Reformation, prepared by humanism and the Brothers of the Common Life, quickly gained ground; and behind it stood William the Silent, Prince of the Netherlands. The ideal of freedom which he served was part of his inmost nature and brought him the direct enmity of Philip II of Spain, visiting Holland after his coronation. Already angered by resistance to his persecutions, Philip was driven to fury by a formal remonstrance, signed by William, Count Egmont and other nobles, against the intolerable conduct of his soldiery. About to board ship and depart, he accused William of thwarting his plans by intrigue; and when William replied that all had been conducted regularly through the Estates, the King seized his wrist and shook it, shouting, 'Not the Estates but you, you, you!' He judged rightly, for William was indeed the faithful servant of his country. With the threat of the Inquisition, resentment grew from day to day. Count Egmont was sent to Spain to seek concessions from the King. The Calvinist nobles combined and submitted a petition to the Regent. From now on, converting an enemy gibe to their need, they called themselves ' Geuzen ' —Beggars. At this time, William the Silent was thirty-three years old.

In 1566 Philip agreed to abolish the Inquisition but in the following year he sent the notorious Duke of Alva to Holland and William had to flee to Germany. Alva arrived in Brussels with 10,000 men and immediately began his reign of terror. Egmont and Hoorn were taken prisoner and the whole population were declared to be traitors. Thousands were beheaded, hanged, or burned at the stake. After William's victory at Heiliger Lee in Friesland, Egmont and Hoorn were beheaded in Brussels in reprisal. Alva triumphed. But out of this holocaust a new Holland was born. When all seemed lost, the men of Holland broke their dykes and sailed in upon the flood water. They returned as founders of a new state. The Spaniards faced with this unbreakable will to resist, left the country. William then sought to unite the Netherlands. In 1579, the seven northern provinces were joined in the Union of Utrecht. Two years later, Holland declared her independence. Five years later William, ' the father of his people ' was murdered in his house in Delft.

In the wars of liberation the Belgians suffered as heavily as the Dutch and had fought with equal bravery. The reason for the separation from the sister country is therefore not as obvious as has often been suggested. Perhaps it was necessary that tendencies common to both peoples should be experienced differently in the following years, in Holland more through action, in Belgium through self-denial. While the people in the northern Netherlands could intervene actively in the course of their future, those in the south had to remain passive and receptive.

The Belgian earth has been the setting for three important spiritual events. In the ninth century, the Ardennes in all probability harboured one of the Grail centres. In the twelfth century, a relic of Christ's blood was brought from Jerusalem to Bruges. The annals of the Duchy of Burgundy also record that part of the cross on which St. Andrew died was preserved in Brussels in a silver shrine. The Order of the Golden Fleece, whose membership included many of the fighters for the freedom of the Netherlands, had been founded in honour of this cross.

An inner connection seemed to exist between the foundation of the Order and the events in the life of Joan of Arc. The Order was inaugurated by Philip the Good, of Burgundy, in 1429. In September of the same year Joan of Arc was injured in battle. It was Philip's Burgundian soldiers who later took her prisoner and thus helped to bring about her death at the stake. The real link between these events may appear obscure, at most to be traced only tentatively. Yet their proximity in time is not without significance, for the soul of Joan of Arc, radiant like the golden fleece of the lamb, was filled with the being of the cosmic Virgin; creative deed and sacrifice.

In the years between 1412 and 1416, around the time of the birth of the Maid of Orleans, the *Très Riches Heures* of the Duc de Berry were painted.* In these miniatures, the beauties of this world and of everyday life are meticulously observed: yet never very far away the spiritual and elemental world hover. A few years after the death of the Maid of Orleans, Memling, the painter of graceful and restrained, yet life-like Madonnas, was born. Hubert and Jan van Eyck—who in the Ghent altarpiece created the first portraits in the modern sense—were active at the same time. It was the dawn of Netherlands art.

While the people of the north were chiefly interested in observation of the world of man and of nature around them, those of the southern Netherlands lived more in the realm of soul. To them the scenes depicted by Hieronymus Bosch were a reality. He could portray the forces of temptation and demons of every kind with a devotion to detail only equalled by the painters of the north in their interiors. Bosch was active at 's Hertogenbosch in North Brabant, at that time a province of the Middle Netherlands. He wanted to show the life and movement of a world that is invisible and yet part of the phenomenon of creation.** (Plate 14.)

Many of the greatest Flemish painters came from the northern Netherlands: Hugo van der Goes from Zeeland, Gerard David from Oudewater, Dierik Bouts and Jan Mostaert from Haarlem. Pieter Breughel the Elder was born near Breda, Pieter Aertsen, who was active in Antwerp, was of Dutch peasant origin, Antonio Moro came from Utrecht. As guests on southern soil, a soil receptive in the highest degree, they became the creators of Flemish painting. Later the art of the southern provinces came increasingly under the spell of the Renaissance.

No country but Holland produced an art of such directness, so completely independent of

---

* See *The New Testament* with 21 illustrations from the *Très Riches Heures*, published by Collins, London, 1958. The *Très Riches Heures* has been described as ' the king of illuminated manuscripts '. (Editor.) *Les Très Riches Heures du Duc de Berry*, partial facsimile (139 plates in colour), from the fifteenth century illuminated manuscript, published in 1969, by Thames and Hudson, London.
** C. A. Wertheim Aymès in ' The Pictorial Language of Hieronymus Bosch ', New Knowledge Books.

the past and of other civilizations, of Gothic no less than of Greece and Rome. Albert van Oudewater, active in Haarlem in the middle of the fifteenth century, was among the first to paint interiors where he could show the play of light. His pupil Geertgen tot St. Jans introduced the naturalistic treatment of textiles into his pictures and also painted several landscapes. He died at the age of twenty-eight. A small painting from his hand shows the cosmic Virgin through whom Isis works, surrounded by angel choirs and seated on the crescent of the moon, supported by a dragon. This picture (*q.v. frontispiece*), light-filled and remote, speaks with deep truth.*

Cornelius Engelbrechtsz (1468–1533) who worked in Leyden was a master of detail. His pupil, Lucas van Leyden, died when only thirty-nine, in the same year as Jacob Cornelius van Oostman, who is chiefly known for his woodcuts. This rapid passing of so many painters is like a preparation for the coming golden age of Dutch art. The following century saw the birth of every outstanding master, the last two Vermeer and Hobbema. The Dutch soul is filled with reverence for all creation, divine or human, and Dutch painting derives its strength from the loving observation of tangible events and physical objects. Every aspect of the world around was made the theme of works of art, to be rendered faithfully, without flattery or a seeking for effect. There was no prejudice or aesthetic convention, only a conscientious re-creation of the existing world according to its own laws. Everything could be portrayed as it was in life. Metal kept its sheen, silk its softness. Animals moved naturally, human faces were sometimes simple and inoffensive, sometimes earnest and dignified. The mood was one of cleanliness and honesty. The obvious was respected, the rest was not the artist's concern. In this distinct phenomenalism lies the originality of Dutch art.

Until that time, painting elsewhere had mainly been concerned with religious or mythological themes. Religion was the source of inspiration. In Holland, painters also worked with great devotion; but every subject was considered worthy. Even the smallest things were, in the last resort, part of creation. Much had been changed by human industry. Silk and wool into clothes, wood into tables and chairs, clay into plates, cups and jugs. Pictures created in this mood became an integral part of a Dutch popular culture in which all could share. But in the many lively discussions of the time about painting, it was only the object that mattered, never the technique or composition. The admiration a picture could arouse depended purely on the theme.

Through Rembrandt, Dutch art could transcend itself. (Plate 15.) To him, all earthly life was but an image, a tragic and human one. He died poor and abandoned, a year after the death of his wife and son. After him, Dutch art withered away. His pictures, dispersed all over the earth, were forgotten for more than a hundred years. The work of Frans Hals who died three years before him suffered the same fate. The great age of Dutch painting did not last beyond the seventeenth century.

The ingenuity and initiative of the Dutch spirit, which had created the very soil of Holland, had founded a state without foreign help, and had inaugurated an entirely new development in art, also opened up new paths in the sciences. Both microscope and telescope were invented within a span of eighteen years in the workshops of two Middelburg glass cutters. About 1590, Jansen invented the principle of the microscope and in 1608, Lippershey submitted his first simple telescope—soon afterwards also a telescope for two eyes—to the Estates General.

---

* Geertgen tot St. Jans. *The Glorification of the Virgin*, Boymans Museum, Rotterdam.

Lippershey was a spectacle maker, and his discovery is said to have been made by his children who, looking into a mirror at distant objects through lenses of different cut, drew their father's attention to the magnifying effect.

Through these discoveries the human spirit learned for the first time to make instruments enabling observation at remote distances or study of the smallest detail. Modern astronomy, botany, zoology, anatomy, mineralogy and other special studies were made possible.

The period of greatest productivity of the Dutch genius coincided with an age when the folk spirit was seeking the spiritual sources of all progress. It was not merely a question of exploring the secrets of matter, but of the whole world. Three times towards the end of the sixteenth century, Dutch navigators tried to reach the Arctic regions. When their attempts failed, they turned towards the Antarctic. Again their journey was in vain; but this detracts in no way from the fact that Dutchmen were the first to penetrate the extreme north and south.

During this period Cornelius Houtman sailed to the East Indies. Almost at the same time, other Dutch seafarers reached America. The people whose interest was directed towards the world around them were thus offered new activities. The East India Company was founded for trade east of the Cape of Good Hope; the West India Company for trade in West Africa and America. Both companies were given customs privileges as well as the right to conclude treaties with native rulers, to frame their own laws and to establish trading centres. By the middle of the seventeenth century the Dutch colonial empire was as extensive as the realms of Spain or Portugal. It was not primarily a question of territorial possessions; what mattered was trade and the setting-up of industries. The necessary bases were gained through agreement with local rulers. Trade extended as far as China and Japan. Bases were established in the Malayan archipelago, in southern India, northern India, Ceylon, Persia, Arabia, and the Cape of Good Hope. The Companies had important trading centres on the west coast of Africa and a large empire in northern Brazil. Their activities also extended to the West Indian archipelago.

A continual stream of natural produce from all over the world reached Holland, though the chief concern was spices. Sumatra and Borneo supplied pepper, the Banda Islands nutmeg, Ceylon cinnamon. In Java, rice, coffee and sugar plantations were laid out and, to protect the Dutch spice monopoly in the Molucca Islands, the large clove plantations of the indigenous population were destroyed.

But the Dutch colonial empire soon disintegrated. First trade in the west collapsed, then in the east. The West India Company was dissolved in 1674; in the years between 1702 and 1747 when Holland was without a regent, the country's position as a major power came to an end.

In the middle of the seventeenth century, impelled by the Sense of Movement which had led the Dutch into the world, Walloon Huguenots crossed the Atlantic in a Dutch ship. The place where they landed later became New York. In commemoration of this event, King Albert of the Belgians was presented by the American government with a gold medal which depicted the landing. No further bold enterprises took their beginning in Belgium after the provinces of the southern Netherlands had recognized the authority of Philip II.

Under Spanish rule the Belgians were to lose their independence. After the wars of the Spanish Succession the southern provinces fell under Austrian rule. Towards the end of the century attempts were made to set up an independent republic, but Belgium had to submit to Austrian domination. Then France, moving against Austria, invaded and held the provinces, until in 1815 at the Vienna Congress they were united with Holland. In 1830 Belgium became an independent monarchy.

Some time later, as if by accident, this small country became a leading colonial power, thereby at last sharing, and developing in themselves, the great Netherlands impulse of the Sense of Movement. In 1870 Gordon Bennett, the proprietor of the *New York Herald* commissioned Stanley to look for the missing Livingstone. Stanley found Livingstone in 1871 at Ujiji, on Lake Tanganyika. Livingstone died two years later, but Stanley went on exploring. In 1876 King Leopold II called an international conference which led to the foundation of the International Association for the Exploration and Civilization of Africa. Later, the *Comité des Etudes du Haut Congo* and later still the Association of the Congo were founded.

After Stanley, who had traced the course of the Congo in 1877, had vainly tried to interest British business circles, he accepted King Leopold's suggestion to return there in 1878. He established bases and concluded treaties of friendship with local chiefs. King Leopold placed the Belgian Congo under the direct control of the crown, and in 1908 it became a Belgian colony. Through the enterprise and initiative of a single man of another nationality, Belgium, incapable of expanding by herself, was freed from a narrowness that had almost become part of her tradition.

In modern Holland the Sense of Movement can be traced even in simple everyday customs. Centuries ago, Pieter Brueghel, Jan van de Capelle, Aert van der Neer and Hendrik Avercamp painted the Netherlands landscape, animated by the movement of the skaters. The landscape of today with its many cyclists is scarcely less lively and gay than the scenes portrayed by the great Dutch masters.

The bicycle is Holland's chief mode of transport. Every family has its bicycles. In the open country and in villages, special paths are reserved for them along the main roads. Even the royal family cycles. It is an activity that corresponds to the need for individual movement. In train or aeroplane, motor car or tram, there is no need or even opportunity to move. The cyclist makes use of his limbs, and thereby becomes pleasantly aware of them.

One may well ask whether simple habits can be of exalted origin, for it is often thought that the realm of the spirit (if it exists at all) begins above the clouds, far beyond our day-to-day existence. But in reality, seemingly ordinary customs and popular traditions are often much purer and more direct manifestations of the spirit than contemporary philosophy. It is indeed a cause for wonder that humanity is still allowed to permeate life on Earth with cosmic impulses through simple activities or pastimes in which even the least brilliant can share. We are apt to think of divine beings as morose schoolmasters whose pride is offended if the children apply what they have learned, in their own way.

But it is quite possible to experience the world of the stars as a loving mother, who follows her growing children on their journey through life. She is pleased that the old tunes she sang to them have not been forgotten, and that they now accompany dance and play. But although the impulses from the constellation of the Virgin can express themselves in small things, they also demand earnest striving. In our age they can become a source of understanding for the secrets of the cosmos, which we must gain for the sake of the future of our planet.

Through knowledge of initiate wisdom, one can perceive how the folk spirit of the Netherlands reflected the creative deeds of the Godhead while the Dutch people established the ground of their country inch by inch. Through painting, the folk spirit created once more what had already been created; and found the means to bring closer to men the smallest unit of creation, no less than the world of stars in its infinity; and made the Dutch the most efficient colonizers in the world.

These activities have come to an end. Colonies were lost; scientific impulses went their ways; paintings sleep in museums. But the destiny of the soil has become part of the destiny of the whole Earth.

When Holland's vast inundated regions were freed from the waters by the work of man, the newly gained land was nursed and cultivated with the greatest devotion. Moon, Sun and stars watched over the well-being of its crops and animals. Though storms might blow the sand away, the sea might attack and the ground subside, nature's strengthening cosmic rhythm never ceased to permeate animals, plants and the soil.

All this has changed in the twentieth century. Animals are made to produce more than they naturally would, and plants and soil are similarly exposed to arbitrary influence. Artificial fertilizers subject the seed to fever and thirst; greedily it absorbs water and produces maximum crops. In Holland, the earth is subjected to chemical fertilizers more than in any other country. In consequence the soil is cut off from the enlivening influence of the cosmos, and the land behind the dunes, enfeebled and without power of resistance, is in greater danger than ever.

The night of the great storm from 31 January to the first day of February 1953, has made the Dutch people sense, though not always in full consciousness, that the greater part of their country can be reclaimed by the sea. The water level of the Atlantic, and therefore also the North Sea, is rising constantly, the soil of the country sinks in more and more and the atmosphere grows increasingly agitated.

The threat of the sea is fought with higher dykes. But to heal the soil, the Dutch people need an understanding for the whole life of cosmic evolution. He who would help nature must seek the mysteries of the Virgin constellation, must look in the direction to which the gaze of the folk spirit turns.

Until almost the end of the twentieth century the fourth corner of the Venus pentagon will point towards the sign of the Virgin and will then pass into that of the Lion. The guiding spirit of the Dutch people lives within sight of great cosmic transformations whose significance begins to be revealed to modern man; he beholds the Virgin secrets of divine alchemy.

The practical application of the wisdom of the Virgin is close to the deeper nature of the Dutch people whose everyday attitude proves that to live in the reality of things is in keeping with national character. But full reality demands an understanding of the spiritual facts of the starry worlds. Because the Dutch respect the world around them, their streets and houses are kept immaculate. Windows and furniture sparkle with cleanliness. This is reverence towards the works of man. Also, consideration is shown, not merely in the conventional sense, but in a vigorous and genuine manner.

A comparatively short path leads from genuine tact and care for dead objects to a realization that plants and domestic animals should also have their inherent needs considered and be kept in contact with cosmic forces. If the Dutch people develop increasingly their interest in the manifest world, they will also penetrate to an understanding of the facts behind the external phenomena. From a feeling for outer creation they can penetrate to the experience of cosmic creation, thereby lifting the veil the Virgin impulses lay before the eyes of the indifferent.

72

Plate 7. *Ancient Coat-of-Arms of Sweden.* A.D. 1360. (*Eric Magnus.*)

Plate 8. *Ancient Coat-of-Arms of Denmark.*

Plate 9. *Ancient Coat-of-Arms of Norway.*

Plate 10. *Hopperstad Stave Church.* (1130). Near the Sogn Fjord, Norway. View from the south.

Photograph by John Fletcher.

Plate 11. *Hopperstad Stave Church.* View from the south-east.

Photograph by John Fletcher.

Plate 12. *Carved Doorway from the west end of the now demolished Ål Stave Church* (1170). Hallingdale, Norway. It is considered the finest surviving Stav church doorway. We feel, on entering the church by such a doorway, that we have to face the image of animal instincts that lie hidden deep inside ourselves.

Reproduced by courtesy of the Universitets Oldsakamling, Oslo.

Plate 13. *Painted Chancel from the demolished Ål Stave Church* (c. 1275). The Crucifixion covers the whole of the east wall above the high altar of the magnificent painted chancel; on the west wall opposite, was painted the *Last Supper*. (The chancel was closed at the west end.) Below the Cross. Left: Mary and Longinus. Right: John, and the Synagogue, losing its crown. (Jewry overthrown.)

Reproduced by courtesy of the Universitets Oldsakamling, Oslo.

Plate 14. *The Wicked World.* By Hieronymus Bosch. (1415?–1516.) Forms a diptych with a panel called *World after the Flood.*

By courtesy of the Museum Boymans-van Beunigen, Rotterdam.

Plate 15. *Christ at Emmaus*. By Rembrandt, 1648. Panel 27 x 26 inches.

By courtesy of the Musée du Louvre, Paris.

Spain and Portugal

THE PEOPLE of the Spanish peninsula are linked with the Zodiacal region of the Scales: and the quality of that region, which brings a Sense of Balance as a particular challenge into their development, is still to be found on early star maps which picture a pendant balance.

The notation in use for the Sign, the astronomical measurement, of the Zodiac— ♎︎ —indicates a sunset, the daily setting beyond the sea. In Europe, by the autumn equinox, when the star ephemeris shows that sunrise is entering the Sign of the Scales, the Sun's activity in nature is drawing to a close. Summer fruits have been harvested, their forces stored in the seed. A feeling of age and maturity, a mood of quiet looking back upon past toil and striving is in the air. The Spanish folk soul is at home in this, for the Peninsula is abundantly rich in destinies fulfilled.

The history of Iberian civilization is ancient, far beyond written annals. The prehistoric early culture has left us cave paintings of outstanding perfection. These works of art from the childhood of humanity were discovered in 1879 by a five-year-old girl, Maria de Sautuola, playing in a cave alongside her father, an archaeologist. Looking towards the roof, she perceived the powerful animal figures. Since then many other frescoes have been found in Spain and southern France.

There are different views about the age and significance of these paintings. They clearly belong to a time before men in general knew how to handle tools or were able to observe nature. The human form as it is today was rarely if ever completely shown, though hands already appear. In the Altamira cave, a sixteen-foot frieze depicts nothing but hands. The priests who performed rituals at such places saw in hands the instruments of future skills and anticipated their dexterity so that it could later become universal. Subsequent tool cultures are a development of these skills.

While the West cultivated manual skill and observation of nature, the priesthood of the East sought another ideal, a human race able to think independently. The priests themselves had to pass through experience which prepared this faculty; the beginnings of conceptual thinking were first foreseen clairvoyantly in the ancient Indian civilization. But while remains of the European cave cultures and some of the tools of prehistoric man survived as tangible proofs and could be discovered, no trace is left of the Eastern cultures of the spirit which were little concerned with handling physical substances.

The two opposite tendencies continued together. The Palaeolithic Age corresponds to the earliest Indian civilization, and during the Neolithic Age the original Zarathustra founded a high Persian culture. The Bronze Age was contemporary with the Early Egyptian dynastic period, the Iron Age with the flowering of Greek philosophy. East and West thus laid their contributions on the scales of human development.

Aegean seafarers went to the Iberian Peninsula for its mineral resources. They were followed about 1000 B.C. by Phoenicians and by Celts from the north. Greek colonists settled later along the coast, and Carthaginians, called by the Phoenicians, penetrated into the interior. About 197 B.C. the Peninsula fell under Roman rule and was given the name Hispania.

In the first Christian centuries the country was invaded by Alans, Sveves and Vandals, against whom the Romans called in the Visigoths. In 415 Ataulphus and his legions crossed the Pyrenees, though a Visigothic empire was not securely established until 530. A struggle now began between the Romans who followed the Catholic-Athanasian creed and the Aryan Goths. At the Council of Toledo, King Reccared finally adopted Catholicism and asked his people, who still adhered to Aryanism, to do likewise. This was the beginning of incessant strife among the Goths and ended in their decline.

On the death of the last king, rivals anxious to secure their own power called in the Arabs who were to prove a heavy burden to the Spanish Peninsula. After only seven years they had conquered the whole country and began to invade France. Though defeated by Charles Martel at Poitiers, they kept their grip on Spain. Towards the end of the eighth century Charlemagne crossed the Pyrenees and pushed the Arabs back to the south. Early historians tell that he carried with him in his campaigns against the Moors the sacred spear of St. Maurice. With the repulse of the Arabs, part of the country was secured for further development and its Scales mission could materialize. In 778 Charlemagne created a Spanish March and his son, Louis the Pious, further enlarged the area. The Peninsula was now ready for the foundation of a series of smaller Christian kingdoms, which gradually displaced Arab influence so that a balance could be achieved between Christians and Mohammedans.

In the northern kingdoms formed in the course of the ninth century, Grail centres probably arose. Monserrat in Catalonia, St. Juan de la Pêne and Montreal-de-Sos are all said to have harboured the sacred vessel. But to the folk soul, the Holy Grail as fountainhead of spiritual progress, as the transforming substance for mankind, was not linked to one particular place.

As the Arabs founded centres of learning in Spain, a highly cultured civilization arose where the knowledge of the Holy Grail met with understanding. Wolfram von Eschenbach declared that his teacher, Master Kyot, had found in Toledo a book in Arabic that told of the Holy Grail. The Mohammedan sages who were connected with the vestiges of Eastern temple mysteries did not reject the Christian mystery wisdom, which by its very nature was open to those of other faiths. Wolfram tells that the Christian knight Gahmuret fought in the service of the Baruch of Baghdad and on his death in battle was given Christian burial and had a cross raised upon his tomb.

Gahmuret's sons were half-brothers: the light Parzival and the black and white Feirefiz, representative of Eastern humanity, whose mother was the Moorish queen, Belacane. Together they came to the Grail, and before the dark Feirefiz returned to his own country he took as his wife a servant of the Grail. Their son was the priest-king, John. Tales of his kingdom illustrate the flowering of Christian mysteries among Eastern humanity.

The origins of Basque mountain tribes in the Pyrenees go back to very early times. Their language differs completely from that of most known idioms. They guarded carefully their close family ties and remained without any cultural impulse. Completely withdrawn, they form the strongest possible contrast to the Arabs, who were full of enterprise and whose universities were unequalled in contemporary Europe. The deeds of the Carolingian king reflected beneficially on the Basques. Already in the ninth century they advanced to the Ebro region where they formed the Christian population of the kingdom of Navarre.

As the Grail movement brought a wider sense of the world, a church was built in the Spanish peninsula where future generations of seafarers would turn to pray before they set out on their voyages. Between 791 and 842, during the reign of Alfonso II, the relics of St. James were discovered and brought at the initiative of the king to Compostella, four miles from Flavia, where they had been buried originally. According to tradition, the Apostle had decided after the Resurrection to seek out all the tribes of Israel to bring them the Gospel. Eventually he came to Hispania.

Cuper, the Bollandist, who investigated the origins of this tradition, found it confirmed in many early manuscripts, amongst them the writing of St. Jerome and St. Isidore. It is also mentioned in the earliest breviary of Toledo and in the Arabic *Book of Anastasius*, Patriarch of Antioch. It is told that St. James returned to Jerusalem where he was beheaded in the year 44. His body was brought back to Spain.

After the foundation of Santiago de Compostella, the folk soul of the Spanish Peninsula stood within a task reflected, not in the hieroglyph, but in the very image of the Scales. In old star maps the pair of scales appears, complete with vertical centre bar, movable cross bar and two bowls.

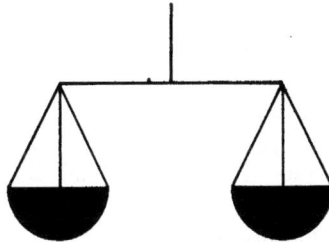

Scales have the characteristic of moving up and down. Translated to the human plane, this means a constant sway in the life of the soul, and throughout history. In the human body the sense of balance governs the relationship between left and right, forward and backward. If the body moves beyond a certain angle it falls. The relation between above and below is similarly ordered by the laws of the Scales. If man did not have within him a force that raises him upwards, he would have to crawl like a snake. If, on the other hand, he were completely at the mercy of the centrifugal force, he would be unable to stand still and would have to keep moving like a dervish. He would live in constant ecstasy. The central force holding him upright between above and below, forward and backward, left and right, is his personality.

Historically it is the mature individuality that keeps the balance of the Scales. In the eleventh century when Aragon began to consolidate, a helper arose for Spain, where the problem of Moslems and Christian living together had become increasingly serious. Roderigo Diaz, born in Burgos in 1030, became a national hero in his lifetime, and in ensuing centuries the subject of the Old Romances under the Spanish-Arabic title of El Cid Campeador—My Lord Conqueror. Bold yet unassuming, he was like the upright central force between opposing tendencies. In him both Christians and Arabs found a friend and helper. When the balance was disturbed by one or other side, the Cid intervened of his own will to help the weak.

His royal master, Ferdinand I, united the territories of Leon, Castile and Galicia and on his deathbed distributed his lands among his children, making them swear to keep the peace. The eldest, however, Don Sancho, attacked and defeated his brother Alfonso and banished him to Toledo where he enjoyed Mohammedan friendship. Sancho then tried to overthrow his second brother Garcia, the lord of Galicia. He was himself taken prisoner, but the Cid came to his aid and fought successfully against Garcia. Then Sancho attempted to take his sisters' lands but was murdered by a traitor from his own side. Alfonso could now return; and although the Cid had held high military office under Sancho, he remained at Alfonso's court until, by an unauthorized venture, Alfonso's distrust of him was renewed and he was exiled.

For several years El Cid then led campaigns for the Moors in Eastern Spain. In Saragossa he found the Mohammedan king, Almuctaman, threatened by his brother Alfabis. A struggle began between Mohammedans and Christians; the Cid fought for the Mohammedans yet took care that no harm should befall the King of Aragon and the Count of Barcelona. After Almuctaman's death there came a reconciliation with Alfonso which broke down. But to meet the invasion of the Almoravides, Alfonso, who knew the Cid's quality, was obliged to recall him. With Alfonso's approval his father-in-law, Benavit, King of Seville, hoping to drive the Moors out completely, had called in the Almoravides, wild African people from the Atlas region.

The new 'allies' attacked Seville and murdered its king. Yusuf, their powerful leader, forced all the Spanish Moors to acknowledge him as 'Lord of all Musulmans'. His Berber legions introduced a fanaticism that had been completely alien to the Spanish Arabs. The Cid now intervened to establish Alfonso's authority in the kingdom of Valencia, the centre of Moslem civilization in Spain. He received written assurance of the right to claim all territory he might in future conquer from the Moors. For several years he went on with the subjugation of Valencia and, through his courage, the city was taken in 1094 with only a small band of men.

He now founded his own principality where, influenced neither by Christians nor Moslems, he became the fair judge and protector of both. Through his own attitude he brought a period of mutual toleration, ruling according to his own law over Christians and Moslems and also over Jews, who had followed the Mohammedans into Spain. All could live in peace. He introduced no new taxes and twice a week he held court and was at everyone's disposal. 'Come to me' he said, 'and I will settle your quarrels, watch over your well-being and advise you as a friend and brother.'

Everywhere he spread confidence and contentment. He turned the largest mosque into a church and appointed a bishop; in this, again, he was acting on his own decision. Ceaselessly but in vain, Yusuf and his hordes attacked Valencia. The Cid died in 1099 and almost immediately his legend grew. It is said that on a journey to Santiago de Compostella, El Cid Campeador once met a sick beggar lying helplessly on the roadside. He put him on his horse, took him to an inn and shared his bed with him. When he woke up, the beggar had gone.

The Cid foresaw that the Spanish people would be at the mercy of great tensions in the future and would need an outlet for their fighting spirit. He therefore walled in an arena in Valencia where he introduced bullfighting. He is himself said to have killed bulls at Barcelona.

To the people the bull fights became occasions of importance. Passions could be roused in the spectators without causing harm. The Catholic Church at first banned bull-fighting, but Church and kings had to yield to popular pressure. Since then, on feast days and Sundays, the Spaniards have experienced fiery enthusiasm for skill and bravery, rage against needless cruelty, and every stage of joy and horror, so that after the performance they could reach a condition of contented balance.

At Cordova, at the court of the Almoravid invaders, lived a famous jurist, Ibn Rashid. His son, Abul Kasim, also won great fame; he was the father of Mohammed Ibn Rashid, called Averroës, the greatest and most universal of all Arab philosophers (c. 1126–1198). Through his brilliant intellect the philosophy that the Arabs had forged with Mohammedan incisiveness out of the Graeco-Oriental Gnosis reached its greatest flowering. He was introduced to King Abu-Yakub Yussuf by the famous philosopher Abn Bekir Ibn Tofeil, who recommended him as the only commentator of Aristotle.

Aristotle had translated ancient Mystery wisdom into concepts. In bringing form and clarity to human thinking he became the educator to freedom, which finds its support in thinking. His work was a milestone on the path of steadily growing consciousness.

But the way Averroës presented Aristotelian wisdom led in the opposite direction. He taught that human thinking could only be passive, although it could draw prophetic power from the sphere of the Moon if man prepared himself through asceticism. All men are one with the Earth and are gifted with an Earth intelligence into which the 'active intellect' works from outside. Only this soul substance, which shines into man for a time, has permanence. At death the individual soul passes into this sea of cosmic thought and the individuality flows back into the universal cosmic reason. Man has no life after death.

The event motivating this line of thought happened long before Averroës' time. It is connected with Gondi-Shapur in Persia, where Mani, the founder of Manichaenism, was crucified in the year 276. Mani, preparing a remote future, taught that the love awakened through the Christ impulse would one day be so great that evil could be transformed by thinking. To his disciples, he set the highest possible task of individual inner development.

When in 529 the Emperor Justinian had closed the schools of Greek philosophy which guarded the traditions of ancient wisdom, many of the teachers went to Gondi-Shapur where they founded an academy. On this basis, anti-Christian circles planned in the seventh century to develop human faculties in the world from the year 666 onwards, thus leading mankind away from its true progress.

The intention was the spiritual conquest of the entire known civilized world in Europe and Asia. The growing Christ impulse in the souls of men demanded that the personality should unfold, so that it could develop higher spiritual faculties through a thinking that understands the course of the world. But Gondi-Shapur, through the gift of visions, aimed to banish man to the Earth and to deprive him of the ability to develop.

77

He was to be taught a wisdom that, while it offered a profound insight into the spiritual nature of man, denied the principle of moral development—the chief impulse of a truly understood Christianity—in humanity. It was a wisdom seeking to turn man into a kind of great cosmic automaton.

Such intentions take time to mature; the spiritual world meanwhile tended to work in the opposite direction. In 622, Mohammed inaugurated Islam, which rapidly swept the East, countering the impulse of Gondi-Shapur—then Djundaisabur—with a force that took away its poisonous sting. The city was conquered by the Mohammedans in 641. Orthodox Moslems despised the study of pagan sciences as a deadly sin against the *Koran*: others drank in the wisdom of Gondi-Shapur. The fierce struggle between strict followers of the *Koran* and the Islam of philosophic universalism acted as a lasting balance against the aims of Gondi-Shapur.

Baghdad, founded in 762 where a centre of trade and travel had existed since Sumerian times, became a new cultural centre whence this two-fold Arabism radiated its magic light. With an intellectualism premature in evolution, Averroës presented the borrowed, mystically attuned Arab wisdom in such a way as to impede human thinking again and again. While he still lived, his works were translated into Latin and brought across the Pyrenees into Europe from Toledo.

Against his vision of the world which later influenced the Catholic Church, Thomas Aquinas and Albertus Magnus were to battle in a life-and-death struggle. From now on the shadow of the crucified thinking faculty hung threateningly over all striving for knowledge and scientific research.

Spain's smaller Christian kingdoms, at first hostile, later combined through marriages. Castile and Aragon, the only independent states left, developed along separate lines. While Aragon's interest was turned abroad, Castile became a consolidating element within the peninsula, gradually creating an inner stronghold, a real ' castle ' wresting Toledo, Cordova, Seville, Cadiz, Algeciras and Gibraltar from the Arabs. Only Granada remained in Moorish possession. In Aragon, Pedro III married Constance of the house of Hohenstaufen, and when Conradin, the last of the Hohenstaufen, was beheaded at Naples at the instigation of Charles of Anjou, Pedro avenged his death with a terrible massacre. In the ensuing peace of Caltabellotta, Naples and Sicily were united with Aragon.

Caltabellotta was the ancient Calot Bobot, an Arabic name meaning ' Rock of the Oaks '. This sombre castle in the wild Sicilian mountains had been captured by the Moors in 840. There was another contemporary ' Rock of the Oaks ', Kalat-el-bellut, near Cordova, and in the ninth century secret links appear to have existed between the two in the anti-Grail spirit of Gondi-Shapur.

It is said that the magician Virgilius, a blood relation of Klingsor, had founded a school of black magic at Naples, where teachers from Spain were active. Klingsor was lord of Calot Bobot. Through the Peace of Caltabellotta, residues of sinister impulses came to life in Spain at a time when the outward manifestations of Arab rule had disappeared.

Spain's power increased enormously. In 1469, Ferdinand of Naples married Isabella of Castile and on his father's death became king of Aragon. They combined their domains to a united kingdon. Two impulses were now active side by side—the one dark and contracting, the other expansive and health-giving—both equally intense. The former was connected with the Inquisition, the latter with the voyages of discovery.

Ferdinand and Isabella, strict followers of Rome, did not hesitate to use the most extreme methods in subjecting the country to Church and papacy. In 1483 Castile resumed the Inquisition which had been introduced once before. In the same year they were granted the right to appoint bishops, and Aragon also set up the Inquisition, which became a royal institution. Heretic Christians and Moors were burned in thousands under the first Grand Inquisitor. 160,000 Jews were expelled. Even the bishops of Segovia and Calahorra had to leave the country because of their Jewish origin. The Mohammedans, who had hitherto lived peacefully next to the Christians in the regions where they had formerly held political control, and also the Jews, were charged, expelled and even killed. On the mosque of Cordova, gold letters had proclaimed since Moorish rule: ' The Caliph of Cordova guarantees the Christians freedom of worship.'

The court of the Inquisition now sat daily under this very inscription condemning men and women to torture and death at the stake for their religious convictions. But the friendship the Spanish Christians had felt for their Moslem brothers was by no means extinguished.

The romances of Granada, which describe the struggle for that kingdom, are a lasting document of understanding and compassion. It is known that they were written by Christians, who could feel completely at one with their persecuted Moslem compatriots. Later, Ginez de Hita incorporated many of these tales into a historical novel about the civil wars in Granada.

Portugal placed conciliation and restitution in the fateful Scales of the Iberian Peninsula. Its first step towards independence had been taken when El Cid Campeador attempted to master the Scales mission. In 1097, Henry of Burgundy, who had come from France to help in the struggle against the Saracens and who eventually married the daughter of the King of Aragon, was granted the region between Mino and the Douro river. He later called himself Count of Portugal.

The country had to assert its independence again and again in fierce and prolonged wars against the Saracens. Throughout these, it had the help of the Templars. The Order of the Templars was founded in Jerusalem in 1119. A few years later the mother of Alfonso I of Portugal gave them Coimbra and Leiria as protection.

King Alfonso himself became a Templar and gave them Souro ' out of love for the Order and because he, as a brother, had shared in its blessings.' With the Templars' help he conquered Lisbon after a long siege. The Moors who remained in the city in large numbers were given a charter promising full protection against Christians and Jews.

When the ruler of the Almohades in Africa and Andalusia sent a vast army against Portugal, the aged king met the enemy at Santarem with a small band of supporters. When he had lost his horse he fought the vastly superior powers on foot. This king stood under special spiritual protection and knew that Portugal's mission was willed by higher beings.* Suddenly he beheld the Archangel Michael's winged arm fighting at his side and leading him and his knights to victory.

---

* Throughout history, certain individualities have had this gift of higher knowledge. (Editor.)

King Deniz was born in 1261 on the day of St. Dionysius the Areopagite. A wise judge and counsellor, he tried to balance all injustice. He fought the abuses of the Church in Portugal, at the same time protecting it against oppression: though he curbed the power of the aristocracy he encouraged their better aims. He supported the Portuguese knights of the Order of Santiago and saved that of the Templars in Portugal by dispersing it in the hour of danger, bringing it to life once more when the threat had passed.

The Templars had been active in the country for nearly two centuries and of their loyalty there could be no doubt. In a papal bull of 1317, King Deniz was asked to attend the Council of Vienna where the wrongful activities of the Templars were to be discussed. The following year the Bishop of Lisbon was instructed to give the most careful scrutiny to their mode of life. The King held the Order to be innocent, but he knew it to be in great danger and therefore looked for ways to protect it without offending against the Pope's command.

His plans were bold indeed. He started legal proceedings against the Order—yet not a single knight was arrested. Instead, the Templars left the country. Their estates were taken over by the crown or, where ownership was a matter of dispute, sequestrated. When the papal bull was eventually made public in Portugal, the Order had ceased to exist. The King was accused of avarice and injustice, but filled with the strength of conciliation, he awaited calmly the course of events. In 1318 a papal bull announced the foundation of the Order of Christ. Its rules agreed in every detail with those of the Templars. King Deniz thereupon declared invalid any legal decision awarding him the Templars' estates. All their movable and immovable goods and all their rights and privileges were granted to the Order of Christ.

The knights of the Order were paid the accumulated revenues due to the Templars, and in addition he presented Castro-Marim in Algarve to the new Order. The first to be welcomed there by the Grand Master, the Master of the Avis Order, were Templar knights. At a chapter held at the house of the Templars in Lisbon when most of the participants were former Templars, the Order of Christ was given new statutes.

The measures taken by the King were to bear fruit in later years. While he was active in saving the Templar knights, he was having firs planted on the hills of Leiria to protect the land from constant sandstorms. These conifer forests later supplied the timber for ships sent out by the Order of Christ. Portugal still had to fight many battles against Aragon and Castile who tried to bring the country under their domination.

The final victory was achieved by King John and his friend Nuno Alvares Pereida in the battle of Ajubarrota. The truly heroic fighters and their small band of supporters lived in the realm of ideals of the Holy Grail and King Arthur's Round Table. Their courage secured Portugal's independent future. Their battle cry was ' St. George.'

John's son, Henry the Navigator, inaugurated the great voyages of discovery. As Grand Master of the Order of Christ he could use the funds of the Order in connection with this task. He collected the nautical, geographical and astronomical knowledge which made possible those journeys into unknown regions. (Plate 16.)

The Portuguese voyages had a religious basis in contrast to those of the Dutch seafarers a hundred years later, who were impelled by the Sense of Movement and an interest in the created world. The members of the Order of Christ carried in their souls the image of the

Priest-King John, whose kingdom they hoped to find. It was as if a call from the Holy Grail had fired their search for distant continents, for the knowledge of the priest-king, son of the black and white Feirefiz, had been guarded by the Templars. An age was prepared when the whole Earth would receive a new impulse through an all-embracing human consciousness.

This future is inscribed as a possibility in the stars of the Scales. Long ago the heavenly Scales were a cosmic altar where the sacrifices of divine light beings could rise to the highest spheres. Through Christ the Earth has become the future altar of the solar system, on which the deed of dedication can be performed by free men as a result of the Mystery of Golgotha.

The Priest-King John exemplified the fulfilment of this ideal for he united three streams of humanity hallowed by the life of Christ. The shepherds in the fields were representatives of the priestly stream. They were receptive to nature, protected their flocks and beheld the angels. The kings, the wise men from the East, represented those whose heads are crowned with the radiance of cosmic wisdom.

Since their time, the acquiring of a deeper insight in full responsibility could become a truly royal deed. The Johannine stream took hold of St. Paul at Damascus, when despite his inner darkness, he beheld the Risen Christ. This is the stream of mercy that makes all men equal before God. The full development of these three streams within the individual, as in the Priest-King John, leads to the spiritualization of the Earth.

The coat-of-arms of the Order of Christ is like an indication of this new Earth. It shows the Earth with north, south, east and west forming a cross that points beyond the Earth, over which runs a broad band. To the Portuguese the voyages were soul adventures, demanding careful preparation. How they would endure the many trials, even where they would land, they did not know. They knew only that their time had come. Even outwardly, their undertaking was an impulse of the Templars, who had fought the Mohammedans and had placed all their gifts in service of Christ. But the Holy Sepulchre that they had guarded was lost again.

About 1300, many leading spirits of the time, among them Raimundus, suggested that an attempt should be made to check the power of the Moslems who not only controlled the Near East and North Africa, but dominated the routes to India. A year before his arrest, Jacques de Molay, the Grand Master of the Order of the Templars submitted a plan to the Pope with this end in view.

A hundred years later, Henry the Navigator took up the same proposals. He sent emissaries to Pope Nicholas V, who then issued a bull confirming Portuguese jurisdiction over all newly-discovered territories as far as India.

Henry settled at Algarve near San Vincento, the *Promontorium Sacrum* of antiquity where a Saturn sanctuary had once stood. There he dwelt at the bay of Sagres, though every trace of his stay was later removed. But even until last century, ships would lower their sails in greeting in passing this spot. (Plate 17.)

In this tranquil place he prepared the great voyages of discovery. Annually he equipped ships to explore the west coast of Africa. In the course of time Portugal could thus acquire Porto Santo, Madeira, the Cape Verde Islands and Senegal. When Henry died in 1460 his work was continued by the Order of Christ, and thirty years later his plans were close to their fulfilment. Bartholomeu Diaz reached the southernmost tip of Africa. Vasco de Gama landed in India in 1498. He had carried on his ship fully armed knights and artillery. During the subsequent defeat of the vast Indian armies, a white knight played an important part. His appearance made the Indians withdraw. The vision was not seen by the Portuguese.

In 1505 Francisco Almeida was sent to India as Portugal's first governor-general. Aden at the entry to the Red Sea, Ormuz on the Persian Gulf, Malacca on the way to China were conquered, and ruled from Goa in India; settlements were established in Ceylon and trading was carried on with China and Japan. All the riches brought back to Portugal were used to equip further journeys.

Spain's discoveries were connected with Portugal but sprang from a different background. Christopher Columbus came to Lisbon where he conceived a desire to sail westward to discover India, the country of mystery. It is thought that his services, offered to Portugal, were rejected. His motives were different from those of the members of the Order of Christ. From Queen Isabella of Spain, he demanded as reward for his prospective undertaking the rank and title of Admiral of the Seas for all the countries he might discover, as well as the title of Viceroy, and a tenth of all the metals found there. In 1492 an agreement was signed between him and the royal house. He intended to find Japan and to establish relations with the Great Khan: instead, he discovered America.

From now on, the Scales destiny of the Spanish Peninsula assumed increasing importance in world history. The Earth was divided into two parts. The Treaty of Tordesillas laid down that all territories west of a certain line in the Atlantic should belong to Spain, those to the east, to Portugal. The demarcation line ran a hundred miles west of the Azores.

In spite of this the Portuguese explorer Cabral landed in Brazil, which became a Portuguese possession. In 1529 the Pope, through the Treaty of Saragossa, fixed another line in the Pacific between these two peoples who, though related, were yet polar opposites. A clear balance was thus established between East and West.

In the East, the Portuguese sector, the voyages of discovery which brought contact with other races and creeds led to no problems that might have endangered Portugal's mission. The destiny of Spain took a different course. Already the companions of Columbus proved rapacious and ignorant. He himself sent the first five boat-loads of Indians to Seville, to be sold as slaves. Later, after Cortes had gained his first victory over the Indians near Tabasco, Montezuma, the Aztec Emperor of Mexico who had at first resisted, sent him a miniature sun of pure gold and other temple treasures.

The Aztecs were at that time looking for the return of Quetzalcoatl, the divine hero of Toltec mythology, and took the new arrivals for beings of a higher world. But to maintain the conquest, fierce struggles took place and many Indians were killed. From now on, the gold of the Mexican temple treasures flowed to Spain and greed for gold took hold of the Spanish ruling house. The originally Christian impulse to navigation and discovery turned to its opposite through the crimes of the conquerors.

In 1495 the successor to the Spanish throne, Joanna the Mad, married Prince Philip, son of the Emperor Maximilian I. It was said of their son, Charles V, that the Sun never set in his kingdom. Philip II, the son of Charles V and Isabella of Portugal, was the first Hapsburg ruler to be born in Spain. The Spanish people accepted him completely. Spanish power,

82

Spanish dignity and Spanish faith were his power, his dignity and his faith. He loved the Inquisition, for he was filled with a blindly ecstatic belief in the Church that stood behind the institution.

To him, life was a brief hour of decision between eternal salvation and eternal damnation, and he wanted to rescue whole nations, indeed the whole of mankind, from the clutches of hell. He strove for the absolute rule of the Roman Catholic Church, then threatened by the Reformation, and for a rebirth of medieval life under Spanish protection. Since he never gave open orders, he generated a creeping fear that spread throughout Europe; the fear of Catholic universal monarchy, the fear of Hapsburg rule.

When the direct line of succession became extinct in Portugal in 1580, Philip had the country invaded under the command of the Duke of Alva. The subsequent union of the two countries and the introduction of the Inquisition were the beginning of Portugal's decline. Though Portugal regained her independence sixty years later, her leading position in the world had passed to Holland. Philip became involved in war with England and in 1588 his fleet, the Armada, was lost. This catastrophe brought relief. Spain had lost Holland, and England and France now stood outside her sphere of influence.

High on a rock in the Guadarrama mountains Philip raised a vast palace and monastery, El Escorial, dedicated to St. Lawrence. It needed great persuasion to prevent the workmen from leaving for a story went round that Satan, in the form of a winged dog, could be heard screaming in the Escorial at night. When the building was finished this King, under whom the Spanish people had seen an age of unparalleled power and world domination, lived as a monk with the others. For hours he would kneel before a crucifix. Amid the sombre magnificence of this setting, he died in 1598.

In El Greco's *Dream of Philip II*, the King is shown kneeling in a dark landscape, between visions of heaven and hell, his two overpowering worlds. This painting is a true Scales picture. It recalls an early Spanish fresco, reproduced on the cover of a Unesco publication about Spain, where the Scales appear with an angel behind one bowl and a devil behind the other. was called *St. Michael and the Balance of Souls* and was painted in the thirteenth century by Valle de Ribes. (Plate 18.) The same book had an even more dramatic Scales picture in which a human figure is shown with the beam—a saw—passing through his breast. Red devils take the place of the bowls.* The wound they make with the saw begins at the head and moves towards the heart. Demonic powers aim to destroy man's individuality. The word 'individuality' is related to *dividere*, to divide: the individuality is the indivisible in man. This picture dates from the end of the eleventh century, the time when El Cid Campeador, through the radiance of his individuality created in the peoples of the Spanish Peninsula the foundation for a healing balance between the Scales tendencies. (Plate 19.)

El Greco, nearly five centuries later, played a similar part. He was born in 1541 in Crete, and he belonged to the Greek Orthodox Church. No one knows why he united his destiny with Spain of the great contrasts. Shortly after his arrival he was officially asked why he had come. His answer was: 'I am under no obligation to tell anyone why I came.'

El Greco tried to create balance to all one-sidedness. As his home he chose Toledo, the

---

* *The Martyrdom of St. Julita.*

' city of races ' and the centre of Spanish fanaticism. He lived in the despised Jewish quarter and even painted a Jew who could have been none other than the secret leader of Spanish Jewry, which outwardly had ceased to exist.

Though deeply religious, El Greco allowed the clergy no say in his work. Almost as a challenge to danger he remained true to himself. He painted ascetic pictures, yet he lived in a house with thirty rooms and slept under a red canopy. He had no ambition to be a saint. He was both a man of the world and an admirer of St. Francis, whom he painted again and again. Working in full independence at the very core of ecclesiastical and secular authority, he took the duality of the Spanish character into his heart and gave it balance. His work was to belong to the people he had chosen and to whose greatness he contributed. Yet he never became a Spanish subject, but wished to remain the alien wanderer who had ceased wandering.

El Greco fully experienced the remoteness of his age from Christ. Many times, he painted the Cleansing of the Temple, with Christ in a glowing flame-like red robe in the doorway, flanked by the young money-changers on the left and the old Pharisees on the right. He also painted the loneliest of all representations of Christ on the Cross. The large figure of the Crucified One hangs on a cross which occupies almost the entire picture. Behind it is nothing but sombre clouds, against an even darker sky. Below, at the sides, are two men, one in white and one dressed in black, the representatives of the Church and the world. Christ's face is turned from both. In his deep suffering, He is entirely alone. Between the two world tendencies, through His death on the Cross He is the healing third. (Plate 20.)

So far, El Greco has been the only painter able to portray in its full significance the Agony in the Garden: the fully conscious acceptance of the cup of destiny from the hands of the angel. El Greco, too, had received from higher hands the task he carried out in courage and humility. He died in 1614.

Miguel de Cervantes died two years later. Cervantes had portrayed the duality of the Spanish character in his novel, *Don Quixote*. Don Quixote, the knight, is idealistic, generous and brave. He lives in dreams that he takes for reality, he fights non-existent enemies and develops courage in overcoming imaginary difficulties. Sancho Panza his servant is only interested in food, drink and comfort. Both are at first ridiculous, but in the course of the story they inspire compassion, and even love.

Don Quixote, translated into every European language, has been reprinted innumerable times. Next to the Bible it became the most widely read book in the world. When a certain line of thought is felt to be of importance by large numbers of people, it usually expresses a reality more significant than first appearances would suggest. Cervantes—perhaps without being conscious of it—looked towards those spiritual beings who tempt the soul into onesidedness.

In a simple humorous manner he touched on the greatest of all such problems humanity has to face in the course of its development. The legions of tempters that influence the individual are not a united demonic world, but chiefly two groups of fallen angels who arouse different experiences within the soul. One group consists of the bearers of deceiving light and illusion, the other of the spirits of heaviness who try to chain man to the Earth. Cervantes portrays both tendencies.

Idealistic striving in Don Quixote is carried to the point of caricature in the search for an illusory world, while Sancho Panza's interests do not extend beyond down-to-earth matters. Through his book the great Spanish poet addressed himself to the universal human gift for keeping the balance between extremes.

His message is moral, yet he does not moralize. All who could share in the adventures of the noble but foolhardy knight and the cowardly, comfort-loving Sancho Panza could thus develop their own inherent courage and calm selfless love. Cervantes led men to a clearer experience of a Sense of Balance.

To stand, fully conscious, between contrasting worlds can mean a profound inner struggle. This is described by the greatest representative of the Spanish spirit in the twentieth century, Miguel de Unamuno, an exile from his own country, who said of himself that his inner reality 'was the reality of the whole Spanish people.' He wrote in explanation of his *Agony of Christianity*:

> What I am trying to put before the reader is my own agony, my struggle for Christianity. The agony of Christianity is within me, its death and resurrection are in every moment of my life . . .
>
> Christ has come to bring us agony, war and not peace. Peace is a peace granted to us in war, just as war comes to us in peace . . . thus it happens that Christianity is in conflict with Christ, in agony.

He looked at historical events and weighed them. In comparing the Sadducees and Pharisees, he saw between them St. Paul. Regarding dogma and heresy, faith and doubt, he showed how the contrasts support each other, for dogma thrives on heresy, and faith on doubt. He saw the working of extremes everywhere. He looked at the life of the soul and wrote:

> Everyone truly human carries within him the seven cardinal virtues and their opposite, the seven deadly sins. He is proud and he is humble, restrained and yet greedy, voluptuous yet chaste, envious yet generous, lazy yet industrious, irate yet patient. And he finds in himself the substance of tyrant and slave, of criminal and saint, of Cain and Abel.

Unamuno also spoke of the cardinal point whence the contrasts of the soul can be kept in balance. He asked: 'What is the profoundest, the most creative, the most real element within man?' And answered:

> He who longs to be truly human. And I maintain that this man who longs to be truly human is the creator within him, that is, in his innermost being it is he who is the truly real human being. And it is through what we longed to be, and not through what we really were that we shall be redeemed or damned . . . The truly real man, the *homo realis*, who is entirely *res*—that is, cause, for only what is active really exists—is the true creator.

Every individual and the whole of humanity stand within the tensions the Spanish people had to bear as historical destiny. Through sharing in the extremes the folk spirit tried to bridge, the Spaniards became a proud people; in Spain's noblest representatives, this pride made them aware and self-assured in their mission. Grown to inner maturity through Spain's past, the worthy son of the Iberian folk spirit can become like an experienced judge who, conscious of the extremes within his soul, is no longer deterred by them.

Britain

BRITAIN BELONGS to the realm of the Scorpion, which was perceived in ancient times as an Eagle, striving in the world of spirit with powerful golden wings.

As the vision from the heights gradually grew dim, the eagle turned into the earth-bound scorpion. But the scorpion too will change: it will become a white dove. The British folk spirit has been faithful to the fulfilment of these changes, patiently accepting them and demanding that its people should not rest content with ancient gifts but should move forward to future tasks.

Yet, when the light of ancient wisdom is abandoned the spirit itself seems an illusion, and death the only reality. This is a state of transition; for out of such darkness can come a new sense of brotherhood that will overcome death. Wisdom, sacrificed, becomes love.

Britain, as the country that accepts death, was the first to develop a natural science for which death is the end of existence. Yet not long afterwards the inhabitants of the British Isles began to learn something else: the transformation of force into a will for reconciliation. The peace that is striven for as a great English aim is only seemingly passive; it is really an active acceptance of those who are different, and in practice takes the form of a readiness to help.

Anyone who has cruised above a lake in an open aeroplane may have experienced the sky above and the water below as seemingly identical worlds; and descending, may have felt the proximity of the sky as he looked at the reflection in the water.

Flying over the region round Glastonbury, we can see images of the Zodiac pictures impressed into the landscape in gigantic forms: the Lion, portions of the Scorpion and the Archer, the Goat, the Waterman and others in the sequence. Aerial photographs reveal them as forming a circle twelve miles in diameter; the fixed star constellations are recognised in water runs, old paths, woods, hills, rammed earth walls, moors and fields.*

The temple priests responsible for these copies did not look up into the cosmos to find inspiration but raised their souls above the Earth, to look down as does the eagle. In the dark realm below of Annwen, the earthly world, they saw Caer Sidi, the Zodiac, reflected, and what they saw they built into landscape forms.

Neither did they find the soul of the cosmos in the stars. They looked for its manifestations on Earth and worshipped it as Ceridwen, who in her cauldron brewed elixirs from all kingdoms of nature. Cosmic memories of creation bubbled in her magic potion and those who drank of it could acquire new faculties. The drink of Ceridwen was the draught of inspiration and poetry.

---

* *A Guide to Glastonbury's Temple of the Stars,* by K. E. Maltwood. James Clarke & Co. Ltd.

Legend tells that King Arthur thirsted for this drink. He still lived in the sphere of the all-surveying eagle consciousness, among the seven stars of the Great Bear. To gain the potion of Ceridwen he had to descend through the realms of the planets, from castle to castle, until he found in deep darkness the cauldron that did not cook for cowards. There, a fiery sword shone towards him.

'King Arthur' was the name given to a degree of initiation that could be held by only one person at a time. There has been a succession of Kings of the Round Table, which is a picture of the circle of the heavens. Tintagel, the royal castle, stands on a rock rising steeply from the sea and is now connected with the mainland by a footpath. Here King Arthur assembled his knights: within their circle he was the Sun and his consort, Guinevere, was the Moon.

Looking down from the height of the rock they could see how Christ, in the working of the elements, was approaching the Earth. His spirit-form appeared to them in the rushing of the wind, the spray of the waves, in the colours revealed by the play of water, air and light. They set themselves the task of protecting the bright and the good and of fighting the evil that lived as dragons and monsters in the darkness of Annwen.

The religious culture of the Celts was led by the Druids. The stone circles where they celebrated their rites, and the dolmens in whose shadow they observed transitions between light and darkness as the interaction of the forces of heaven and earth, were distributed all over the British Isles, from Wales and Southern England to Scotland and Ireland.

The Romans called the Druids 'Apollo's people'. Diodorus reported of the island that it had been the birthplace of Apollo and that its inhabitants therefore worshipped Apollo above all other gods. He tells of a beautiful Apollo temple on the island, round in shape, and of a city likewise dedicated to the god. Most of the people played the harp and their temples resounded with music and song in praise of Apollo. The vast round temple may well have been Avebury or Stonehenge. (Plates 21, 22.)

This Sun culture found outward expression through the Bards, who preceded the Druids. They spread their wisdom in the bardic *Triads*, poems in three parts, containing the sacred truths. But these were not written down until very much later. It was said in them: There are three branches of wisdom: wisdom connected with God, wisdom relating to man, and wisdom towards oneself. Three things are part of never-ending growth: fire or light, understanding or truth, the soul or life. These three will conquer everything and the state that was at the beginning will then be no longer. The Triads, part word, part music, were the fruit of a deep knowledge of body, soul and spirit.

The victory of peace over lawlessness and brute force through the power of song and poetry was the highest aim of the Bards, as it was the aim of King Arthur's knights who were also Bards. It was through the Bards that the legends about King Arthur were chiefly spread.

The most important and hidden European Mysteries were those of Ireland, Hibernia. The priests of those Mysteries could unite their souls with the trinity of all existence. Later, when the Holy Child was born in Palestine, those Irish temple priests were able to read the event in the spiritual aura of the earth, and the whole people celebrated with them.

St. Patrick was able to unite what had been active in Ireland's past with his own Christian experience. After him a universal Christianity, unparalleled elsewhere, awakened in the island. Through St. Columba this Christianity found its way to Scotland. Today, the ancient Celtic crosses rising against the sky in Ireland, Scotland and northern England survive as monuments of those times. (Plate 23.)

From the Irish monasteries, which were great centres of learning, monks were sent out to the heart of Europe. Like Christ and the Apostles, like King Arthur and his Knights, they were always one and twelve, the image of the Sun and the Zodiac.

The travelling monks were taught to fix the time of Easter by the position of Sun and Moon. Like their brothers in Ireland, they celebrated Easter in days when, after the spring equinox, the Earth is lit day and night by Sun and Moon. By the sixth and seventh centuries, the ancient clairvoyance was already dying and the Irish could not realize that the light of the Christ no longer radiated towards man and nature from outside, but was increasingly seeking to enter the human soul in order to shine into the cosmos from the Earth. The festival of Easter is therefore no longer dependent only on external light.

The nature of this change from the worship of Christ in the heights to that of Christ on Earth was understood at the centres of the Holy Grail in the ninth century. The Grail vessel, in the form of the waning moon, could be experienced as the image of Earth, illumined from within by the light of the Risen One. The Grail impulse came to England in the reign of King Alfred whose mother, Judith, had been the daughter of Charles the Bald, the grandson of Charlemagne. Probably through this connection Alfred came to know Scotus Erigena, the Irish sage, to whom he offered lodging at Malmesbury.

Scotus was the last to survey the world in majestic eagle consciousness. In his book, *De Divisione Naturae*, he speaks of the Godhead where all beings originate, from the highest hierarchies to the lowliest creatures. Through the Logos as intermediary, they will all return to God. Scotus died in 877, murdered at the altar of St. Michael's Chapel in Malmesbury. It is said that monks stabbed him to death with pins.

His martyrdom marked the beginning of Britain's drama which unfolded historically in dynamic scenes and powerful images. The British Isles, placed in front of the European continent, became the stage of a world theatre, where the transition from pre-Christian vision to Christian insight was performed through all its phases.

The Drama

English history represents the gradual establishment of conditions necessary for the creation of modern consciousness. The scientific trend of thought familiar to everyone in our time was first introduced into the world through the English people.

The materialistic tendency of natural science was a basic preparation for the individual experience of freedom which has to be reached in the course of human evolution. Step by step, historical events in the British Isles led in this direction.

The ancient clairvoyance was rooted in the blood that had flowed through past generations. In Britain the blood had to be mixed, and freed from the forces of the past. The first loosening began through Anglo-Saxon invasions in the sixth century and continued through Norse invasions in the ninth. In 1016 King Canute the Great of Denmark occupied almost the whole of England; after the death of the King of Wessex he gained control of that region also, for a generation. Half a century later, the Battle of Hastings brought the victory of the French Normans.

In 1154, Henry II, then aged nineteen, ascended the throne of England. Of both French and English blood, he was not bound by an ancient, one-sided spiritual inheritance. But remains of Druid spirituality were still active, particularly in Scotland, Wales and Ireland. In a half-dreamy state as if looking down from heights, people still felt related to the life of nature where they could find poetry and inspiration. The disappearance of this link with the cosmos was experienced as a great tragedy. Before the loss of this consciousness could take full effect a point of rest had to be established—a visible place of sacrifice and worship that could turn into a source of strength and inner concentration. This spiritual rock was the shrine of Thomas à Becket.

Immediately after Henry's coronation Becket became Chancellor through the influence of Bernard of Clairvaux. When the Archbishop of Canterbury died, Becket succeeded him, again through the influence of St. Bernard. After having been the King's friend and adviser for many years, now he had to oppose him. He was forced to flee to France, his life threatened. Aware of his mission, however, he decided to return to Canterbury and there he was killed on the steps of the altar on 29 December, 1170.

The sword with which he was killed later became one of the nation's relics and the shrine where he was buried was for hundreds of years a famous centre of pilgrimage and was loved by those who saw in it a place not worshipped from inner vision, but because a historic event had occurred there and because it harboured the remains of a man who had suffered martyrdom on English soil.

It is said that in the reign of Henry II, King Arthur's grave was found and his body dug up and scattered to the winds. The impulses of the Round Table could now be considered destroyed. But in the death of an ancient tradition there was already germinating the British Parliamentary system. Formerly the knights had sat with King Arthur at the Round Table, hearing stories of the troubles and distresses of the times; and then they would go out to put things right. As if from distant memory, people in Britain still love to sit in a circle to discuss events near and far and to achieve common understanding for opposing points of view.

This attitude became decisive in the development of Parliament, which grew into an instrument for settling differences and a centre where king, Church and barons on the one hand, and knights and citizens on the other sat together and discussed every aspect of administration. Parliament could thus act with the full will and authority of the people.

In the way the English Constitution developed, the Arthur impulse could once more assert itself. When the knights of the Round Table prepared for action their decisions were made out of a reverence for the laws of the cosmos which for them were direct experience. In a similar way the Constitution accompanied the consciousness of the English people as a purely spiritual reality, a central force from which the social organism drew its strength.

In the thirteenth century a pioneer of coming tasks appeared. This was Roger Bacon who was born about a year before the signing of the Magna Carta and who died in 1294. He was no bringer of glad tidings but a morose and sinister personality, displeased about everything he encountered. Though he himself still had roots in tradition, he yet rejected all past and contemporary thought. Accepting only physical observations he became the pioneer of experimental science, standing out against his time in lonely greatness.

In the Hundred Years' War Britain tried, against her true destiny, to gain lasting dominion over France. The secluded insularity of Britain's character was essential to her mission. St. Joan of Arc, who became the personification of French courage, brought about this isolation.

Meanwhile the blood relationships which had been the vehicle of ancient clairvoyance lived on into the fifteenth century. But so much of the blood of the aristocracy was spilt through the Wars of the Roses that these outlived faculties were greatly weakened. Nothing now stood in the way of the rise of modern England.

The Scorpion age first entered an active phase in the sixteenth century. The action of the drama that now began appears like a mythological tale, full of horrors and grandeur. In the light of esoteric wisdom it becomes clear that the British archangel was resolved to complete the sacrifice of the old to give room to new and vigorous impulses.

When mythology, the image of divine plans in the form of stories, turns into historical event, the feelings and intentions of earthly men work into the process. There are often great souls whose physical and emotional constitution enable them to play parts on the stage of history, parts understood and taken on in the life before birth, in the realm of choice and vision. Through the quality thus given to an earthly life, such men—now no longer consciously— carried out their aims. Sometimes, unknowingly, they brought about their own destruction.

Mary, Queen of Scots, beheaded in Shakespeare's time, was the representative of the spiritual element of Celtic Scotland. With her death the British people had to lose their nature-given spirituality. Female experiences are connected with the past, with realms to be preserved. Mary Stuart was the mother of King James VI and I, whose son suffered a similar fate. But the masculine head of Charles I looked to the future and not the past.

With his execution the British folk soul brought a sacrifice that related to the intellectual head forces. Charles had proved himself an early representative of the age of natural science. He was interested in vivisection and loved to watch Harvey's experiments. After his father's death, he placed all the animals in his deer parks at Harvey's disposal. But intellectual investigation based on curiosity rather than on reverence and wonder contains an aggressive element, which in the last resort provokes hostility. Compassion, the basis of peace, is alien to it. This cold, head thinking had to be overcome if love and wisdom were to triumph.

To us, who have passed through modern education, it is difficult to see more than accidents in historical events. To Shakespeare they were still means of educating the human race, through the moral experience inhering in the royal dramas in which the heads of consorts and advisers fell under the axe. King Henry VIII who had divorced Catherine of Aragon had married Anne Boleyn in 1533. Sir Thomas More, the Lord Chancellor and the King's friend and adviser for many years, was beheaded two years later. The beheading and the marriage were closely connected. Anne Boleyn was beheaded on May 19, 1536; the next day, Henry was betrothed to Jane Seymour and two days later they were married. Again there is a link between these two events. On July 28, 1540, Thomas Cromwell, Sir Thomas More's successor, was beheaded. The same day Henry married Catherine Howard. The execution and the marriage coincided. After Catherine's execution Henry married Catherine Parr, who survived him.

90

What took place here as outer events recalls the experiences man has to undergo within his soul in an inner training. When he tries to transform inherited gifts and virtues, which inevitably carry the seed of pride, into humbler, but self-acquired characteristics, he feels at first as if his thinking, feeling and willing were beheaded. The mystic beheading is the preparation of the soul for its marriage to the moral self. The British people, who had to overcome the inheritance of the past, had to go through this experience as historical event.

Shakespeare knew that evil, too, has its task in the course of history; it has therefore to be beheld and understood by man. Many of his tragedies are distinct pictures of initiation experiences and show stages on the path towards a pure marriage of soul and spirit. Through his plays he was able to strengthen in the spectator the sense for a more profound insight. Above all, his plays prepared a faculty of perceiving in given situations what is materially intangible.

In the first quarter of the seventeenth century important events centred around James I, who encouraged the rise of science. At the Union of the Crowns, he retained the physician of Queen Elizabeth, William Gilbert, who had applied the methods of experimental science to the realm of static electricity. Gilbert, the author of a book on magnetism, taught that the Earth itself was nothing but a magnet in the cosmos. The discovery of electricity and magnetism made possible the rise of modern technology, the most outstanding contribution to Earth intelligence. The offspring of these discoveries is a machine civilization dominated by electricity.

Afterwards William Harvey became Court Physician. From his observations of the working of the heart in living animals he deduced that the heart was a pump, as indeed it is in the case of a mortally wounded animal. He was the first modern scientist in Europe to cross the barrier of reverence for the living creature. He thus brought an entirely new mood into the search for knowledge: in course of time, this was to lead to a complete lack of regard for and consequent violation of natural processes.

The general philosophical direction for the age was given by Francis Bacon, Earl of Verulam. He saw the task of philosophy as the discovery of practical application rather than the search for truth. To him, truth and utility were identical. Dominion over nature—' *imperium homini* ', ' the empire of man '—was in his view a truly worthy aim. But in the last resort the urge to discover the secrets of nature in order to exploit them in the service of human selfishness leads to the atomization of all substance and the destruction of the Earth.

James I is a mysterious figure and presents historically an open question. Shakespeare, with his living grasp of history, welcomed the King's accession as a sign of new and better times. His attitude was general in contemporary England. Everywhere men expected a change for the better: but nothing startling happened. James went his own way, which no one understood. He was little concerned with parties. His whole being was orientated towards peace. His teacher had been Tycho Brahe's friend Buchanan, and when James went to bring home his bride from Denmark, he visited Tycho on the Uranienburg—the ' star castle '—on the island of Hven. He also maintained secret contacts with other leading men of his time. He had courage and never yielded to external pressure. Though urged constantly to enter the Thirty Years' War, he resisted firmly till his death.

He was free from personal ambition. All his advisers were chosen from men unburdened with the political training of the past. To those around him, his decisions seemed based on factors unknown to them. Before his reign, England had been almost constantly involved in war and wars almost immediately followed his death. It was he who kept in check the forces striving for war.

James I had inwardly renounced the ancient warlike Mars forces. The martial gifts that seek outward expression were to be transformed into impulses of peace. Gradually the forces of courage should be freed for purely spiritual struggles. James had enough wisdom to understand this: voluntarily he sacrificed the forces of the head to those of the heart. Had he not developed sufficient patience to live through his mission, which history failed to understand, Britain could not have evolved tolerance and understanding. His untraditional attitude made new social impulses possible.

Britain was now ready to play a leading part in world history. As the last in the chain of liberators of the British people from the dreaminess of the past, Cromwell appeared. He banished all the visual arts; only music was allowed. Puritanism swept like a scourge of God not only across England, but also through Ireland and Scotland.

When Cromwell, the victorious Lord Protector, died in 1658, the conditions for the development of modern England seemed secured, except that London, raised on ancient Druid centres, remained unsuited to become a modern city. Here the English mission received drastic resolution: in September, 1666, within four days the whole of the city was burned to the ground.

Within a comparatively short time, Christopher Wren submitted plans for a new London. Although his first scheme, in which wide streets radiated from a centre, was not accepted, he subsequently built fifty-three churches, the halls of twelve livery companies, gateways, the Monument, the Royal Hospital and the Royal Observatory at Greenwich, where his own instructions regarding instruments and lenses were carefully carried out. He also built the dome of St. Paul's, with a spiral staircase of 365 steps.

His contemporaries marvelled at the boldness of his art, at his accuracy and his practical sense. He was not only an outstanding architect, but also a great scientist and a co-founder of the Royal Society whose president he became. Many inventions are owed to him. To Wren, astronomy stood above all other arts. Originally he had been professor of astronomy at Gresham's College in London. At his installation ceremony he said that astronomy in its glory was as high above all other sciences as the heavens are above everything below them. Astronomy became to him a higher astrology that could show the connection between earthly organisms and the world of the stars. Such astrology, he stressed, had nothing to do with the cheap and popular version.

In the distant past the Druids had built their vast star temples at Glastonbury and Avebury out of divine inspiration. Wren possessed a star knowledge of a different kind which he could translate into architecture. Trained in natural science, he could harness the winged force that strives to the heights for the service of a new city and a new age.

While he searched for ways of turning the forces of the Eagle into those of the Dove, Locke, Berkeley and Hume united themselves with the Scorpion forces and denied the universality of the spirit. John Locke, born in the same year as Wren, 1632, stated that the soul was incapable of any real experience, passive, like a slate on which the world outside recorded itself. He experienced the world of human thought trapped in the cave of material surroundings. George Berkeley, also Wren's contemporary, held the opposite view. He sought to prove that all outer appearance was only seemingly objective and did not exist at all physically. The soul, he held, is tied to its inner impressions and cannot know anything of any objective surroundings. David Hume, born when Wren was already an old man, found that most human evidence about the world was based on habits of thinking and related to nothing but observations of the senses and their logic. No statement was justified, so he held, that went any further.

When Isaac Newton, one of the greatest English scientists, died in 1727 he took his picture of the world with him to the realm of the stars, as does any human soul. In spite of his sensibility to a 'great ocean' of undiscovered truth, his scientific picture was of a dead universe, governed only by the force of gravity. His world of colour was cold and soulless, one of undifferentiated experiences where even the distinction between white and grey was blurred. To the spiritual worlds the image that rose from the Earth through Newton was utterly alien. It appeared to them as doubt in man's being.

When, thirty years later, William Blake descended to earthly life, he carried within him the question of the significance of such a development; and he strove to give a healing answer through his own life. In his apocalyptic drama *Jerusalem*, which he engraved himself, with endless patience, on a hundred large sheets, colour and form mutually supporting each other were the direct expression of spiritual experience. The soul was expressed in colour, the intention by form. He called the human soul 'Jerusalem'. Throughout his work, it descends from the world of the stars to Earth, where it has to face the trials and horrors of demonic forces. It seems doomed to die, yet is finally redeemed. With it suffers Los, the human spirit, who in the end builds the new city of peace.

Through this poem Blake replied to the dead picture of the universe which was then beginning to take form:

' Fear not, my Sons, this Waking Death: he is become One with me.
Behold him here! We shall not Die! we shall be united in Jesus.
Will you suffer this Satan, this Body of Doubt that Seems but Is Not,
To occupy the very threshold of Eternal Life? if Bacon, Newton, Locke
Deny a Conscience in Man and the Communion of Saints and Angels,
Contemning the Divine Vision and Fruition, Worshiping the Deus
Of the Heathen, The God of This World, and the Goddess Nature,
Mystery, Babylon the Great, The Druid Dragon and hidden Harlot,
Is it not that Signal of the Morning which was told us in the Beginning? '

Jerusalem, IV, 93

Blake was aware of the great perspectives of human evolution. A mood of reverence before the mystery of death fills his work. In *Jerusalem*, Albion says to Jesus:

. . . ' O Lord, what can I do? my Selfhood cruel
Marches against thee, deceitful, from Sinai and from Edom
Into the Wilderness of Judah, to meet thee in his pride.

I behold the Visions of my deadly Sleep of Six Thousand Years
Dazling around thy skirts like a Serpent of precious stones and gold.
I know it is my Self, O my Divine Creator and Redeemer.'
Jesus replied: ' Fear not Albion: unless I die thou canst not live;
But if I die I shall arise again and thou with me.
This is Friendship and Brotherhood: without it Man Is Not.' . . .
Jesus said: ' Wouldest thou love one who never died
For thee, or ever die for one who had not died for thee?
And if God dieth not for Man and giveth not himself
Eternally for Man, Man could not exist; for Man is Love
As God is Love: every kindness to another is a little Death
In the Divine Image, nor can Man exist but by Brotherhood.'

Jerusalem, IV, 96

Blake called his people to awareness.

> England! awake! awake! awake!
> Jerusalem thy Sister calls:
> Why wilt thou sleep the sleep of death
> And close her from thy ancient walls?

When William Blake was forty years old, he experienced inwardly a tragedy which still remains a possible future for the world. Out of powerful imaginations he wrote and painted the fifteen large pages of *Europe: A Prophecy*. It was the warning of a lonely genius who was at the same time a seer, a warning which, in the second half of the twentieth century, many people all over the world may understand through their own vision of events that may yet come to pass through destructive human inventions. In the frontispiece to this Prophecy, the Ancient of Days leans down to the Earth, to measure with his compasses those regions of space to which the Prophecy is addressed. After the Prelude, storms and tempests, horror, terror and despair appear. Deep winter comes, war ceases, and all flee shadow-like to their abodes.

Then Los, the Spirit of Man, withdraws to the Moon. Wakening the thunders of the deep, Urizen, the great Demon, glows in the arctic sky. Famine and plague! ' The midnight clock has struck! and hark! the bell of death beats slow!—Heard ye the note profound?' (Plate 24.)

Mildew blasts the cornfields: Man's sustenance is destroyed. For a long time he is such stuff as dreams are made of. The Prince of the World now is that demon, Urizen, whose brazen book was copied by the whole world's kings and priests. Every man is fettered. Spectres throng the shadows.

On the doors is written that iron curse: ' Thou shalt not,' and over hearth-stones, ' Fear.' Town-dwellers walk with leaden feet, the bones of countryfolk are soft and bent. Only the lowest forms of life, and spiders in their webs survive the desolation. Red-limbed, the Angel of the Last Judgment thrice essayed presumptuously to wake the dead with his tormenting trump of doom: but no sound came. All such attempts were made in vain till the nights of holy shadows and of human solitude came to an end.

When, after long ages, the earth once more was habitable, morning awoke in the east, and Los, clad in thunder, lifted his head with a cry that shook nature from pole to pole, calling all his sons to the strife of blood. Once more the Spirit of Man could work in human bodies, could work in the warmth of the blood.

*   *   *

British natural scientists of the nineteenth century were the first to interpret the kingdoms of nature from the point of view of evolution. Darwin, Wallace, and Lyell introduced this entirely new element into scientific thinking. Through an extraordinary coincidence they were diverted from the comprehensive concept.

Between 1831 and 1836, Darwin had taken part in a scientific expedition. On his voyage he had been deeply impressed by the great fossilized animals of South America and what appeared to him to be their living descendants. In his own words: ' In October, 1838, that is fifteen months after I had begun my systematic enquiry, I happened to read for amusement Malthus on *Population*, and being well prepared to appreciate the struggle for existence which everywhere goes on, from long-continued observation of the habits of animals and plants, it at once struck me that under these circumstances favourable variations would tend to be preserved, and unfavourable ones destroyed . . . Here then I had at last got a theory by which to work.'

Thus, quite suddenly, Darwin felt convinced he had come across proof that the different plant and animal species owed their survival to the natural selection of the fittest in the struggle for existence.

A. Russel Wallace, a young naturalist working in Borneo, had occupied himself for three years with the problem of the existence of the many different varieties. In February 1858, during a heavy attack of intermittent fever, he remembered Malthus's *Principles of Population* which he had read earlier. ' Then it suddenly flashed upon me the fittest would survive.' Immediately Wallace wrote to Darwin about his ' discovery '.

Sir Charles Lyell, the famous geologist and Darwin's older contemporary, came across the tracks of evolution on his voyages to America. He was made President of the Geological Society of which Darwin assumed the office of Secretary. Lyell too became a follower of Darwin. Later, on one point, Wallace always differed from Darwin; he could never accept that man himself was nothing but the outcome of the struggle for survival. Other factors, he maintained, were also at work.

Malthus's theory was the result of his studies of social conditions in nineteenth century England, the first country to experience the transition from agriculture to industry. Applied to natural history, such theories were alien though fateful intruders with far-reaching consequences. The twentieth century is no longer content to ask how things came about, but also asks where evolution is to lead and what aims it serves.

The answer to these questions cannot come out of the head, for anything can be proved intellectually. The paths of life lead in a different direction, to deeper realities. Britain's own history is proof that the creative factor is not the struggle for existence, but forces that aim at transforming this very struggle into a peaceful metamorphosis so that new social conditions can come about.

Britain was to become a conciliatory element between continents and races, no less than between philosophies. To fulfil this mission, the British people needed more than the possibilities offered by every-day intelligence. Britain could create this new bond, because her people had walked fearlessly the path from the Eagle forces through the Scorpion experiences, taking upon themselves patiently the consequences and relying on the ordering and healing influence of time.

The British people were to develop a sense, comparable to the sense of smell on the physical plane, that would allow them to perceive the sources of influences which, though undesirable, must nevertheless be respected because they manifest hidden processes that cannot be fought directly. They reckon with the realities governing the world situation and can sense scarcely noticeable but highly significant symptoms. This awareness also explains a unique police system, which combines the utmost efficiency in the discovery of hidden crime with respect for the individual.

One of the legacies of the early days of modern science is the British will to freedom that finds expression not so much in the conscious striving for freedom of the spirit as in indignation against interference with personal liberty. The spirit of indignation became a constructive element in the social order because the right to personal freedom was acknowledged in others.

A community resulted in which every conceivable ideal of government could exist side by side as long as each one accepted the principle of toleration. Monarchy, aristocracy, democracy and socialism helped and encouraged each other. In the Church of England religious streams are represented from Anglo-Catholic to near-Rationalist. The conscious acceptance of those who are different makes it possible to weather difficult situations with dignity. The British wait and observe, to gain the insight necessary for the next step.

The British Empire was largely the result of world-wide colonization. As it grew, new opportunities were offered to other races. The destruction of the Spanish Armada in 1588 was important to the later development of the United States, for Spain had been firmly established in the New World for nearly a century. Had the Armada been victorious, Spain, with the sanction of the Church, could have prevented the foundation of an independent heretic state on the Atlantic by the Pilgrim Fathers. British ' might ' also protected the new settlements threatened by the advance of French colonization from the St. Lawrence river towards the Ohio river and the Mississippi. This French expansion formed a kind of wall which might have cut off access to the Pacific for the English-speaking settlers. Through the victory over the French at Quebec, the path to the West was freed.

In the following century Napoleon amassed an army in the West Indies to invade America. Jefferson, the creator of the Declaration of Independence, warned Napoleon that he would meet with the utmost resistance if he were to land in New Orleans. Napoleon thereupon changed his plans and offered for sale to the Americans the area of Louisiana, which equalled in size the whole of the United States of that time. Jefferson was able to accept immediately because English banks were willing to advance him ninety per cent of the purchase price. All this was a preparation for the later development of North America.

Twenty years after this transaction Russia tried to make use of the Holy Alliance, founded by the Tsar against the world's democratic governments, to further her own expansion in

North America. Russian immigrants had reached Oregon via Alaska. Along the coast of the Pacific, to California, they had set up fortified posts. Already the Bering Straits were declared a *marc clausam*. Canning therefore proposed to President Monroe that they should jointly declare that the United States and Britain would resist all outside intervention on the American continent. This put an end to the Tsar's schemes.

In the administration of her colonies, Britain followed her own convictions. Thus in 1833 she dared to free the slaves in the colonies and to abolish slavery—then universally accepted—altogether. Some 800,000 people were freed. When disturbances broke out in Canada, Lord Durham was sent out to investigate. As a result, between 1846 and 1849, Canada was granted internal autonomy; the same principle was applied in Australia and New Zealand a few years later. In 1867 Canada became a Dominion, that is, her provinces were united: and three years later, New Zealand which had always been unified, was given a constitution. After the Mutiny of 1857-8, India passed under the British Crown and at the same time, assurances of political rights and religious toleration were given. On January 1, 1877, Queen Victoria was crowned Empress of India.

At the turn of the century as the curtain went up on another act in the drama of history, Britain stood at the height of her power and proud self-awareness. But then followed the impact of two World Wars; and history demonstrated that it is possible to surrender both power and possession through a realization of the needs of an age. Britain was to give up her Empire. The task was enormous, demanding calm and patience that the great changes might come about peacefully.

Down to the very language the English character is self-aware. In English ' I ' is the only pronoun spelt with a capital. Education had been increasingly directed towards an individual sense of well-being that found its natural fulfilment in a consciousness of national greatness. But the colonial peoples demanded complete equality. They longed to be independent. If the Empire dissolved, education for the assumption of authority would lose its meaning. To allow these changes meant a kind of death.

Britain's soul made the decision to grant independence even at the cost of great sacrifices, and to create a solid foundation for peace. The decision grew into a deed, performed with greatness and dignity on the stage of history. The British Empire died. But out of renunciation the Commonwealth of Nations was founded, a world-embracing community where free peoples and those on the road to freedom can begin to make the brotherhood of man a reality.

World domination was no more. But the monarchy remained untouched, although its significance changed. The crown was now deprived of all arbitrary power, though it was thereby also freed from ancient burdens. The ceremony of coronation and anointing were not altered. The king or queen now represented the ideal of a human being, standing entirely in the service of humanity and hence revered by millions of people. This reverence is a source of unity.

Britain will probably pass through still greater changes in the second half of the twentieth century. If further outward losses are accepted out of a deeper insight, then the Scorpion forces will be increasingly deprived of their sting. Willing renunciation opens the gates to new inspiration and leads to the source of positive deeds, to which the British folk spirit longs to guide its people. For this, Britain must will to carry out her decisions, and fulfil the tasks she has taken upon herself, despite storm and danger.

The great drama is not yet finished. The attitude of the British towards the results of their own natural science is the same as in all other situations: expectancy, and a realization that the last word is yet to be spoken. The forces of death hold no terror, for the British folk spirit has lived through them, its innermost being untouched. In every situation the aim is to preserve human dignity in the face of all the attacks against it from science, mechanization and automation. It is not for nothing that people in England greet each other with their heads erect. Always there is a determination to be self-assured, firmly established in the personality yet at the same time tolerant of others.

The drama unfolding in the British Isles is also the drama of the human race. At the end of the century Pluto will pass through the Scorpion. The working of Pluto within the folk soul is only a small part of his mission. Pluto longs to awaken historic responsibility in all men, though he does not coerce. He warns: ' Individuality—or atomic destruction '. The choice lies with the human race.

At the beginning of a new millennium, the third corner of the Venus pentagon points to the Sign of the Scorpion, showing the human ego the path to realization of the mystery of truly creative and healing deeds. If man accepts the challenge of the times with patience and acquires new insight, then he furthers the transformation of the Scorpion into the Dove which is the symbol of peace. If he fails he becomes an ally of the dark Scorpion forces, undermining his own future and that of the world.

France

THE KEY to a true understanding of France lies in the cosmic language of the Archer, which speaks of the hard struggle of man's ascent, of the loneliness of the soul in striving towards true humanity. For through the intervention of demonic forces, man sank deeper into the abyss in the course of his evolution than the gods had intended. The upward path is long and painful but can be ascended because Christ has united Himself with human destiny.

His coming was foreseen in France long before His birth. He was carried by the world soul that brings cosmic wisdom to bear upon our humanity. At Chartres, the principal sanctuary of the Druids who lived in France in pre-Christian times, Celtic priests experienced the world soul as the *Virgo paritura*, the 'Virgin who is to give birth'. They saw her descending from the heights, carrying her Divine Child down to Earth. Her light-permeated being, walking above the world waters, shone like a radiant star; an altar was built for her and she was worshipped as the highest deity.

When the first heralds of Christianity reached France after the events in Palestine, they were filled with wonder that the Druids had already long worshipped the Virgin who was to bear the Christ Child, and even knew of the event that had meanwhile taken place on Earth. On the altar of Chartres stood the Madonna with the Child.

The news of the actual event appeared as a natural fulfilment to those western initiates. Though the shrine in the grotto at Chartres remained secret for generations, the worship of the Virgin mother lived on at many centres throughout ancient Gaul. In 861 the mantle of the Madonna was brought to Chartres, the scene of the cosmic revelation of the world soul. The Byzantine Emperor had sent the garment, worn by the Madonna at the Annunciation, to Charlemagne; afterwards, according to tradition, it passed into the hands of Charles the Bald of France and was preserved at Chartres, where from that time onwards a school of wisdom began to grow.

This school was founded by Fulbertus (c. 1000) and soon developed into one of the most important centres of learning in Europe. Fulbertus taught the Liberal Arts, which had been cultivated in ancient Greece: Grammar, Dialectic, Rhetoric, Arithmetic, Geometry, Astronomy, and Music. He sang the Virgin's praise in many hymns: ' She who is to give birth to the sun of justice, the King of kings, Mary, star of the seas, today this star shines forth: rejoice, ye faithful, to behold the Divine Light! O wondrous birth, O birth miraculous! O glorious Child! At the moment of thy birth, angels proclaim peace to the Earth!'

In 1150 the Madonna with the Child, hidden for so long in the crypt, was represented in sculpture above the west portal of the cathedral, visible to every pilgrim. (Plate 25.) She was surrounded by the seven Liberal Arts. All the teachers of Chartres imbued their pupils with the love of Greek learning and with the confidence that they could ascend to the World Mother, the Sacred Sophia. The school reached its greatest importance in the twelfth century. At the beginning of the thirteenth, when all its great teachers had died, its influence, based on the working of past impulses, gradually faded.*

The power of Arab intellectual thinking had meanwhile reached France from Spain. The teachers of Chartres did not formulate concepts that could have withstood the intellectuality of the successors of Averroës, for their world had consisted of invisible beings active in the human word. To the Arabs on the other hand, the word was merely a name, arrived at by no more than accident.

Only the Scholastics could challenge Arabism. Their centre was the University of Paris and their leading personalities were Thomas Aquinas and Albertus Magnus. With crystal clear logic Thomas Aquinas demonstrated that descriptions and names of things are related to their spiritual background. He thus gave to the course of thoughts and their formulation in speech a clarity that was soon to be lost; but his Realism energetically countered the increasingly superficial Nominalism of Arab thinking.

The teachers of Paris were like kings, living in a daylight consciousness that had drawn strength from Christian sources; just as the teachers of Chartres had been shepherds of souls and guardians of tradition. Living predominantly in thinking and feeling however, neither had directly attempted to influence social life. In the course of its ascent the soul must also progress towards the purification of will and in southern France this evolution produced the movement of the Cathars or Albigenses. The first Cathars had already appeared at Limousin while Fulbertus of Chartres was active.

In the twelfth century, under their influence, a culture unequalled in its day developed in the region of Toulouse, then extending over an area from the right bank of the Seine to the Garonne valley. Nobody carried arms. All the arts flourished and were cultivated by both knights and commoners. The *troubadours* or *minnesingers* who set forth from here on their journeys and the sculptors of Toulouse were active far beyond their native province.

In translating Manichaean books in the *langue d'oc*, the Cathars became acquainted with the idea of reincarnation. They could see humanity struggling against adversary powers and sought a strengthening of the will. They carried St. John's *Gospel* with them wherever they went, and knew that Christ had descended from the stars. The Earth where they lived flourished, and the state of Toulouse became the wealthiest and most fertile region in Europe.

But the Church was worried by a Christianity with so direct a message. On 21 July, 1208, Pope Innocent III proclaimed a crusade against the Albigenses to be preached throughout France. Simon de Montfort undertook the execution of this scheme. Already during his first attack, 20,000 people were murdered at Beziers. Seven thousand were burned to death in

---

* See *The Mysteries of Chartres Cathedral* by Louis Charpentier. London, 1966.

the church of St. Madeleine. The persecutions lasted for over thirty years. Documents were destroyed. Mercy was often promised to those willing to recant, but the Cathars resisted and threw themselves singing into the flames.

The path of the Archer does not lead upwards in a straight line but makes detours. Occasionally, therefore, short cuts are attempted; where they succeed, it means that many human beings must stay behind while the few ascend more swiftly. The hand of destiny has often allowed such short cuts to be interrupted; and human courage would indeed falter on the long and painful journey if there were not some among the vast legions, able to keep the flame of progress alight through deeds of sacrifice.

The destiny of the French Templars resembles that of the Cathars. Through their spiritual insight they too could carry their influence into social life. Through their contact with the East they were acquainted with an ancient wisdom and, free from egotism, could combine it with practical foresight and with compassion. They possessed great wealth and held the administration of gold to be a sacred trust so long as it served the well-being of all and not personal advantage.

Their integrity and unselfishness gained them wide respect; but the independence and wealth of the Order aroused the envy of the Church and of King Philip the Fair. When the King was in serious danger during a riot in Paris, he found refuge with the Order; and in the ' temple ' where he sheltered he saw a vast amount of gold and thereupon decided to destroy the Order and make its wealth his own.

In 1307 he had the knights arrested on charges of heresy and idolatry, and confiscated their goods. From that time onwards the ' temple ' became a prison and many of the Templars were subjected to torture and were burned. The Grand Master Jacques de Molay and the eighty-year-old Grand Prior, Guido de la Normandie, were slowly burned alive. Before Jacques de Molay died, he asked Philip the Fair, Pope Clement V, and Philippe de Nogaret who also bore a large share of responsibility for the persecutions, to arraign themselves for judgment before God. Within six months, the King, the Pope and the Grand Inquisitor died.

The curse laid on the French royal house by the theft of the Templar gold lasted until well into the nineteenth century. The reigns of the French royal families, Capet, Valois and Bourbon ended similarly with three sons who ascended the throne but died without heirs. First came Philip's own sons who each became king and died childless. The sons of Henry II and Catherine de Medici suffered a like fate. At the end of the eighteenth century the course of the stolen gold once more turned against the ruling dynasty. Louis XVI was imprisoned and eventually beheaded in the ' temple ' where Philip the Fair had fallen prey to his greed for gold. Eventually his two brothers were to ascend the throne and died without heirs. The circle of destiny of the French kings thus came to a close.

From the twelfth to the fourteenth century, while the Cathars and Templars were active and undergoing persecution, the French soul created in the north of the country the literature of the *fabliaux* and the *bestiaires*. Anonymous story-tellers spread anecdotes among the people characterizing base human qualities, usually as animals, in allegorical pictures, with the object of combating men's subhuman instincts. The story of the fox, *Renard-le-Contrefait*, was a collection of tales in which animals behave like human beings. The two most important characters were Isengrim, the wolf, who was always hungry and Renard who got the better of everybody.

The theme of this struggle, which was to recur again and again in France, was woven into French life by the folk spirit. On ancient star maps, the Archer was a centaur. Head and chest were human, his hands held a bow and arrow or a lyre; the rest of the body was that of a horse. In some respects this representation of the Archer is the most universally human of all the star signs: it is not the concern only of one particular people or of one historical age, but of every individual human being. The image is not the ideal conceived in the creative thought of the Godhead, but of man as he has become and of the obstacles facing him. The Archer appeals to an increased sense of truth so that what is genuinely human can be distinguished from the purely nature-bound.

Today it is a matter of course to see a link between man and animal. Man's evolution from the animal kingdom belongs to the most elementary scientific education in schools. Yet there is equal justification for trying to imagine that before any hardening processes had set in, the animal species split off from the human kingdom. If this be so, then man has gradually placed outside himself the characteristics likely to impede his progress. Soul elements detached from him have assumed animal forms. But in this connection it would be quite mistaken to equate what is now the life of instinct in animals with human egotism as it is today. The animal is never evil: for its actions are impersonal and they but express the needs of the group. Nor is it capable of change. This gift is reserved for man alone, who can know his own weaknesses.

Before humanity became self-aware, centaurs were experienced as beings of wisdom. The myth of Heracles tells that his teacher in the arts, Chiron, was a centaur. It was during the flowering of Greek culture that the attitude towards the half-human condition changed. The centaurs began to symbolize the man bound to passion and instinct. On one of the friezes of the Parthenon, the temple dedicated to Athena, each centaur battles with a warrior who is shown in the beauty of his complete humanity. (Plate 26.) The future was to belong only to the fully human.

The lower instincts will not be overcome without great difficulties, but when the cleansing storms have passed across the Earth, spiritual vision will no longer behold man as a centaur but as a white horseman on a white steed. He will be master of himself down to his bodily nature, and his true being will at last be realized. Such true humanity has been striven for everywhere throughout the course of Europe's evolution and the *fabliaux* served this specific task of the French people.

At the beginning of the fifteenth century France was in danger of losing her true destiny. King Henry V of England, who ascended the throne in 1413, conquered most of the French mainland, and Charles V of France, who was feeble-minded, acknowledged him as his successor. Both kings died, almost simultaneously. At their death, the heralds proclaimed: ' *Vive Henri de Lancastre, Roi de France et d'Angleterre!* ' In 1428 it seemed unlikely that France would ever become independent again. The other European states had fully accepted her defeat.

But the division of Europe into responsible and independent peoples could be part of a Divine plan, and could be known as such to those having access to knowledge derived from the wisdom of the Mysteries. On the sixth of January 1412, a girl was born into a family of simple shepherds in a remote village of Lorraine. When Joan was twelve years old, a great light appeared to her and she heard the voice of the Archangel Michael, who said: ' Go to France, raise the siege of Orleans, and lead King Charles to his coronation at Rheims!' She hesitated: ' I am a poor girl, I know not how to manage a horse, far less can I conduct a war'. ' I come from God to aid and guide you, Joan. Be good and God will help you.' Such experiences recurred hundreds of times. Other spirits, angels and archangels, also appeared to her and taught her.

After four years, she went to Chinon to the Dauphin and persuaded him to make her Commander-in-Chief of the army so that Orleans could be liberated. It took her eleven weeks to carry out her plan. The English army in Patay was defeated and the Dauphin led in triumph to Rheims where he was crowned as Charles VII. In full armour Joan rode ahead of the troops, carrying her banner inscribed *Jésu-Maria*. Generals, advisers, the Archbishop and the Dauphin himself did all they could to stop her, but she seemed guided and carried by an invisible power. She alone was the cause of this victory.

In 1430 she was captured by the Burgundians and might still have been returned to France for a ransom. The suggestion was transmitted to King Charles, but nothing was done to rescue her. In consequence she was delivered into the hands of the English and burned alive at the stake in Rouen by the Inquisition. She was only eighteen at the time of her death. Shortly before it, she prophesied that the English armies would have to leave French soil within seven years. Her forecast proved correct.

Joan of Arc died a martyr's death not only for France, the country that betrayed her, but also for England whose authorities had surrendered her to her executioners. She died also for Germany, which later could throw off French and English influence and develop a different spirituality. Like a shining beacon, Joan's sacrifice marks the beginning of modern times. (Plate 27.)

As France became increasingly independent, outward successes followed. The next century saw the reign of Francis I, who with Charles V brought absolutism to Europe. France was now strong enough to conclude agreements everywhere: with the German Lutherans, with Suleiman the Great, with Henry VIII. Treaties were made and broken, reconciliations and quarrels followed closely upon each other. While the King supported the German Lutherans, the Calvinists were massacred in the interior. The monarch ruled *à bon plaisir*.

Rabelais, the great commentator on the life and manners of his people, was a contemporary of Francis I. With incomparable boldness, outstanding learning and a vast sense of humour, he placed before the French a mirror of their innate weaknesses. He clothed his observations in the fantastic story of the powerful giant Gargantua and his son Pantagruel.

These giants were placed within the contemporary French landscape so that everybody should feel quite at home with them. Rabelais greatly praised their follies, exaggerating them with seeming admiration to incredible extremes. As he used it, language was richer than ever before or after in French literature, though he was no respecter of grammar. It was as if his vocabulary had been picked up not only in the street, in taverns and at fairs, from peasants, soldiers and pirates, but also from politicians, doctors, judges, nobles, princes and kings.

The philosopher Pierre Galland, who lost his life in the Massacre of St. Bartholomew's Eve in 1572, called Rabelais a sly fox who swore, scribbled, growled and barked at the older philosophers like a dog. Boileau called him ' reason wearing a mask '; Lafontaine considered his work ' the most perfect example of narrative art '. ' Rabelais has more sense than any of us ' was the general comment.

The centaur theme runs throughout his work. He speaks of the earliest ancestor of the giant family, who lived before the flood and was too big to enter the ark.

> . . . he sat astride of it with one foot on each side, as small children do on hobby-horses . . . In this fashion, by God's aid, he saved the Ark from danger. For he kept it balanced with his legs, and with one foot turned it whichever way he wished, as one does a ship with a tiller. The people inside sent him abundant victuals through a chimney, to reward him for the service he was doing them . . .
>
> Have you thoroughly understood all this? Then drink a good draught without water. For if you do not believe it—indeed I don't!

It is said of the childhood of Gargantua, who was all his life a good horseman, that a beautiful wooden horse was made for him:

> . . . which he made to prance, leap, curvet, plunge and rear at the same time, to pace, trot, canter, gallop, amble, go like a nag, a trotter, a camel or a wild ass. He made its colour, as monks do their tunics, according to the Saints'-days: bay, sorrel, dapple-grey, mouse-dun, deer-coloured, roan, cow-coloured, zebra, skewbald, piebald, white.
>
> He himself made a hunter out of a large log, and another for everyday out of the beam of a winepress: and he turned a great oak into a mule with trappings for his room. What is more, he had ten or twelve more for relays, and seven for the post. And he put them all to sleep near him.

Later, as a youth, on waking up,

> . . . he turned and stretched and wallowed in his bed for some time, the better to rouse his animal spirits, and dressed according to the season . . .
>
> Then he yawned . . . coughed . . . sneezed . . . and breakfasted, to protect himself from the dew and the bad air, on fine fried tripes, good rashers grilled on the coals, delicate hams, tasty goat stews, and plenty of early morning soup . . .
>
> After having taken a thorough breakfast, he went to church, and they carried in for him

a great basket, a huge slippered breviary, weighing, what with grease, clasps and parchment, eleven hundred and six pounds.

There he heard twenty-six or thirty Masses . . .

As he left the church they brought him on an ox-wagon a heap of rosaries from Saint Claude, each bead as big as a hat-block, and as he walked through the cloisters, galleries or garden, he told more of them than sixteen hermits.

Then he studied for a miserable half-hour, his eyes fixed on his book but—as the comic poet says—his soul was in the kitchen . . . Being of a phlegmatic nature he began his meal with some dozens of hams, smoked ox-tongues, botargoes, sausages and other advance-couriers of wine. Meanwhile his servants threw into his mouth, one after another, full bucketfuls of mustard, without stopping. Then he drank a monstrous gulp of white wine to relieve his kidneys and after that ate, according to the season, meats agreeable to his appetite. He left off eating when his belly was tight. For drinking he had neither end nor rule.*

With superb humour Rabelais, the great educator of his people castigated the gluttony of his compatriots. Ronald de Carvalho wrote that his laughter is that of a people who had invented two invisible weapons: the innocent heroism of the Maid of Orleans and Gargantua's endless pranks. Rabelais' laughter was not that of a detached novelist but of a true human being, triumphing over reality through the discipline of joy.

While Rabelais battled against the animal body of the centaur, Descartes glorified his head-organism. In attempting to understand the world and himself through entirely independent thinking, he became the father of modern philosophy. His starting point was doubt. Finally, he even doubted the reality of his own existence. To discover truth, he determined to reject all the concepts of the past and to destroy his own intellectual world. Like a marksman in the dark night, he searched for a solitary bright spot which he could aim at and accept as real. On 10 November, 1619, he had his sudden illumination: *Cogito ergo sum*. I think, therefore I am. The idea that one-sided intellectual thinking could replace the power of human self-knowledge took firm hold of him.

The experience was followed by three over-powering dreams. In the first, he saw himself paralyzed and in the midst of a great storm. In the second he heard thunder and felt himself surrounded by flames. In the third dream he opened a book at random and his eyes fell on the line of Ausonius' poem: *Quid vitas sectator iter?* What is served by this splitting up? He was deeply moved, saw himself warned, and prayed for help to the Virgin, promising her a pilgrimage to Loretto.

There were rumours at the time of a Rosicrucian circle where truths, unknown elsewhere, were preserved. The journeys Descartes took led him across Europe and wherever he went he appears to have tried to meet Rosicrucians. When he finally returned to Paris he was himself

---

* *The Histories of Gargantua and Pantagruel*, by François Rabelais, translated by J. M. Cohen. Penguin Books, London, 1955.

taken for a Rosicrucian although, greatly to his sorrow, he had never been able to meet members of the Order.

Through his work, Descartes liberated biology from ancient metaphysical links. In his last book *The Passions of the Soul*, he tried to justify ethics through physical laws. In his earlier years already, he had expressed the view that animals were without a soul. He believed that it would be possible with the help of artificial organs to construct a machine that could not be distinguished from a live animal. Yet he also stated most decisively that man himself could not be imitated by any machine. To imagine him as a machine would have been impossible for Descartes, in whose soul, beside the search for the certainty of his own existence, there still glowed the longing to serve the future development of humanity.

A century later, Julien de la Mettrie published *Man as a Machine*. He led the one-sided head-thinking of the centaur to its extreme. In doing so he claimed to base himself on Descartes, with the reservation that 'the strong analogy between man and animal must force all scientists and competent judges to admit that the proud and vain creatures, distinguished rather by their arrogance than by the name of Man, are fundamentally only animals and machines crawling along upright'.

Severe trials of consciousness now beset the French soul. Descartes' dualism, which still recognized the existence of body and soul, was for convenience replaced by monistic materialism. The distinction between body and soul was set aside: the soul was now merely part of organic matter.

Julien de la Mettrie was the central figure of the school of mechanistic biology. Diderot and his collaborators continued along the same lines. Buffon wrote in his *Traité des Animaux* that soul and body were one in the animal kingdom. Cordillac spoke in his treatise about the dependence of animals on automatism. The materialists of the Enlightenment further concluded that the whole cosmos and its organic and inorganic content were the result of mechanical processes.

When Descartes died in February 1650, Lafontaine was in his thirtieth year: his friend Molière was only six months younger. In both, the star impulse of the folk soul emerged in a fully human fashion. Both were loving observers of the world, true artists and teachers of a life-affirming self-control.

Lafontaine possessed the gay and penetrating spirit of the *fabliaux* poets. He was simple, unassuming and of great integrity. He kept away from the court and its intrigues and died in loneliness and poverty. His fables were originally published by himself, in three volumes of twelve books each. They were soon widely read for they had universal appeal. Human faults and weaknesses appear in his fables as fox, wolf, lion, eagle, gazelle, rabbits, raven, mice and so on. With a tolerant smile but at the same time with merciless severity, he brought to light everything that impedes true humanity. In his own life he was gentle, conciliatory and calm.

Molière worked in the same spirit. He pointed to the corruption threatening the French soul and fought every kind of excess, as well as the narrow-mindedness and intolerance of sects and academies. He was close to the earth, unlike his contemporaries who kept aloof from everyday life in their work. He appealed throughout to truth. The sole theme of his plays was man in his relationship to his fellow men. He was completely free from orthodoxy and not restricted by any formula. His expression was precise; the instrument of a free mind and an intelligence of childlike innocence. Outside his work, he was often melancholy, yet kind and fearless. Lafontaine and Molière judged the moral quality of contemporary society and individuals with an awareness that is normally experienced only in the Moon sphere after death.

Spiritual knowledge tells that for every soul, expansion in the Moon sphere after death is a preparation for higher stages. The soul becomes for the first time really conscious of its failings and judges itself with a truthfulness that is almost impossible on Earth.

France is the Moon country. In the seventeenth century, an age of great splendour and power for France, the French mission often seemed hidden. But behind the outer scene the folk soul, striving towards great aims, constantly faced searching self-criticism: ' Am I worthy? Is my people faithful to its mission? Does it really count in the evolution of the world, and is it capable of developing? '

Louis XIV, blinded by splendour and self-glorification, made answer, ' Yes, for I am the *roi soleil*, the great monarch. I have absolute power and a love of culture: France has become Europe's leading power.' In the French people the longing for ' la gloire ' grew increasingly. There is not really an adequate translation for *la gloire*. The word expresses love of power and ambition; and contains a deeper, almost melancholic undertone, a longing for an all-pervading beauty and humanity that can find recognition before the soul's own great tribunal.

The taming of the will had been furthered by Rabelais, Lafontaine and Molière, the increasing independence of thinking by Descartes. The balance of feeling was achieved by the French people through love of art, which gradually penetrated all spheres of culture. Help came through the spiritual link with ancient Greece.

According to tradition, Dionysius the Areopagite, St. Paul's Greek pupil, visited Paris. The district of St. Denis is named after him. Greek thought was cultivated at Chartres and the Scholastics spread the teachings of Aristotle from Paris.

Corneille, Racine and Voltaire adapted the Aristotelian principle of the unity of time, place and action to their plays. Greek themes were used once more. Corneille and Voltaire wrote Oedipus plays, Racine about Alexander, Andromache, Iphigenia and Phaedra. In *Les Plaideurs* Racine bases himself on Aristophanes. Among Voltaire's titles were *Artemis* and *Oreste*.

The name of Paris recalls the mythological story of the origins of Greek culture. Paris, the Trojan hero, tried to win Helen, the beauty of Greece. Paris, the city, also strove for beauty: and came to be known as the fairest city of modern times.

French architecture and interior decoration dictated European taste. But other spheres of human activity were also affected by the French sense of beauty. The concept of a ' bel-esprit ', an increased sensitivity for intellectual liveliness, is the outcome of the influence of beauty on human thought. The delight in giving free rein to thoughts and emotions often proved stronger than the feeling for down-to-earth reality.

Language also passed through the school of beauty. It was considered essential for the man of culture to speak beautifully and with self-assurance. Manners became more refined, and the fashions of all civilized nations fell under the spell of French taste. Everywhere, directly or indirectly, the Sense of Taste, whose metamorphosis was part of the French mission, became manifest.

Great attention was given to cooking. Meals became ceremonial, and their preparation was treated as important. Richelieu, who founded the *Académie Française* in 1635, who destroyed the power of the nobility and the Huguenots, and who assured the French state its dominant position in Europe, knew how to cook. His successor, Cardinal Mazarin, like Richelieu, invented dishes which were named after him, as did even Louis II of Bourbon, *Connètable* of the Condé and an outstanding general. Another famous cook was the statesman Colbert, the founder of the *Académie des Sciences*, and superintendent of the arts, buildings and factories. To him, cooking was a noble pastime. Montaigne wrote a *Science de la Gueule*, a ' science of the mouth '. Later, Grimod de la Rèyniere became the great French authority on cooking; he wrote eight volumes for his *Almanac des Gourmands*. Carême, Talleyrand's cook, and his book *Le Pâtissier Pittoresque*, were famous. Brillat Savarin's *Physiology of Taste, or Meditations on Transcendental Gastronomy* was published in 1825. The preoccupation with food had become both art and science.

A new attempt to cleanse French morals was made at the beginning of the eighteenth century. Three outstanding individuals appeared as the heralds of new impulses. Rousseau tried to prepare the way for a more natural mode of life, Voltaire strove for the freedom of the spirit, and Montesquieu developed the concept of the threefold state. None of them realized that a disastrous whirlwind would use their work to fan the flames of the Revolution.

Jean Jacques Rousseau, though born in Geneva, was essentially French in temperament. He loved to go on long walks, for it was then that he could think best. His most radical ideas came to him, in 1749, when he had spent eight days in the forest in almost trance-like walking. Earlier in the same year he had already had a decisive experience on a walk from Paris to Vincennes. Quite suddenly, he was filled with the thoughts which were to become the starting point for all his later work.

His earnest and loving devotion to nature could kindle similar feelings in others. He placed nature above everything else in his attempts to reform the social conditions of his time. Longingly he dreamed of a state not unlike that of primitive peoples, from which, he imagined, universal freedom and happiness would result. He spoke a great deal about freedom: ' Man is free, but he lives in chains '. Freedom, he believed, could be found if men were untouched by civilization. Rousseau thus placed the ideal of freedom, which is the culmination of human development, at the beginning. Almost inevitably he came to advocate libertinism. His work is the glorification of the animal aspect of the centaur nature.

Voltaire, who developed in his thinking the archer aiming at his target, wrote after reading a book by Rousseau: ' Never was the case for turning us into beasts stated more brilliantly; one really feels like walking on all fours after reading this work! ' Louis Claude de St. Martin, the philosopher and theosophist, said of Rousseau and his followers: ' Like him and his friends,

I want man to follow his natural laws, but we differ greatly, for they demand that man follow the natural law of the animal, while I have in mind the law that distinguishes him from the animal. That is the law that illuminates and guides his steps, in fact the law that is derived from the light of truth itself'.

Voltaire, too, was a fighter against oppression. With brilliant wit, he unmasked claims to authority in spiritual matters and mocked every form of superstition. Throughout his long life, he was like a personification of the French people, of the longing to find access to freedom through logical thinking.

He stood in the midst of the rationalism of his time, and represented the 'enlightened' stream of philosophy, directed towards materialism. Yet he was far too truthful to exclude all other aspects from the new picture of the world. His hatred and contempt were confined to the forces that kept the soul enslaved. Despite the tendencies of his time, he tried again and again to save a trinity which he called God, Freedom and Immortality. He coined the phrase: 'If God did not exist, He would have to be invented'.

Montesquieu's *L'Esprit des Lois* appeared in 1748. Here an attempt was made to bring the ordering power of a threefold system to bear on the organization of the state. Equality was to be assured through well-planned laws and constitutions, by dividing the state into legislature, the law and the executive.

Thirty years later his *Trias Politica* was to prove revolutionary. Immediately before the Revolution, pamphlets appeared passionately demanding changes in the legal and social system. The reorganization of social life seemed to have become the concern of every Frenchman.

The reason for the great impact of Montesquieu's work lies in man's own nature. Every individual represents a trinity of body, soul and spirit, which manifests itself in the life of the soul as thinking, feeling and willing. The unity of the body is similarly based on three physical systems; the nervous system, the rhythmic, or heart and respiratory system, and the metabolic system. Man's own creation, the social system, is also basically threefold. Its realms are: the spiritual life, the life of the state and the economic life.

To each of these the French people had made unique contributions. In the spiritual life, they had created in the eighteenth century an almost universal culture of the intellect, whose symbolic expression was Diderot's encyclopaedia. This earliest of all encyclopaedias had brought knowledge within everybody's reach, while the splendour of the court became so typically French that it led to an increased awareness of beauty everywhere. The general enthusiasm for cookery was, inevitably, linked with the production of food and therefore with the economic system.

Parallel to this development of a threefold culture which followed a natural urge, small circles cultivated the aims that could have given a new direction to the gifts of the people. With great reverence, the ideals the French soul was striving for, liberty, fraternity and equality, were carefully guarded. But there was also no illusion about the great dangers threatening France.

In George Sand's *Countess of Rudolstadt* (first published in 1844) the hero is made to say:

'Hear the call: long live the republic! hear the vast crowd proclaiming freedom, brotherly love and equality. Alas, these were the words talked of in our mysteries with subdued voices, and only the adepts of the highest degree would speak of them with one another. Now no secrets are necessary any longer. The sacraments are for the whole world, the cup for everybody, as our fathers, the Hussites told us.' But suddenly he burst into bitter tears: 'I know, the message had not yet penetrated far enough! Not enough men carried it in their hearts or took it into their spirit! What horror,' he continued, ' war everywhere, and what a war'. He wept for a long time. We did not know what visions unfolded before his eyes.

Since the time of Philip the Fair, France had been threatened with the possibility of having the healthy impulses of her mission diverted. The fateful years when all might still have been turned to good were during the last quarter of the eighteenth century. This was the time when the Comte de St. Germain, like a cleansing comet, tried to arouse a sense of responsibility everywhere. In aristocratic circles he warned of the coming catastrophe that could be diverted by the right measures. Elsewhere also he advised, and tried to spread calm.

At that time only he knew in what measure the impulses behind freedom, equality and brotherhood could clear the path towards the future: Freedom, in which the spirit could shed the fetters of an outlived civilization; Equality that guards the rights of every individual in the state; and Brotherhood in the use of the blessings of nature and in everyday life. The realization of this threefold ideal meant the solution of the social problems of the new age.

The Enlightenment could still prove a blessing. The educated class took the ideals of freedom seriously, the bourgeoisie tried to guard its rights against arbitrary interference by the state, and the peasants became owners of their land. Everywhere there seemed a growing readiness to introduce an orderly revolution. On the fourth of August 1789, the National Assembly, in a night of session, declared the words Liberty, Fraternity, Equality, basic to the inalienable rights of man.

The peaceful glow of these three ideals caused even leading German spirits like Goethe to welcome the Revolution. At the time it seemed as if the innermost substance of her destiny, to the cultivation of which France had devoted herself throughout the centuries, would be experienced as a healing element in Europe.

But the ancient struggle between man and his lower self, between aims of true progress and untransformed instincts, was not yet won. The Revolution degenerated into tyranny and crime. By 1793 the slogan had become a cruel threat: ' Liberty, Equality, Fraternity—or death!'

The impulse towards a threefold order, whose practical application was a dire need for France and the whole of Europe, became homeless but travelled on. There are tasks that long to be fulfilled even if the first efforts fail. The mission one people is unable to fulfil may be adopted elsewhere.

Again as the result of historical events, though this time through the death of a country, the idea of a threefold social order was taken up by great Polish thinkers who, recognizing that the threefold ideal is written into world history, spoke of the future institutions it would inspire. For a third time, again in the wake of historical events, the same impulse appeared in Central Europe, this time worked out in full awareness of historical responsibility. But it was not to materialize. Now, the call for a social order where freedom, equality and fraternity can find expression in a healthy way no longer goes out to nations, but to individuals, those who are fully awake throughout humanity.

For France the moment for a thorough renewal had passed. The Napoleonic wars and all later outward successes merely fed the longing for a never-ending greatness, *la gloire*.

But today, glory and greatness can no longer be confined to any particular nation. They become the glory of individual man who, despite innumerable obstacles, holds in humility to the Archer's aim of true humanity.

Plate 16. *Henry the Navigator*. (1394–1460.) Grand Master of the Order of Christ. Detail from the famous St. Vincent panel.

By courtesy of the Museum of Antique Art, Lisbon.

Plate 17. *Sacred Promontory* (*Promontorium Sacrum*). Bay of Sagres near Vincento, Portugal. Where a Saturn sanctuary had once stood.

Plate 18. *Holy St. Michael with the Scales.* By Valle de Ribes (13th century).

By courtesy of the Museo Episcopal, Vich, Spain.

Plate 19. *Martyrdom of St. Julita.* End of the 11th century.

By courtesy of the Museo de Arte, Barcelona.

Plate 20. *Christ on the Cross.* By El Greco (1547–1614).
Painter, sculpture, architect, musician and writer.

By courtesy of the British Museum, London.

Plate 21. *Avebury, Wiltshire*. (Reconstructed.) In its own way Avebury is just as unique as Stonehenge. A great circle of one hundred stones, many of them weighing up to forty tons. Within the large circle were two smaller circles. The north circle contained thirty stones. In the centre were placed three huge stones arranged on three sides of a square. The south circle contained thirty-two stones.

From a drawing by Alan Sorrell. 'Crown Copyright,' reproduced by kind permission of H.M. Ministry of the Environment. (From the Official Ministry Guide Book.)

Plate 22. *Stonehenge, Wiltshire.* (Reconstructed.) Dated between three main periods, 1800–1400 B.C. This very special circle must have been very important in the ceremonies and planetary calculations of the ancient Initiate Priests.

From a drawing by Alan Sorrell. 'Crown Copyright,' reproduced by permission of H.M. Ministry of the Environment. (From the Official Ministry Guide Book.)

Plate 23. *The South Cross, Ahenny, near Waterford, Ireland.* The Ahenny crosses are the earliest true High Crosses in Ireland. (Circa 735–790.) The sandstone cross is eleven feet high. Together with the North Cross, they stand in a deserted churchyard.

Photograph by John Fletcher.

Plate 26. (above) *Lapith and Centaur.* (Circa 445 B.C.) From the south metope of the Parthenon. Athens.

By courtesy of the British Museum, London.

Plate 24. (left) *Europe: A Prophecy.* By William Blake. (1794.) 'The midnight clock has struck! and hark! the bell of death beats slow!'

By courtesy of the British Museum, London.

Plate 25. *The Royal Doors (West Facade)* 1150. *Chartres Cathedral.* On the typanum of the south door of the Royal Doors, is a statue of the Madonna and Child. The artist was inspired by the ancient wooden statue, called the *Virgo paritura*, 'The Virgin who is to give birth', originally in the crypt, destroyed by fire in 1793.

By courtesy of Maison de l'Asne-Qui-Vielle, Chartres.

Plate 27. *Joan of Arc* (1412–1431). By Dubois (1896). In front of the west entrance of Rheims Cathedral.

By courtesy of Buch-Künstverlag Ettal, Switzerland.

Plate 28. *The Last Judgment*. By Michaelangelo. From the Sistine Chapel, the Vatican, Rome.

By courtesy of the Vatican, Rome.

Plate 29. *St. Michael Overcoming the Dragon.* By Raphael. Painted when he was eighteen.

By courtesy of the Musée de Louvre, Paris.

Plate 30. *Melencolia.* Engraving by Albert Dürer (1514).

By courtesy of the British Museum, London.

Plate 31. *Goethe.* Aged 41. Copper engraving by Heinrich Lips (1791).

By courtesy of Zentralbibliothek der Deutschen Klassik, Weimar.

Plate 32. *The Madonna Elëusa of Vladimir*. Icon.

By courtesy of the Ikon Museum. Recklinghausen, Germany.

Italy

ITALY'S MISSION is connected with the formative impulses of the Goat. His horns of light curve upwards, but on medieval star maps his body is shown with a fish's tail plunging into the depths. The Goat knows both the heavens and the earthly abyss and is the gateway to a realm of gods where violent battles take place.

When the new Europe was being prepared in the ninth century, Italy already possessed the great legacy of her Roman past. External Rome had been the creation of Romulus; Numa Pompilius gave it the breath of life. He was the founder of the Vesta cult, the guarding of the eternal flame through virgin priestesses. The fire of the Sun was to burn in Rome for all time and Numa was the first high priest, the *Pontifex Maximus*.

Rome pressed other peoples into service and cast a shadow across whole continents, demanding as the *Imperium Romanum* tribute and recognition.

Into this power-hungry civilization impulses of love were placed with the birth of Christ. St. Peter, the first Christian *Pontifex Maximus*, confirmed his office by death on a cross. Love to the Sun-Being, the Christ whom all hierarchies serve, was henceforth to be decisive in place of outward power. The will to take and hold on leads to rigidity; to give and to receive helps the forces of metamorphosis.

Healing impulses began to be active in Rome. When Attila the Hun was at the city gates with his hordes in 542, Pope Leo faced him in his robes of office, and the attack did not take place. During the preliminaries of appointing Gregory I as Pope, Rome was ravaged by plague. Gregory organized help and precautions, and ordered a procession to gather for prayer. Tradition has it that at the close,

> . . . the Archangel Michael appeared over the mausoleum of Hadrian sheathing a sword, which announced the cessation of the plague . . . Another relates that Gregory heard the angels singing the Paschal Anthem: *Regina coeli laetare, Alleluia; quia quem meruisti portare, Alleluia; resurrexit sicut dixit, Alleluia;* to which Gregory added on the inspiration of the moment: *Ora pro nobis Deum, Alleluia.**

The plague came to an end. Gradually the old warrior impulses weakened in the Roman empire. People after people came to Italy through their own decision and were absorbed and transformed by the Italian soil.

---

* St. Gregory the Great, by Abbot Snow, 1924.
  [Rejoice, O Queen of Heaven, Alleluia; for He whom thou wast favoured to bear, Alleluia; has risen as He said (foretold), Alleluia; . . . Pray for us to the Lord God, Alleluia.]

The region of the Goat has powerful formative tendencies and radiates the crystallizing forces which once helped to give the Roman empire its character. Rome was the focal point through which the nations were held together. In the ninth century the city again assumed the task of unification and worked for Europe's independence from the influences of the East, to which she was still spiritually linked. The ancient clairvoyance rooted mainly in Asia was still weaving in European souls and it was Rome's mission to overcome it.

Throughout thousands of years the time had been prepared for, when humanity would have to pass through the trial of godlessness, so that inner strength should grow out of this combat against darkness. It was the task of an emergent Europe to bring about this condition.

Pope Nicholas I (858–67) viewed the future with deep concern. At his court were many outstanding personalities, among them his friend Anastasius Bibliotecarius, whose great insight into the problems of his age made him share the Pope's anxiety. Nicholas felt it as his responsibility to find ways of making the inevitable easier to bear, and the forces of the Goat helped him to create a vessel, sufficiently firm to hold concentrated spiritual truth, and rendered untouchable through the power of the Roman Church.

Through Nicholas the wisdom of the cosmos hardened into dogma that could be accepted without being understood. A faith arose which rejected all vision, and made it superfluous. Even the ritual became part of dogmatic concept, reduced to mere symbol and carried by faith.

Pope Nicholas was a courageous fighter with statesman-like gifts, moral strength and great will-power. He achieved the increase of Rome's power throughout the West. But he saw great danger to his aims in two spiritual movements. With sorrow he looked upon the exalted spirituality of Western Europe. In Ireland, France and Spain esoteric schools still existed through which men could look into the spiritual world, and where Christianity could be taught through visionary experience. This he could not countenance, and so when John Scotus Erigena, who was of Irish origin and represented the radiant spirituality of the West, offered Nicholas his translation of Dionysius the Areopagite's work on the Hierarchies, the Pope refused it. The translation was then entrusted to the care of Anastasius the Librarian.

Nicholas similarly attacked the esoteric cult of the eastern Christians who saw in the Holy Sepulchre the source of their strength. To the Eastern Church he explained that the Roman Papacy was founded on the rock of St. Peter as the guardian of Christian unity. He made clear that no decision could be taken in Constantinople without his agreement. In nine letters he demanded that the entire Eastern Church and its leading personalities should bend to his will and make it manifest.

An important event of the time was the conversion of the Bulgarians. In 865 King Boris I adopted Christianity. Though he had been taught by Greeks, he turned to the Pope who answered all his questions in a manner that made Greek influence appear as unnecessary and calculated to mislead. The supreme authority of the Apostolic See was proclaimed and the Bulgar king declared himself the servant of St. Peter. Nicholas also looked to Moravia, where Cyrillus and Methodius, the great missionaries, were active at the time. He called the two apostles of the Slavs to him to render their account. But by the time they arrived in Rome the Pope had died.

In due course Arabian abstraction was to enter this dark void; and consequently a materialistic Europe arose which became for the soul a dark valley, full of error and guilt. But the spiritual vacuum which set in from the ninth century onwards allowed the folk spirits to evolve undisturbed the cosmically rooted twelvehood of the peoples of Europe.

Italy has three distinct historical zones: the north, Rome, and Naples with Sicily.

Northern and Central Italy developed dukedoms and cities with a progressive culture where Italy's soul could flourish. Rome had the ability to incorporate what others had created, without losing its own character, and remained the Eternal City, *Roma aeterna*.

In southern Italy Pythagoras had been active in pre-Christian times. He spoke of the journey of the soul from incarnation to incarnation, of mathematics and astronomy, and of the cosmos resounding with the music of the spheres. The east of Sicily still reflected the sunlike radiance of the deed of Empedocles, who threw himself into Etna to prove to his Greek contemporaries the immortality of the soul. But the west of Sicily was the scene of decadent mysteries, whose influence profoundly affected Europe.

In the ninth century when Pope Nicholas was creating new foundations for the future, and when the knights of the Holy Grail were guarding the flame of the immediate presence of the spirit at carefully hidden centres, an enemy appeared who was known to the followers of the Grail as the greatest of all adversaries. Wolfram von Eschenbach later called him Klingsor. His main sphere of activity at the time was southern Italy and Sicily, Capua and Calot Bobot.*

The fortress of Calot Bobot stood high on a rock in Sicily's south-western mountains. Here schemes were put into action resulting from the union of Klingsor with Iblis, the Queen of Sicily. The name Iblis is Arabic and means Lucifer. Klingsor was in the grip of satanic powers. Not far from Calot Bobot—Caltabellotta—stood the ancient Temple of Erix which had once been dedicated to Aphrodite and where utterly decadent ceremonies were now performed.

Its presence increased the dangerous influence of Calot Bobot considerably. It is said that Klingsor was lord of the Terra de Labur or Terra di Lavoro. He reigned from Capua and his historical name was Landulf II of Capua.** His power was vast. The Emperor Ludwig raised him to ' third man in the Empire ' and heaped so many honours upon him that Landulf wanted to make Capua an archbishopric, with himself as archbishop. He had called the Emperor to Italy ostensibly to fight the Arabs who had been enticed there by his own brother in 840. Landulf was their secret ally, and with their help he maintained his connection with Calot Bobot. When in 873 he openly concluded a treaty with them, he was excommunicated by the Pope. For a moment, the fog hiding his aims divided.

Modern historians have written of Landulf's relationship to popes and emperors: Muratori, Amari, Lokys, Harmann, Stein and others. Their writings leave no doubt that Landulf and his friends stood behind all the intrigues of the age. Many important documents were falsified, among them the pseudo-Isidorian Decretals, which justify the intervention of the Church in secular affairs. Pope Nicholas appears to have been presented with them by Rothard of Soissons. At first he rejected this document, but later he made use of it.

Klingsor's influence was probably also behind the decisions of the eighth Ecumenical Council, held at Constantinople in 869, when it was laid down that man consisted only of body and soul. The trinity within man's nature was to be forgotten.

---

* Compare the chapter on Spain and Portugal.
** Compare W. J. Stein, *Das neunte Jahrhundert*, 1966.

The following centuries in Italy saw incessant warfare between the popes and the German emperors who, since Otto I, had wished to be crowned in Rome. They hoped to make Italy a western centre to hold together their own empire. To the popes, Rome was the rock from which they could defend their power. In the struggle, Rome remained victorious.

In Pope Innocent III the spirit of the *Imperium Romanum* found a new instrument. As ancient Rome had forced Roman law on other nations, so the Pope now claimed for himself the right to act as supreme judge of the West. Ancient Rome had established its authority through the power of arms. The Pope spread his through the force of dogma or, where it seemed necessary, by excommunication, fire and sword. He made the teaching of Transubstantiation a basic principle of faith which had to be blindly accepted, and introduced oral confession to gain control of mens' souls.

Before being crowned, Otto IV had to promise to surrender all goods demanded by the Church and to refrain from intervention in ecclesiastical elections. When he later tried to free himself from this enforced promise he was excommunicated, and Frederick II was raised to the rank of German Emperor in his place. The French king, Philippe Auguste, was forced by the Pope to re-marry his former wife; and Pedro of Aragon in order to be crowned had to promise to make his entire realm pay tribute. King Sancho of Portugal also paid heavy dues.

When King John of England insisted on the independence of his country he was excommunicated; until eventually he gave England to the Pope, receiving it back from his hands, as a vassal. After losing his country to Rome he was called 'John Lackland', John without land.

Pope Innocent inaugurated the crusade against the Cathars, which ended in their extermination. He personally preached the crusade against Constantinople. With the help of his friend, the powerful Doge of Venice, Enrico Dandalo, who joined the crusade for egotistic motives, he was able to defeat Byzantine Christianity. At the time of the conquest of Constantinople, the cold and calculating Venetian stood nearly at the end of his very long life. Dandalo destroyed Byzantine rule and set up a Latin empire. But based as it was on selfishness and lust for power, it lacked the strength to withstand attack by the Turks in the following centuries. The Christian Constantinople was lost.

Into this situation created by Pope Innocent, St. Francis of Assisi carried the message of love and compassion, which Buddha had once taught and which had become reality in Christ.

His activity was the spiritual antithesis of all power impulses. Instead of wanting to rule, he chose to serve, in place of wealth he preferred poverty and suffering. He did not bring judgment but comfort, he blessed instead of cursing.

He was completely without fear. The scourge of his time was leprosy, then virtually incurable and highly infectious. St. Francis looked for the lepers in the caves where they had been banished. There he lived with them: he comforted them, nursed them, and surrounded them with his great love. Since he was filled with moral power he could sometimes heal. The images of the events in Palestine lived with timeless reality in his soul.

His love extended also to animals and plants. The flame was a sister to him, even when it burned his hut. In his all-embracing love he included the elements and the stars, for these represented his soul before the Godhead. He loved the harsh and ascetic destiny he had created for himself. He was the *Pater Seraphicus*, the servant of the Spirits of Love.

St. Francis lived in loving observation. He had eyes that drew in the sufferings of others, so that their burden should become lighter. Thus he united himself with death and sorrow, for what the eyes can see, and the Sun shine upon, is subject to the laws of death. Those radiant eyes weakened and lost their light. It was while he was blind, lying in his dark hut in terrible pain, that he wrote his hymn to the Sun, hoping his monks would one day sing it throughout the world, like troubadours.

> Most High, All Powerful, God of Goodness:
> To Thee be praise and glory, honour and all thankfulness.
> To Thee alone, Most High, are these things due,
> And no man is worthy to speak of Thee.
>
> Be Thou praised, O Lord, for all Thy Creation,
> More especially for our Brother the Sun,
> Who bringeth forth the day and giveth light thereby.
>
> For he is glorious and splendid in his radiance,
> And to Thee, Most High, he bears similitude.
>
> . . . . .
>
> Be Thou praised, my Lord, of those who pardon for Thy love
> And endure sickness and tribulations.
>
> Blessed are they who will endure it in peace,
> For by Thee, Most High, they shall be crowned.

When he was near death, he added to the *Canticle of the Sun* a praise of death, for death is an expression of the Sun who burns physical matter to liberate the spirit.

> Be Thou praised, my Lord, for our Sister, Bodily Death
> From whom no man living may escape.
> Woe to those who die in mortal sin.
>
> Blessed are they who are found in Thy most holy will
> For the second death shall not work them ill.
>
> Praise ye and bless my Lord and give Him thanks,
> And serve Him with great humility.

On 14 September, 1224, two years before his death, St. Francis received the Stigmata which he bore in silence to the end. The marks on his hands, his feet and his side, were formed in the presence of a Seraph. Brother Leo told how for forty days between the feast of the Assumption of the Virgin and St. Michael's day, St. Francis had passed through a deep struggle in solitude.

Between his receiving of the Stigmata and his death on 3 October, 1226, fell the birth of an even greater and completely different individuality. Thomas Aquinas (1225–1274) did not have to take any outer martyrdom upon himself, for St. Francis had performed the great sacrifice of direct physical spiritualization for his time.

Like St. Francis, Thomas Aquinas worked from within the Church, rather than against it. Thus he could let the redeeming power of clear thought shine forth from it. He forged earthly intellectual concepts into a vessel for the invisible. Problems that had hitherto been solved by supersensible vision he brought into the sphere of human thinking, basing himself on man's innate ability for dispassionate intellectual judgment. His thinking was conscientious and disciplined to a degree unknown before. With mathematical certainty he linked idea to idea, conclusion with conclusion.

But he saw that only to a certain extent could he penetrate the mysteries of Christianity. Thinking could lead him only to an understanding of the working of the Father God, who is manifest in all creatures. The mystery of the Son could not be fathomed with such methods. Here, knowledge had to be supplemented by faith.

It is told that shortly before his death, Thomas Aquinas, at prayer in the church of his monastery in Naples, was seen floating above the ground, his features reflecting the radiance of the light of Christ, Who spoke: ' You have written well of Me, Thomas. What do you seek from Me? ' ' Thee alone, O Lord,' answered Thomas. He experienced the Divine within man; but his burning wish to be allowed to reveal the glory of the Son even through human thinking was not granted to him. Only when Christ Himself penetrates the power of thought can vision and faith turn to knowledge.

Whereas Thomas Aquinas, through the clarity and vigour of his thinking,, renewed and increased contemporary knowledge, Brunetto Latini experienced the forces active in the cosmos in inner visions. He was one of the last to do so at the end of the Middle Ages. He had been sent as an ambassador of the Florentine Guelphs to King Alfonso of Castile. His journey back led him through the Valley of Roncevalles where Roland, Charlemagne's favourite paladin, had died and where Grail memories were still alive. Here his spirit withdrew from normal consciousness: his experiences in this state he later wrote down in *Tesoretto*.

He passed through the gate to the Godhead. In a wood he met the ' Goddess Natura ' of whom he said that no words could describe her adequately. Innumerable creatures belonged to her and all of them began and ended, lived and died, as she told them. Heaven was her veil. At her command, the skies divided; whole worlds were enclosed within her arms. Sometimes she smiled, sometimes her features darkened in anger or sorrow. She explained to Brunetto the seven days of Creation, the birth of Christ, the mystery of the divine Mother. Heaven and sea, the air and the angels drew their strength from her and begged her permission to carry out their task. Finally, she ordered him to walk on alone. After many experiences he learned of a community whose head was the God of Love. He then penetrated, with Ovid's help, to a sphere where the human spirit makes free decisions for his future development.

Brunetto Latini became the teacher of Dante Alighieri, the great exponent of the Italian people's genius.

Though the work of outstanding individuals is linked to a certain place and period, it is also universal in its influence. As Shakespeare still speaks to us like a contemporary, and Molière both encourages and admonishes us through his wit, so Dante can be a beacon at the gate of death that leads to the Godhead. His great poem was constructed in three parts, the *Inferno*, the *Purgatorio* and the *Paradiso*—and in them he describes the life of souls after death. The closing lines of each of the three books point to the stars. Emerging from the Inferno, he says:

> We climbed, he first, I following his steps
> Till on our view the beautiful lights of Heaven
> Dawned through a circular opening in the cave;
> Thence issuing we again beheld the stars.

The *Purgatorio* concludes with the words:

> I returned
> From the most holy wave, regenerate,
> E'en as new plants refreshed with foliage new,
> Pure and made apt for climbing to the stars.

And the final words of the *Paradiso*:

> Here vigour failed the towering phantasy:
> But yet the will rolled onward, like a wheel
> In even motion, by the Love impelled
> That moves the sun in Heaven and all the stars.

What he represented as hell is the experience of souls trapped in earthly desires which they have to discard with great pain after death. His purgatory is the next step in the gradual adaptation to higher spheres. Finally he found spirits in the land of the spirit, in bright cosmic worlds. He led the reader upwards from the depths, from fate to fate, from soul to soul, as if ascending through a wondrous dome which had its foundations far in the darkness below, and yet rose into extreme heights of Divine creation: it embraced the whole of humanity which, through its individual members, shares in all its parts.

Dante was soldier, statesman and scholar. His friend Giotto was painter, sculptor and architect. While Dante went back to the wisdom of the past, Giotto's work points to the future. His portrait of Dante is one of the first life-like paintings of the late Middle Ages. Giotto no longer used the gold background beloved of the Gothic; he was the first to paint the sky blue. He is the forerunner of the Renaissance, which is the product of the observing eye.

In the fifteenth century three outstanding men appear, forerunners on the road to naturalistic representation; Brunelleschi, Ghiberti and Donatello. The discovery of Greek and Roman statues coincided with their efforts to make soul forces visible in idealised, yet life-like figures.

Churches and palaces rose everywhere. To walk through the streets of Italian cities, or to kneel before the great altar-pieces of the time, was to share through the eyes in the artistically rich substance of the nation.

The Italian folk spirit looked up to St. Michael who, as representative of the Sun, furthers man's ascent from the depths to the heights. But other forces working against his aims were also active. During the great flowering of art in the Renaissance, the very families which encouraged this general awakening were dominated by the lust for wealth and power. In Florence the Medici had already in the thirteenth century striven among themselves for leading positions. One rising followed another, palaces were stormed, looted and burned whenever their owners incurred popular—or their rivals'—wrath. Slander, confiscation and executions were daily occurrences.

The Medici stopped at nothing when it was a question of strengthening their power. But they were by no means alone in their use of treachery and murder. All the leading families employed these methods. But skilful intrigues demanded great discretion and presence of mind. Crime, courage, love of beauty, and friendship for those who distinguished themselves in science and art went hand in hand.

At the turn of the sixteenth century, the darker side of the Renaissance had its chief representatives in the Borgia family. Guicciardini wrote that all Borgias were false and shameless, without any sense of good faith or loyalty, and avaricious to the point of barbarism. Roderigo Borgia bought himself the tiara and became Pope Alexander VI. Half Europe was at that time the property of the Church and paid vast tributes to Rome.

Pope Alexander was as greedy for gold as his predecessors and like them, he also knew how to give. He was proud in the extreme and loved splendour and ostentation. He was the first pope to speak openly of his children. Cesare Borgia was his favourite son. Messer Pieretto, his father's *protégé*, was stabbed by Cesare while he sheltered under the Pope's own mantle. At Cesare's instigation, his brother the Duke of Gandia was murdered and thrown into the Tiber. Later he caused the murder of all the nobles of the Romagna.

It needed courage to be evil on such a vast scale in an age that believed so strongly in hell and purgatory. Cesare was of Spanish origin, but his life was spent entirely in Italy, the country of the Italian soul which could experience alike beauty and ugliness, the exalted and the diabolical.

In 1502 an emissary appeared at Cesare's headquarters in the Romagna. He was of medium height, with a small head, black hair, thin lips and sparkling eyes. This was Niccolo Macchiavelli. The impression Cesare Borgia made on him was overwhelming: he became to him the ideal of a prince. Macchiavelli admired his ruthlessness, combined with his calculated use of cruelty, his avoidance of half-measure and his self-assurance. In his letters he expressed the view that Cesare's methods of conquering and consolidating a new state, as well as his treatment of false friends, were highly commendable. Later, in *The Prince*, which was based on the character of Cesare Borgia, he analysed the means for an ambitious ruler to gain absolute power. Beginning with the study of humanity, he stated that everything could be ascribed to natural causes or to the play of fortune.

These views underlay his *Science of Politics*. Political success was placed above all ethical considerations, above all economic measures, above the well-being of the individual and above art and science. He considered even religion as subordinate to the state, which was to be guided by an all-powerful ruler.

Passions are inscribed in the human face: to perceive them in full objectivity requires great inner strength. Leonardo da Vinci possessed this strength. His innumerable, meticulously drawn caricatures, one more horrible than the other, are no play of imagination but works of scientific accuracy. Vasari tells of him that he would follow an unusual face for days to study it in detail. Often he invited strangers, met in the street; offered them food and made them drunk so that he could study their expressions of greed and coarseness. In order to create the terrible head of the Medusa he bred poisonous toads and snakes, which he irritated to fury. He learned in this way to characterize the sub-human.

It was the same Leonardo who painted Madonnas of heavenly perfection; who portrayed the twelve Apostles in the *Last Supper* with such deep realism, and yet transcended it. His ideal of the Christ was so high that for many years he felt unable to paint the sacred features.

Leonardo's character is unfathomable, like the smile of the Mona Lisa. He had incomparable gifts as a sculptor, architect, musician, anatomist, botanist and engineer, and was a master of astronomy and astrology. Above all he was an inventor. He constructed mechanical mills and machines that could drill tunnels or drag loads. He invented methods of draining swamps and suggested that the Church of San Giovanni should be raised and placed on a platform with steps. He also studied the problem of flight. His experiments of every kind cast their shadow far into future centuries.

Leonardo was handsome, his body well-formed and powerful. He was rich, and kept servants and horses: princes and kings were among his friends. Yet a dark cloud lay above his life. He remained mysterious, a spirit who had decided to keep his real destiny hidden from curious eyes.

Two great works of Michaelangelo can claim comparison with Leonardo's *Last Supper*: his *Creation* and his *Last Judgment*. When he painted the Sistine Chapel he called the remote past to life with titanic strength; it seemed as if the ceiling had been pierced to bring world memories down from the cosmos. He gave them form, as clear and precise as the Prophets had experienced—and again as they had breathed stormily through the souls of the Sybils. He takes us through the generations from the beginnings of man to the time of Christ. The past becomes present before human eyes.

Michaelangelo's name means Michael's Angel. Through his creative gifts he tried to lead men to an awareness of their divine origin and human dignity. In the *Last Judgment* he painted an apocalyptic vision of humanity's future. Here, those who have followed the Christ on Earth are shown coming towards Him. Others, through demonic power, are falling into the depths, towards an Earth of which nothing is left but hardened remains. (Plate 28.)

Through these frescoes, Michaelangelo spoke to his contemporaries with the courage of one who has no illusions about men's attitudes to their individual destinies. Yet he worked not merely out of personal awareness, but drew from the very depth of the soul of his own people, to whom heaven and hell were realities.

Italy at the time of the Renaissance had innumerable painters. It was the general practice for students and assistants to complete the pictures of their masters. Such productivity was supported by the interest of all classes, from merchants and lower ranks of the nobility to princes; convents and even whole cities watched impatiently the growth of major works.

Raphael Santi painted for all, although his most extensive work was carried out at the Vatican under the patronage of the Pope. His representations of the trinity of religion, science and art cover whole walls on the stanzas, the new rooms in the Vatican; they took three years to complete and were finished when Raphael was twenty-eight.

Raphael's countless paintings of the Madonna were created out of the infinite harmony of his soul. Her features are the same on all of them, as if he had seen her with his own eyes, as if she had stood before him constantly. She is the *Immaculata*, full of wisdom and gentleness. His love, his devotion and his great art were entirely dedicated to her.

In the High Renaissance, the urge to make the invisible visible was particularly strong in Italian art. As the heavens closed to man, this longing increased. No earlier school of painting had gone so far in giving the Divine human features. The Madonna is perfect in her humanity and yet entirely divine.

One of Raphael's early works, painted when he was about eighteen, shows Michael's fight with the dragon. St. Michael, in full armour and with radiant shield, stands in the midst of hell. His sword is raised, his foot rests on his vanquished adversary. Though his determination assures him victory, his face is as gentle as that of the Madonna on Raphael's later paintings. (Plate 29.) It is like a portrayal of Raphael's own nature—a fiery, yet gentle spirit, who amid the passions surrounding him could find the tranquillity to translate heavenly purity into human features. He was born on Good Friday; and he died on Good Friday of 1520. He was so entirely a servant of Christ that he was allowed to die on the day Christ's death is celebrated. His last picture was the *Transfiguration*. When it was finished, his own life was completed.

The great spirits of the Italian Renaissance were entirely devoted to the beings they portrayed; but in character they differed greatly. Leonardo's life was under a mysterious shadow which even wealth and gifts of mind and body could not lift, and Michaelangelo stood amid the storms that rage between earth and heaven. In Raphael, storms and sadness seemed to have long passed, they had become transformed into the harmony of his genius. All three had in common their creative vision. Italian culture owes its existence to the eye, to the Sense of Sight.

The eye is sun-like. In ancient times, it was built into the human body by the Sun; it is the product of Sun activity. But the ability to see was prepared by the Godhead long before the development of this physical eye. The sense of sight is rooted in the creative sphere of the heavenly Goat, and through this the visions of the exalted Spirits of Love, the Seraphim, were transmitted to the archangels.

The relationship between the artists of the Italian Renaissance and their contemporaries appears like a memory of those earliest days of creation. The creative eye directing the hands of the great painters made manifest their mighty visions, which thus appeared before those unable to bring them forth from their own strength. As nature can be perceived by means of the Sun, this art linked to the eye could give form to the spiritual beings of which Christianity speaks. What was faith to the people was placed before the senses as painting and sculpture.

The love for what is Sun-like inspired the strange politico-philosophical work of Thomas Campanella in the seventeenth-century, *Civitas Solis*, the *City of the Sun*. The power of sight was felt as something majestic and splendid that could be intensified into spiritual vision; and it was thus expressed in the beautiful words of the philosopher Giordano Bruno:

> Foundation, Cause, the Thou—eternal One,
> From whom flows endless life, existence, motion,
> Through Heights and Widths and Depths—a boundless Ocean—
> Where Heaven, Earth and Hell are Thine alone.
> With spirit, sense and reason I behold
> Thine endlessness, immeasurable One,
> Whose All is Midst, and whose Beginnings none:
> My being lives in Thee, by Thee ensouled.
> If blind illusion, common wrath, and hearts
> Grown cold with senseless greed and ruthless arts—
> Should they be wed with these dark days' desire,
> They ne'er could triumph, nor becloud the air,
> For still, despite them all, mine eyes are clear,
> Unveiled, and see my Sun's resplendent fire.

In another poem he writes:

> O Thou, who has lodged in the breast of the mortal the splendour
> Of immortal flame, burning in me with its glowing and glory,
> That star-ward aspiring and spurning the shadows with courage,
> O'ercoming the fettering load and the massive inertness,
> I may soar through the vastness, freed from the bondage of senses,
> Light, Light that's creative, all-seeing Light, giving me vision . . .

Even to mention such things was considered heresy during the transition from the sixteenth to the seventeenth century. Giordano Bruno was the first to prove that God can be found in nature through the activity of the eye. He was killed for his deed. His brilliant powers of observation were the specific gift of his folk spirit. In boundless devotion to the visible world, he took the step from passive to active vision.

' The sense of sight does not deceive ' he wrote, ' it records as much as it can with its inherent radiance.' He was the first to think deeply about the activity of the senses and described four stages of vision leading to the Divine.

The first stage is sense perception. The second is reached when outer perception ceases and is retained in memory. As memories deepen, man can approach the truth about the world of the senses more closely. He ascends from outer nature to the formative thoughts which flow towards him from the spiritual world. These thoughts are more complete than outer phenomena; the third stage has thus been attained. The fourth stage Giordano Bruno calls ' reason ', the working within the realms of the spirit.

Such vision leads to the experience of the presence of the Divine: ' Each image we perceive in the universe embraces by its very nature the soul of the whole cosmos.'

He taught that spirit is revealed in the forms of crystals, plants and animals, and that what appears in outer nature as form is active within the soul as thought. Both the world of nature and the world of human thought are the shadows of divine ideas. Man lives within this divine world in thinking about nature, no less than in looking at it.

Boldly he broke through the medieval concept of the closed crystal heaven. He was aware that this placed him within the struggle for new forms of knowledge. He allied himself with the evolution of humanity and was a fighter against the forces hostile to progress. Prophetically, he experienced the fulfilment of Christ's words: ' Is it not written in your laws: ye are gods? '

The force that makes possible universal knowledge and universal vision is love. Love opens the spiritual eye. Because Giordano Bruno looked at the world with such great love, permeated by the Spirits of Love, he could see also the image of the Godhead in outer phenomena. Although sensing that this would lead to his death at the stake, his courage did not fail him.

Giordano suffered martyrdom for the future common task of humanity: the metamorphosis of the senses and their permeation with the Christ impulse. In 1600, after seven years in the prisons of the Inquisition, he was publicly burned alive.

The devoted interest in the visible world lived on in Italy with Sun-like power. It was to become a source of strength and inspiration to visitors from many countries. To Goethe, his Italian journeys brought a new unfolding of his faculties. In the Botanical Gardens of Palermo, he could rise for the first time from outer observation to the spiritual experience of the archetypal plant.

Italy had become a gateway to a metamorphosis of the senses. Now he knew with absolute certainty that an archetypal force was active in the plant world, and he recognized this so clearly that he could demonstrate it to Schiller afterwards with a few lines.

Schiller exclaimed: ' But this is not a reality: this is an idea! ' Goethe hesitated for a moment, before he replied: ' In that case I welcome the fact that I have ideas without knowing it, and that I can see these ideas with my own eyes.' He had learned in Italy to look at the divine ideas in the manifestations of nature.

Many thousands of people have experienced Italy as a source of strength and liberation. The wanderer across the St. Gotthard Pass would feel that he could and even should now forget everything for a while, to prepare himself all the better for new impressions. If he could stay for some time in this landscape with its deep, clear colours, then he might begin to feel like a young bird, sheltered in the warmth of the egg, his wings just beginning to grow. He would gain the strength to burst through his shell. Italy has helped many a tired wanderer to discard the burden of the past, and to have confidence in the future.

This redeeming mood was strengthened further in the nineteenth century through the manner of Italy's liberation. Garibaldi, through whom it was achieved, was the image of selfless courage. At the age of eighteen, when he visited Rome for the first time, he realized what his mission was. An Italian in the fullest sense, Garibaldi lived entirely through the experiences of his eyes. When in his youth his ship was approaching the coast of South America, he saw his future wife through a telescope. She was sitting in a boat headed towards the shore, where he also decided to land. Throughout his campaigns his eyes played a most important part. He was never without his telescope: while his troops were resting he would watch the distant hills for many hours.

When he thought the right moment had come, he took up the struggle for Italy's liberation from Sicily. He was so selfless in his aims that he could unite without danger with the almost savage descendants of the Arabic–Sicilian population. His volunteers obeyed him out of respect for his humanity. They were ready to die with him for his cause. His mission achieved, he rejected all offers of reward and position. He was courageous not only in battle but in renunciation.*

The Italian who looks into the future and tries to find for his people new seeds of strength and insight needs to contact the courage that lives in his folk spirit. Not tradition, but courage and ever new courage creates the forces of redemption that carry man, as with angels' wings, over the abyss of the dark years.

---

* Rudolf Steiner describes Garibaldi's karmic connections in *Karmic Relationships*, 1924; Vol. I, Lectures XI and XII. Rudolf Steiner Press, London.

Germany

GERMANIC PEOPLE brought forth the word *Ich*—I. It consists of the Greek initials of Jesus Christ: I–CH. With this word, man speaks of himself as the being he can become—a Christ-bearer. The word *Ich* was created by Ulfila, Bishop of the Goths who came from Cappadocia. For his translation of the Gospels he adapted the Greek alphabet to Gothic sounds, supplementing it with Latin and Germanic runic signs. What has become *I* in English, *Je* in French and *Io* in Italian has remained as *Ich* in the German language throughout the centuries.

During the great migrations large numbers among the Germanic tribes actually died into the peoples of southern and western Europe. It was the task of the eastern and western Goths to unite the Germanic soul element with that of the Latin peoples by whom they were absorbed. What was to develop later as French and Italian culture had at its roots those Germanic forces that had streamed into the west and south.

An independent Germanic section remained in the heart of Europe. In order to transform soul-nature ultimately into spirit-nature, these people had to enter into an intimate and personal relationship to Christianity. A powerful impulse was given for this in the ninth century through the author of the *Heliand* epic. The *Heliand* was begun between 814 and 840. In spite of the keenest investigation from the Elbe estuary to the Rhine and from Normandy to England, the author and place of origin remain unknown, defying discovery, like the resting-place of the Holy Grail. The poem tells of the King of Peace who is active, not in Palestine, but in Germany, who walks the German countryside and lives in German castles. He unites himself completely with the German people into whose soul he is received.

Another epic, Muspilli—*The Conflagration of Worlds*—sets forth with the same free and original freshness the vision of the great world struggle; the battle of Good against Evil, of the Angels against the Demons, of Elijah against Anti-Christ.

> When the blood of Elijah shall drip on to the Earth, then the mountains will be consumed with fire, then no tree will remain upon the Earth, the waters will dry up, the swamps will shrink away, the heavens will blaze with flame, the Moon will fall, the Earth, the whole world, will burn . . . Then no man will be able to deliver his neighbour from the Muspilli . . .

These early writings originated in the inmost nature of the German people and so belonged entirely to its peculiar character, but later they were forgotten.

The history of the German *Imperium Romanum*, of the Holy Roman Empire, begins with Charlemagne. On 25 December in the year 800, Charles the Great attended the celebration of High Mass at St. Peter's in Rome. As he knelt, the Pope unexpectedly set the Imperial crown upon his head. Charles's biographer and contemporary writes: ' It was then that he received the title of Emperor and Augustus, which was at first so repugnant to him that he declared he would never have entered the church—even on that day of festival—had he known beforehand of the Pope's intention.'

To avoid any similar situation for his son Ludwig—Louis I, King of Aquitania—who in 813 was to be made his associate in the Empire, he bade him take the crown from the altar himself and set it upon his own head. In 843 the three sons of Louis I divided the great realm between them; the youngest, Louis the German, became ruler over Central Europe. In 911, the generations of the Carolingians came to an end.

The actual founder of the Holy Roman Empire was Otto I, who had himself crowned by the Pope in Rome. He had married Edith, a daughter of King Edward the Elder of England.* She went from Malmesbury to Germany and was accompanied by the Chancellor of her brother Athelstan, first Lord Paramount of Britain. It was at Malmesbury that Scotus Erigena was murdered in the Chapel of St. Michael; and it is historically known that from this place originated in Middle Europe the idea of the creation of cities. Through Edith this plan— really a spiritual inspiration—was brought to the German Emperor, who was afterwards known as the ' City Founder '. Edith may be regarded mythologically as the soul of cities.

When she died, still young, Otto married the widowed queen, Adelaide of the Lombards. Through this marriage he styled himself ' King of the Lombards ' and received the iron crown of the Longobardi in 951. He consolidated his empire by strengthening the frontiers and the bishoprics in the Slavonic East and by repulsing the Magyars at Lechfeld.

While Edith had introduced western tendencies into Central Europe, an eastern element came in through Otto II's Greek wife, Theophania. Maria of Aragon, who married Otto III, brought southern influences.

The Saxons were followed by the Franks, under whom the great struggle between the Empire and the Papacy started in the quarrel over the question of Investiture in 1077. Pope Gregory VII undertook ecclesiastical reforms. Although at the Concordat of Worms peace was finally concluded for two centuries, the opposition between emperors and popes remained a fact of major importance.

The Holy Roman Empire embraced a thousand years, again and again overflowing the boundaries of the German language. These years may appear like a lake, into which in the ninth century a stone was thrown, causing waves that circle out across time.

In outer history the destinies of the German emperors caused comparatively small ripples, but within a greater movement more powerful waves rose and fell. The cause lies in the very nature of the German people. They belong to the realm of the Waterman. The sign used in astronomy for this star image consists of regular waves that indicate a pulsation, of a cosmic nature 〰〰 . What the German folk soul has to experience through the Waterman impulse is in earthly terms a contradiction. If we think of water, we have a picture of even flow. But in the German people lives the Sense of Warmth: and fire is a constantly changing state which devours what is there and creates space for the new.

---

* King of the West Saxons from 901–924.

Through constant inner struggle this people destroyed its own creations. The loss of Italy, the wars of the Reformation, the later dissolution of the Empire, were blows that affected German destiny far more profoundly than the comparatively gentle ripples of dynastic change.

And even mightier were the waves of spirit during that thousand years. Their movement did not coincide with the rhythm of outward success but rose highest, indeed, when Germany's political power was at its lowest. It was at the time of the *minnesingers* and the great mystics that Germany lost control of Italy. When Johann Sebastian Bach inaugurated a new age in music, the German people had just passed through the catastrophe of the Thirty Years' War, and when the German poets and musicians of the Romantic age were at their most active, the German Empire had come to an end. The waves of German culture reached a peak at the time of external ebb.

From the end of the twelfth century onwards, the songs of the minnesingers, the minstrels of memory and of love, rang through Germany. The minnesingers were sometimes knights attached to the different courts; often, also, they travelled from place to place, thus spreading a musical and poetic culture. More than three hundred minnesingers are known, every one of whom wrote his own music and his own songs. Wolfram von Eschenbach, himself a minnesinger, contributed greatly to the knowledge of the Holy Grail throughout wide circles.

In the middle of the epic, *Parzival*, Wolfram speaks of the experience that gave him the strength to create it. The second part (Book IX) begins with a conversation between the poet and Dame Adventure, who commands:

> ' Open up! '
> To whom? Who are you?
> ' I want to come into your heart to you.'
> Then it is a small space you wish.
> ' What does that matter? Though I scarcely find room, you will have no need to complain of crowding. I will tell you now of wondrous things.'*

Dame Adventure was the Muse of the minnesingers, the spiritual being who helped Wolfram to put into words what his own reason could not comprehend. Because he opened wide the door of his heart, the different sources of this tale could flow together in his work. As precisely as was possible at the time, he described the path Parzival had to travel so that the experience of the Godhead in his soul could become a reality. His work was rightly called the ' Epic of the Soul '.

From 1193 to 1230, Albertus Magnus was living in Germany. He and his great pupil, Thomas Aquinas, worked on the thought edifice of Scholasticism, to permeate Aristotelian wisdom with Christianity. Scholasticism in Germany was followed by mysticism.

Meister Eckhart was convinced that he spoke of the same God as Thomas Aquinas, but in his striving to deepen the experience of the Divine through the life of feeling, he encountered, unknowingly, memories from pre-Christian times. He held that everything that had been learned had to be discarded: ' When I come to the fount of the Godhead, none asks me whence

---

* Translation of H. M. Mustard and C. E. Passage, New York, 1961.

I come and where I have been and none doth miss me, for here there is an "un-becoming".'
(*Entwerden.*)

Master Eckhart's contemporary, Heinrich Suso, also allowed himself to be guided towards mystic experiences through the genius of his soul. He not only demanded the complete renunciation of all sense experience, but even the rejection of visions which were then still comparatively widespread: ' . . . An immediate beholding of the Godhead, that is right and pure truth without all doubt: and every vision, the more reasonable it be and without pictures . . . the purer and nobler it is.'

The third great mystic of the time was Johannes Tauler, who could already transcend pure mysticism. He was an outstanding preacher, the greatly admired ' Meister Tauler from Strasbourg ', who had absorbed much wisdom from books. One day an unassuming man who called himself ' the layman ' came to him. He was the *Gottesfreund vom Oberland.* Tauler became his pupil and was then led through a severe inner discipline; he even had to give up preaching until he had become completely transformed and was himself a ' Friend of God '.

When, after two years, he stepped before his congregation again his sermons were so full of the power of truth that he could open the gates of inner development to others. His word was now no longer based on mystic feeling but on his own insight into the working of the hier-archical choirs. In a sermon held on St. Michael's day, he described the relationship of these heavenly powers to man.

The Archangel Michael, leader of the Divine angel choirs, was throughout centuries the Germanic folk spirit. Michael calls humanity to overcome what is cold, ruthless and hard. He carries cosmic dynamism into Earth existence, and in the soul of the German people he created warmth and the gift of enthusiasm. Yet throughout this experience a deep melancholy was active: Dürer has portrayed this melancholy in one of his engravings. (Plate 30.)

Warmth is fire, living fire in the warmth-borne human organism and dead fire in outer nature. When the soul glows in inner warmth, it can expand and draw in outer phenomena. But the nature of heat is to dissipate. It must be re-created constantly and again and again be given off. Warmth is a force in constant movement; unresting, it has to be kindled all the time. This fleeting element is a basic trait of the German character. When the German has attained some end, he hastens on to further achievement. It is not the fulfilment that matters to him but the experience of striving.

In struggling to understand the peoples of Europe in their fundamental characteristics, we realize only too painfully that ordinary language is pitifully inadequate to describe these cosmically-rooted gifts. At the best only a very remote picture can be given. In the case of Germany the problem is all the greater. Even quotations from the great German poets and philosophers are insufficient to transmit a real understanding of the national destiny, for even they did not express in words the all-uniting element.

To do justice to the German people, one must allow their words to resound within one's own soul. It is necessary to become German, to live in striving, in transforming action, in renunciation of temporary fulfilment: the world has to be experienced and painfully absorbed by the heart. It must be felt what it means to long to overcome the cold constantly because cold means death, and to try to wrest new life from death, for warmth is also spirit and therefore imbues death with spiritual life.

Natural science does not see warmth as an independent element but as an aggregate condition of matter. But warmth is both material and spiritual: it is transition from the earthly to the cosmic state, and is not a tangible substance. The warmth basic to the German soul is similarly not easy to define. It is active—yet it escapes.

If one considers what appears as specifically German to ordinary observation, one finds nothing that is not also apparent as the day-to-day bourgeois virtues of industry and efficiency elsewhere. Even closer study of the German character will not reveal anything that could not be found in others. Reliability, honesty and good faith exist throughout all nations. But in penetrating further into the very nature of the German people, one comes to the inexpressible factor, for want of a better term called warmth, the intangible element that presses towards the very source of creation. It is there where men have ideals, it grows where they strive for the goals of humanity, it is the flame that would rise from the altar of the Earth—or it is missing. When it is present it works towards the fulfilment of our humanity.

This intangible factor can grow into magic idealism, into the devotion to an ideal, so intense, so warm and so complete that this ideal can be realized by others in later centuries. Magic idealism is so unearthly that it appears to ' rational ' minds as an illusion, and so real that it is a guarantee to the spirits of nature that the Earth will become the planet of love. Magic idealism is the fire of the soul out of which the new Earth will blossom when the last fruit of the old tree of life will have withered.

But he who is speaking of this intangible warmth speaks no longer of Germany alone: it is a language addressed to the world of the stars, that has flowed into man so that he may renew it and return it as a quickening draught. It might be possible to imagine a German people, successful and triumphant, though without any true Germans, just as there might be a physical mankind devoid of all the humanity that can be a source of renewal for the whole of creation, a mankind grown rigid in the struggle for wealth, power and long life. Renewal can flower in every soul, anywhere on Earth, just as our innate humanity cannot perish because it is eternally rooted in the individual, in those who suffer and struggle unnoticed.

To transform love into exalted impulses, what has been acquired in the past into future attainment, takes time. Nothing can be achieved at one stroke. But within a comparatively short time man may gain some idea about his mission if he develops towards self-knowledge, devotion and perfection. Nor does it take long to decide to make full use of every possibility of further development. But to reach the stage when not only soul and spirit long for the good, but even the body is transformed down to the very blood, requires a long time. What was good enough yesterday will by no means suffice tomorrow. That it is possible to transform existing attainment to a higher stage, old into new, sickness into health, is a healing process through which humanity is mercifully guided. The individual human being takes part in this healing metamorphosis through his repeated incarnations.

Lessing, the critic and poet, wrote at the close of his long life a short work on history, *The Education of the Human Race*. It ends with these words:

> Go thine inscrutable way, Eternal Providence: Only let me not despair in Thee, because of this inscrutableness. Let me not despair in Thee, even if Thy steps appear to me to be going back. It is not true that the shortest line is always straight.

Thou hast on Thine Eternal Way so much to carry on together, so much to do: so many side steps to take! And what if it were as good as proved that the vast slow wheel, which brings mankind nearer to this perfection, is only put in motion by smaller, swifter wheels, each of which contributes its own individual unit thereto?

It is so! The very same Way by which the Race reaches its perfection, must every individual man—one sooner, another later—have travelled over. Have travelled over in one and the same life? Can he have been in one and the self-same life a sensual Jew and a spiritual Christian? Can he in the self-same life have overtaken both?

Surely not that! But why should not every individual man have existed more than once upon this World?

Is this hypothesis so laughable merely because it is the oldest? . . .

. . . . . .

Why should I not come back as often as I am capable of acquiring fresh knowledge, fresh experience? Do I bring away so much from once, that there is nothing to repay the trouble of coming back?

Is this a reason against it? Or, because I forget that I have been here already? Happy is it for me that I do forget. The recollection of my former condition would permit me to make only a bad use of the present. And that which even I must forget *now*, is that necessarily forgotten for ever.

Or is it a reason against the hypothesis that so much time would have been lost to me? Lost?—And how much then should I miss?—Is not a whole Eternity mine?*

Germany belongs to the realm of the Zodiac's Waterman, whose impulse is world-wide. Its greatest representatives were Goethe, Schiller and Novalis, but it permeated others also with intimate and at the same time universal aims.

Goethe's friends designated as one of his most important works his unfinished poem *Die Geheimnisse—The Secrets*, or as given often in English, *The Mysteries*—which described an encounter with a Rosicrucian centre. He speaks of the mood of veneration enveloping the settlement. Above its entrance there was a triangle and within it a black cross with red roses. ' Who added roses to the cross?' It was the Grail Christianity, working in silence, that had joined the roses to the cross to speak of death and rebirth. Goethe himself had been touched by the Christianity of the Holy Grail.

In the transforming forces of nature and of man Goethe recognized the Divine. Trained by his sense of metamorphosis, he could commune intimately with nature. In following her creative processes he arrived at his Theory of Colour, at the concept of the archetypal plant and of the archetypal animal. He also gained an awareness of man's own importance in creation:

Being placed at the peak of nature, man sees himself as the whole of a nature that has to attain once more a peak, out of its own strength. Thus he ascends by permeating himself with every virtue and perfection, with choice, order, harmony and significance, until he

---

* Translation. W. F. Robertson, 1883.

finally rises to the production of the work of art, which occupies an exalted place next to his other deeds and works.*

He saw one of the highest manifestations of art in music:

> The dignity of art appears in music perhaps at its most eminent, because there is no material substance that has to be deducted. It is entirely form and content and ennobles everything it expresses.**

From the beginning of Creation, the cosmos was sound. Resounding deeds of Creation had in the Waterman their instrument of action. The Spirits of Harmony lived in the heavenly tones that filled the cosmos, and the Earth as it came to life was an instrument which they could make resound according to the laws of the music of the stars. Angels implanted these workings in mankind by penetrating it with the intentions of the Godhead. They thereby laid the foundations of reason which allows man to search in all things for the archetypal harmonies. These deeds of giving by divine beings are indicated in medieval representations of the Waterman, where an angel pours water from a jug.

Man is no longer conscious that everything he is was once ordered by the music of the stars. Pythagoras could still experience it and spoke of 'sphere harmonies'. The knowledge of the link with the Waterman sounds was already lost to him, although—like many other Greeks and also the ancient Celts—he sensed that life and heavenly music flowed into the soul from the direction of the Sun, where cosmic forces are gathered.

Later, the Sun also grew silent for the inner sense. But at the end of the eighteenth century Goethe could suddenly speak of cosmic music. (Plate 31.) With vigour and self-assurance he placed at the beginning of the first part of *Faust* the Archangel's words:

> The sun-orb sings, in emulation,
> 'Mid brother-spheres, his ancient round:
> His path predestined through Creation.
> He ends with steps of thunder-sound.

Something completely new had happened. Star harmonies and the music of the Sun were still inaudible to physical ears, but in the mirror of human warmth—and the word 'mirror' is inadequate, nor would 'echo' describe it precisely—out of a re-melting process in human warmth, a new kind of experience emerged. This was music, which now began to unfold its earthly glory. This music was entirely the child of Europe, where the star harmonies had died to re-awaken in human hearts and to resound victoriously in the world. It was a real 're-sounding' that began.

The works of the great classic composers became an untold joy and source of strength to millions. The Orientalist, Fosco Marsini, wrote of this art that in it the spirit of an entire

---

* From the essay on Winckelmann.
** *Maxims and Reflections.*

civilization had reached its greatest heights; that it contained also the torment, the passion and the heart of Europe, and even if Europe were to go under in some terrible catastrophe, this music would still proclaim her greatness.

Many Europeans—Spaniards, Englishmen, Frenchmen and Italians—shared in the rise of this musical culture. In 1685 were born Johan Sebastian Bach and Friedrich Händel who began to open the gates of humanly-toned, cosmically flowing music. They were followed by the titans of that European music which could take form through the German spirit of warmth and which found its greatest fulfilment in them.

All these musicians were contemporaries of Goethe.* Bach, Gluck, Händel and Haydn were older than he. Bach died when Goethe was a year old; at Händel's death Goethe was ten; when Gluck died, Goethe was thirty-eight. Haydn was seventeen years older than Goethe. Mozart, Beethoven and Schubert were born and died during his lifetime, as were Johann Strauss, Mendelssohn and Schumann who survived him. Wagner was nineteen when Goethe died and Bruckner eight, while Brahms was born a year after his death. Goethe's age is the age of sound assuming earthly perfection; and all this resounding world was not only experienced in the depth of the heart, but was also written down.

There is something wonderful about the written language of music: it can largely be derived from the signs used for the Waterman and for the Lion facing it. The horizontal lines used to indicate the position of the notes are the Waterman waves at rest.

The treble clef is the Lion sign in reverse: the bass clef is its direct metamorphosis.

---

* Goethe: 1749–1842.

In astronomy the meetings of two planets in the heavens are written with the sign ☌; for example ♀ ☌ ☉. These conjunctions are in the first place events in time. Where the duration of a note is indicated in the language of music, this is done with similar signs: half note ♩, quarter note ♪.

Again, in the language of music, notes float up or down according to the height or depth of the sounds. If the courses of the planets are observed from the Earth, a similar up-and-downward movement becomes apparent. The sign ☌ indicates a solar or planetary meeting, high in the cosmic ocean on the crest of a wave, or deep cosmic space below the earth. A meeting far away from the Earth resounds through space quite differently from one in its proximity. The sign is in a certain sense a cosmic form of musical writing, for every meeting between planets is an event with reverberations.

Written notes too are an experience in sound. According to their succession upwards or downwards, they awaken in the soul different experiences of the world of sound. As an example, to demonstrate the Waterman waves in musical writing, the first bars from Wagner's *Parsifal* are given below.

The poet Novalis knew of the relationship between sounds, lines, and the world of cosmic harmonies. He wrote in his *Fragments*: ' Cosmology: all things are symptomatic of each other. Notes and lines are, as that outward phenomenon which allows the widest possible formation, variation and arrangement, the most convenient way for the delineation of the universe.' Novalis brought to bear on every realm of human thought the force of the imagination that flows from heavenly sources; even now many volumes of his aphorisms have remained unpublished. He had been trained as a mining engineer. At the age of twenty-seven he was appointed an inspector of mines. He made tours of inspection lasting many weeks and wrote extensive reports about the local coal-mining industry, hoping to achieve considerable technical improvements. But this was only a small part of his activity. In 1799 he wrote—within a few months and in addition to his official work—the *Spiritual Songs*, the *Hymns to the Night*, the essay *Christendom or Europe*, *Klingsor's Fairy Tale* and a fragment of a novel, *Heinrich von Ofterdingen*.

He lived a completely ordinary life and at the same time he transformed earthly appearances to their spiritual significance.

He who is completely at rest within is the true seer. As earthly beings we strive towards spiritual development—indeed to spirit. As spiritual beings, towards earthly development —indeed towards earthly form. Only through morality can we attain both these ends.

If you cannot make thoughts immediately perceptible, then try to make outer things indirectly perceptible . . . by transforming them into thoughts. Both operations are idealistic. He who has both completely in his control is the magic idealist.

To those who live in it the world becomes more and more infinite, hence there can be no end to the interplay of the manifold, no state of inactivity for the thinking ego. Golden ages may appear but do not bring an end—man's purpose is not a golden age. He shall exist eternally, be a well-ordered individuality, and persevere—this is the tendency of his nature.

The Waterman is the star image of the fountain of life. The early Greeks saw in it the goddess Hebe, cup-bearer of the Olympians, who handed them the draught of eternal youth. The German spirit longs to lead from the old to renewal. 'What is old?' asks Novalis, 'What is young?' And answers that young is where the future prevails, old where the past predominates. To God we move in reverse—from old age to youth. He sees all life as an exuberant process of renewal having the appearance, only, of a destructive process.

In *Klingsor's Fairy Tale* Novalis encompasses the whole evolution of the world within a few pages. The child Fabel—the moral imagination—overcomes the wicked spinning women and their ally, the mean and petty scribe, through presence of mind and awareness. A new world can thus arise where Eros and Freya, love and freedom, reign under the protection of Sophia. The singing little Fabel is as Sun-like as Michael himself: like Michael, she overcomes the dragon.

In *Christendom or Europe*, Novalis says:

> Have patience; it will, it must come, the sacred time of eternal Peace, when the New Jerusalem will be the capital of the world; and until then, be cheerful and courageous, you my companions in faith. Spread the Divine gospel and remain faithful unto death.

Out of the richness of his experience he wrote, in *The Novices of Saïs*:

> We sit at the fountain of liberty, watching. It is the great magic mirror in which the whole of Creation is revealed, clean and pure: in it bathe the gentle spirits and images of every nature, and all chambers are opened to us here. What need is there to walk through the clouded world of visible things? The purer world lies within us, in this fountain. Here the true meaning of the great, many-coloured and confused spectacle is revealed.

He told of a rare child who had stayed among the novices for a short while. He was bright to the very skin and his voice penetrated the heart, so that all the others longed to give him their flowers, crystals and feathers. As soon as he had come, the Teacher had entrusted his work to him. He then smiled with infinite seriousness, and all felt a strange happiness. When he left the Teacher said: 'One day he will return and live among us; then the lessons will finish.'

Goethe's Faust, too, ascends after passing through a state of renewal. At the beginning of the drama he is old, later he grows young. Only through inner rejuvenation can 'all things transitory' become but a symbol, preserved for eternity.

Schiller spoke of the healing process of rejuvenation in his *Letters on Aesthetics*. He, the servant of freedom, wrote these memorable words: ' Man plays only where he is human in the fullest sense of the word, and he is only entirely human when he plays'. Studying the human disposition he sought the realm where man is truly free in his creating. Freedom lives only in art, and art is like the play of a child. He who is playing does not impose restrictions on himself; he pieces things together as he pleases. He overcomes all compulsion of necessity for the order he creates is his own invention. This ability to play, this free imagination, is in all of us, and can therefore be achieved even in everyday life. When it is awakened, the life of the senses appears to man filled with the expression of such beautiful spirituality that reason, too, is satisfied. A higher man thus evolves out of the ordinary man, and the slave turns into a true human being, rejuvenated through the artistic urge to play and able to experience the Divine within himself.

Out of such freedom springs joy. It is the joy whose praise Schiller sang in his great *Ode*.

> Joy, thou Goddess, fair, immortal
> Offspring of Elysium,
> Mad with rapture, to the portal
> Of thy holy fane we come!
> Fashion's laws, indeed, may sever,
> But thy magic joins again:
> All mankind are brethren ever
> 'Neath thy mild and gentle reign.
>
> . . . . .
>
> Sense of wrongs forget to treasure,
> Brethren, live in perfect love!
> In the starry realms above,
> God will mete as we may measure.

Beethoven incorporated this hymn in his last work, the Ninth Symphony. He carried Schiller's chorus into the cosmic sea of his music, where it continues to resound through time and space. In whatever place or century men may perform this symphony, this song of brotherly love will be an experience of the heights. The songs glide on as if rising from sacred symphonic waters, until they join in a crescendo of joy that rings out in the majesty of one single vast chorus.

When Beethoven wrote the Ninth Symphony he was completely deaf. His sense of hearing contributed in no way to his musical creation, which was rooted entirely in cosmic sound. In the intense warmth of his soul, he transformed the world-harmonies into a quickening draught for mankind. It is said that he always had before him on his desk the words of the great Isis: ' I am what was, what is, and what will be—no mortal has ever lifted my veil '.

All great Germans were moved by the urge to experience thoughts fully within themselves. They would find the answers to their manifold questions within the heart.

Fichte, who wanted to gain all certainty out of the impulses of his ego, searched for aware-ness of self in the innermost soul-foundation of the will. This will was to him part of the world soul. He found that even the ego was only present through a decision of the will. It can only discover its mission out of its own forces. According to its nature it desires a moral world order, and the peoples too only exist to pursue moral activity.

Hegel also placed in the centre of his picture of the world what the soul can experience through itself. He searched above all for clarity and precision of thinking, and for objectivity, as sharp as a mathematical concept. Though this produced only abstractions, it could affect the soul to its very depths. He took up the study of history and penetrated his subject with logic.

Schelling experienced the world spirit as world artist. He came to the view that the essence of the element of feeling is also present as substance. Matter was to him enchanted feeling that waits for a redemption through man.

We can pass from one great German to another and invariably we find the same heartfelt identification with thoughts. It was so in Luther's case. He had been moved to the very depth of his being by the corruption he found in Rome, and from the fire of his immediate thought experience his glowing words kindled the Reformation. He thus achieved what was needed at the time. A people that feels within itself the pulsation of all metamorphosis is in danger of losing itself. It longs to, and indeed must, protect itself against the danger of stream-ing away into nothing. Before Germany's great flowering in the Romantic period, the Reformation had to give inner strength to the individual through personal reading of the Bible. The Catholic rite in the Latin language raises the soul out of everyday life; but it was this sober everyday life the German needed and a sober religious service, to build a safe foundation within him.

The innate desire for firm comprehension remained in the German people; and explains why the German can work so pedantically. He can elaborate in volumes what could be said on a few pages. He analyses the abundance of his material, and organizes it to master it. Often he falls into extremes of pedantry, clinging to his data and definitions. Where he does not keep faith with his own folk spirit and does not master the art of inner development, he is like Faust's assistant:

> Ah, God! but Art is long,
> And Life, alas! is fleeting.
> And oft, with zeal my critic duties meeting,
> In head and breast there's something wrong.
> How hard it is to compass the assistance
> Whereby one rises to the source!
> And haply, ere one travels half the course
> Must the poor devil quit existence.
>
> (*Faust*, I, 1)

The art of printing was invented in Germany. That too is a means for fixing what would otherwise disperse and it brought about the tendency of our civilization to acknowledge as a safe and valid source of knowledge only what has been printed and can be read somewhere. Spiritual experience is choked in words.

Novalis could see the consequences of this development:

> Everything we experience is communication. Thus the world is indeed a communication—the revelation of the spirit. The time is past when the spirit of God could be understood. The meaning of the world has been lost. We have stood still at the dead letter. We have lost what is to be recorded, in the recording. Forms, and nothing but forms. (*Formularwesen.*)

In Goethe's *Faust*, Mephistopheles tells his pupil:

. . . . .
> On *words* let your attention centre!
> Then through the safest gate you'll enter
> The temple halls of Certainty.

Student:
> Yet in the word must some idea be.

Mephistopheles:
> Of course! But only shun too oversharp a tension,
> For just where fails the comprehension,
> A word steps promptly in as deputy.
> With words 'tis excellent disputing;
> Systems to words 'tis easy suiting;
> On words 'tis excellent believing;
> No word can ever lose a jot from thieving.

> (*Faust*, I, iv)

Liberation from the power of the platitude, the word grown rigid, comes through the gift of silence. Through the renunciation of superficial talk an inner strength arises which unlocks the gate to spiritual abundance.

Just as the world of sound is neither good nor evil, national gifts are neither good nor evil. Only by men are the star impulses that radiate selflessly into the peoples turned into healing or to sources of sickness for the rest of humanity. Anything, however exalted, can be perverted in the realm of Earth, where it may take many forms.

When the flowing Waterman element is active in the soul and spirit it strives towards a true internationalism, as in Goethe's time. The movement towards German unity, born out of German Idealism, aroused no hostility among other nations: German Idealism was admired without a trace of envy. Even Eastern Europe began to open to it. At the beginning of the nineteenth century, German philosophy and literature were earnestly studied in England and France, and German music was joyfully received into the cultural life of other nations.

But gradually an alien element evolved in Germany. When the Holy Roman Empire ceased to exist, under Francis II, Germany disintegrated into a number of small states among whom Prussia, with her strong army, soon dominated. After the troubles of the Napoleonic wars Prussia, which had already acquired a section of Poland, was enlarged again. The year of the Vienna Congress, 1815, saw the birth of Count Otto von Bismarck. In 1866, Bismarck fought a decisive war against Austria and thus created an entirely new political situation. As a consequence of the Franco-Prussian war (1870-71) the separate small German states united as the German Empire, and William I, King of Prussia was crowned German Emperor in the Palace of Versailles.

This German Empire, the so-called Second Empire of the Germans which was the product of military and dynastic considerations, developed in the nineties into an outstanding economic power. But since it was an imitation of already conventional western economic and colonizing tendencies and a fundamental contradiction of the German character, it aroused the resistance of other nations—and not only that of other nations. In Germany, Nietzsche wrote of the ' extirpation of the German spirit for the sake of the German Empire'. The flowing Waterman element now turned into purely external activities and produced the urge for ceaseless creation of material wealth. A wild race for markets began that aroused the fear and hatred of others. Germany's exports rose to a flood which her neighbours tried to stem.

The German Empire collapsed in 1918. It had lasted four times twelve years. Schiller spoke the words: ' World history is world judgment '. The course of historical events proved that it is not the true mission of the German people to dissipate its strength in outward success. World history points to restraint.

The German people is a vigorous people, full of vital forces. These can be used for progress or fatally abused. Such misuse was practised by Hitler with his so-called Third Empire. In the German folk spirit lived at that time the demand for the overcoming of traditional restraints that bar true advance. Hitler misunderstood. He broke with tradition and tried to storm into the future but without any regard for the conditions for true community. He could therefore merely renew age-old traditions of one-sided domination by force. Again, world history answered as world judgment and broke up what had to be destroyed, for the sake of Germany and of humanity.

The physiological function of the Sense of Warmth consists in differentiating between the warmth of the body and the temperature outside. It is well known that the German is much more sensitive to external temperature than, for example, the Englishman. He feels cold very quickly and consequently fills his home with the most complicated arrangements to protect himself against cold. In soul activity, the Sense of Warmth furthers the cultivation of the inner life.

The German who carries his people's mission within him has the gift of taking the aims of other peoples into his own heart to further them. He can become responsible in his full individuality and guide the flow of the Waterman forces into the direction he chooses. He can apply them outwardly or within. If outer locks are temporarily closed, then the gate opens to the experience of the spirit. The heart is enabled to collect and order the manifold rhythms and tones of human existence. The first sounds of a great new Earth symphony begin to rise within the soul.

In the loud disharmonies of today's external world events, these intimate experiences are apt to pass unnoticed. But as apocalyptic Earth destinies approach, the triple chord of the new Earth symphony may attain through the human ego to outer form.

Russia

THE RUSSIAN FOLK SOUL still lives in the purely spiritual world, separated from its children who have a long path yet to travel. In its depths, immeasurable possibilities for the future lie waiting. To all that lives dream-like in the Russian earth, all that approaches from other peoples, all that rises from the souls of men, the Russian folk soul listens, childlike and longing for the future; longing for the mission that must be sought in times to come when Russia's true nature will be found.

It is hard to form clear concepts about the future, since our words are mostly inadequate; but what has already happened contains the seeds of what will come, though they are still young and threatened. In two thousand years the Slav peoples will have become the leaders of evolution,* able by then to carry wisely the burden of such responsibility. Many people living in Russia will then behold in their hearts the pure image of heavenly wisdom, the divine Sophia; and thus led, they will consciously strengthen the spiritual bridges between the earth and the cosmos and will experience fully the being of their folk soul as it weaves between the cosmic realm of the Fishes and the Russian earth.

Of the twelve directions of the Zodiac, it is in the realm of the Fishes that the folk soul finds the archetypal image of man in his cosmic dignity. Looking beyond his appearance on the present earth into the remotest past, when his evolution, still held in divine thought, was the highest ideal of creation, it listens—with a gift of devoted listening that comes from this realm —and prepares the people for their task. They have a special connection with the Sense of Hearing; and a devotion to Christ and to heavenly wisdom is deeply rooted in their nature.

Ceaselessly, in infinite patience, the Divine Wisdom must guard all that has yet to be realized, through world days of action and world nights of maturing; and likewise the Russian archangel demands far-reaching patience from its people, giving it the task of sharing in a mission that only the help of the Logos and of the Divine Sophia—Isis—can bring to fruition.

There is an ancient Egyptian legend indicating that memories of the deeds of Isis-Sophia and her son are hidden in the star image of the Fishes. Pursued by the god of the nether world, they were saved only by being transformed into two fishes.

Until 1918, every Russian home had an icon in the corner of its best room, a picture painted on wood; most often it represented the Mother of God. A light burned in front of it, and below was a shelf with flowers. Visitors would turn towards this sacred Sophia and bow, before greeting anybody else; throughout the whole of Russia, the first, most reverent greeting

---

* A comprehensive list of lectures referring to Russia by Rudolf Steiner, with contents indicated, is given in *Russia, Past, Present and Future*, compiled by John Fletcher. New Knowledge Books.

141

was reserved for the Divine. Carried down, not simply as an abstract sentiment, but into the very gestures of human existence, as a deed springing from a foundation of feeling and will, this Divine Sophia remained a reality for the soul, long after she had been forgotten in Central and Western Europe. (Plate 32.)

Sometimes the love of the Russians for their icons had a primitive force. Baring tells of an atheist who tried to prove to the peasants the non-existence of God. He took a sacred icon and said: ' I will spit on this image and break it to pieces. If there is a God, He will send down fire from heaven and will kill me. If there is no God nothing will happen to me.' He spat on the icon, broke it up and said to the peasants: ' Now you see—God did not kill me.' ' No,' they replied, ' God did not kill you, but we shall.' And they did.

On one occasion a peasant, a *moujik*, was taking a stranger across the country. The German said, ' You all practise idolatary! You worship icons and bow before them like pagans.'

' We are supposed to worship icons?' answered the Russian, ' Never! '

Some time later as they continued on their journey, the Russian pointed to a tree and asked: ' Do you think we worship this tree?'

' No, certainly not,' the German admitted, and they went on. When they reached their destination a house painter was sitting on the doorstep. The *moujik* pointed to the paint pot and asked the traveller: ' Were you going to say that I worship a pot of paint? '

' No, certainly not.'

' But you say that I worship icons, which are only painted wood. And you don't realize that these are only an aid for me in praying to the Godhead.'*

Recent attempts to alienate the Russian people from divine guidance could partly succeed despite this attitude. But deep in the Russian heart, Sophia will work on; an endless longing will keep many souls united with her, and love will flare up all the more intensely as the Slav realizes that the wisdom of the Divine Sophia can become his wisdom. She will come to live as a knowledge of cosmic truth, illuminating the stars and the earth, in a way already prefigured in the life of Vladimir Soloviev. Nicolas Zernov tells that in the poem ' Three Meetings.'

> . . . Soloviev stated that three times he had had a revelation of the glory and unity of the created world. This knowledge was given to him in visions of Sophia, the Divine Wisdom, who appeared to him as a woman of unsurpassable beauty. He saw her first in Moscow on Ascension Day, during the celebration of the Holy Eucharist, when he was a boy of nine; the second time in the reading room of the British Museum whilst he was working there on his post-graduate thesis; and again the same year in the desert in Egypt whither an inner voice had called him to await the vision.
>
> For Soloviev, these meetings were the cardinal facts on which he built up his entire outlook. His philosophical works were an attempt to systematize the meaning of these meetings; his religious and social activities were the outcome of his desire to relate them to the daily course of his life. Neither his thought nor his personality can be understood without constant reference to this wellspring of his creative inspiration. Soloviev himself

---

* Maurice Baring (1874–1945).

142

never doubted the reality of his encounters with the Divine Wisdom, a privilege which he found some other mystics claimed to have shared.*

What has faded from human consciousness may arise more victoriously in the future.

But to achieve a true humanity—a cosmic dignity surpassing anything yet comprehended as dignity—man must in growing freedom seek to revere the divine wisdom in his heart and to experience love as a social force. Only thus will the condition be created into which Sophia can enter and work, as the life substance of coming generations. Thought forms must arise fitted to contain her being, which is spirit and soul.

Wisdom is by no means the same as intellectual development, and under the influence of their archangel the Russian people were in a certain sense intellectually held back. It is not their task to evolve clearly defined concepts but to ascend to the spiritual from depth of feeling. Clear concepts must come as a gift from the thinking of the West and that of Central Europe, trained for centuries in natural science. As the West has gained an understanding of nature, it must also learn to place the realm of the spirit before humanity in clear pictures.

That is the only way for East and West to unite so that they can join hands as brothers. Vladimir Soloviev longed for such a union, and in his Paris lectures he appealed to the West to seek a synthesis of its best elements with eastern Christianity. Otherwise demonic forces of both East and West would unite and disaster would follow disaster. The fanaticism of the East will come as punishment for the increasing materialism of the West. Shortly before his death he wrote his *Anti-Christ*,** a profound warning to all who are concerned with the future of our humanity. (Plate 33.)

In the ninth century two centres, round which Russia could take form as a people, arose through the Swedish Normans. Rurik, who with his brothers had penetrated along the waters to the interior, was elected Prince of Novgorod by the local Slavs in 862. Two years later two other Normans reached the hills of Kiev, where they were declared rulers by the inhabitants. Kiev and Novgorod were the beginnings of Russia.

When Rurik died his son was still a child. Kiev was built during the boy's minority by a regent who made a treaty with Constantinople. Russia, the first impulse of whose creation had come from the north-west, now began to listen towards the East.

Rurik's Norman daughter-in-law, Olga, had herself baptized at Byzantium in the presence of the Eastern Emperor, after her husband's death. Folk songs speak of her grandson Vladimir as Russia's beautiful red sun. One of Vladimir's twelve sons became lord of the whole of Russia. In 1037, Yaroslav the Wise built the Church of the Holy Sophia in Kiev and in 1045 his son Vladimir also raised a church to the Holy Sophia in Novgorod.***

Thus Kiev and Novgorod were not only the beginnings of a geographical Russia, but starting-points for the education of the Russian soul. Veneration of the Holy Sophia was to turn the Slav character towards inner contemplation.

Divine wisdom, unlike human knowledge which is quickly gained and can be immediately

---

* Quoted from Nicolas Zernov, *Three Russian Prophets*. S.C.M. Press, 1944.
** Reprinted by the Christian Community Press from *War and Christianity*, V. Soloviev. (Constable, London, 1915.)
*** The three most sacred churches dedicated to the Divine Sophia are at Constantinople, Kiev and Novgorod. (Editor.)

applied, works only gradually into humanity and the Russian people will therefore have to wait in patience. To begin with Russia absorbed what came from Byzantium as eastern culture. Yaroslav built cities, schools and churches and brought Greek and Byzantine scholars, architects and artists to Kiev. Kiev vied in beauty with Constantinople. Roads were built, palaces raised and public squares laid out complete with monuments. Money was minted and laws and customs were recorded.

But Yaroslav's descendants fell out among themselves and the country was soon weakened and disunited. In the year 1222 the Mongols under Jenghis Khan invaded Russia, bringing destruction, slavery and death. Kiev, said to have possessed six hundred churches, was captured. An Italian traveller, visiting the region ten years later, found neither cities, villages nor people, only the bones of men and horses scattered on the ground. Those who had escaped death had taken refuge in the forest where they lived on wild honey and by hunting. Coal tar and furs were their only media of exchange.

The sister church of Kiev, that of the Holy Sophia in Novgorod, survived. Novgorod's coat-of-arms shows two silver fishes on a blue ground. Above them is an empty golden throne, guarded by two bears with sceptre and cross, surmounted by three flames. The Russian soul sensed that it would have to wait into the distant future for the true Russia.*

Fig. 1. *Ancient Coat-of-Arms of Novgorod, Russia.*

A sect called the ' Strigolniki ', destroyed before 1500, existed in Novgorod for a short time, like a presentiment of a much later development. Lazarev confirms that its followers were active in Novgorod in 1314. Sins were not confessed to priests but to the Earth; and if no water was available for washing the hands before meals, earth was used instead. The Earth itself was experienced as the substance of the Christ.

The rest of the vast country was shattered, the people dispersed into the northern regions. Intimidated and impoverished, they could survive where the long hard winters, the impenetrable forests, the swamps and rivers offered some protection against the Mongols. Gradually people were allowed to return as slaves to their wasted homelands, to rebuild towns and villages for the new masters. Even princes were tolerated if they were willing to pay tribute to the Mongols and accept their sovereignty, but as a result of this degradation they began to fight one another.

---

* *The Mission of Folk Souls.* (Lecture 10), by Rudolf Steiner (Christiania. June 1910).

In those apocalyptic times, St. Sergius of Radonesh, the 'architect of Russia' was born. His whole being was directed towards the Transubstantiation and the Christ mystery of the Resurrection, and his personality carried such conviction that the quarrelling princes followed his advice and made peace. For the first time they united to fight the Mongols over whom they won a victory in 1380. Though new Mongol hordes followed later, Sergius had kindled the hope and courage that were to lead to Russia's liberation.

Ivan III the Great, who extended his empire to east and west, married the Greek princess Sophia and following her wishes, introduced the splendour of the Byzantine court in Moscow. Ivan IV the Terrible, under the lingering after-effects of Mongolian influence and, partly, imitating the customs of the Byzantine Empire in its decline, founded Tsarist absolutism. All this had nothing in common with the true Russian character. His military ambition to extend his rule to the Baltic failed, though his name is associated with the first expansion of Tsarist Russia towards Siberia and the overcoming of the Russian fear of Asian tribes. (Plate 34.)

Following his death in 1584 Russia's expansion makes a story of two fishes, one gliding eastwards, one westward; and what they heard outside reached Russia as through dream. In the Zodiacal sign the Fishes are linked by a band.

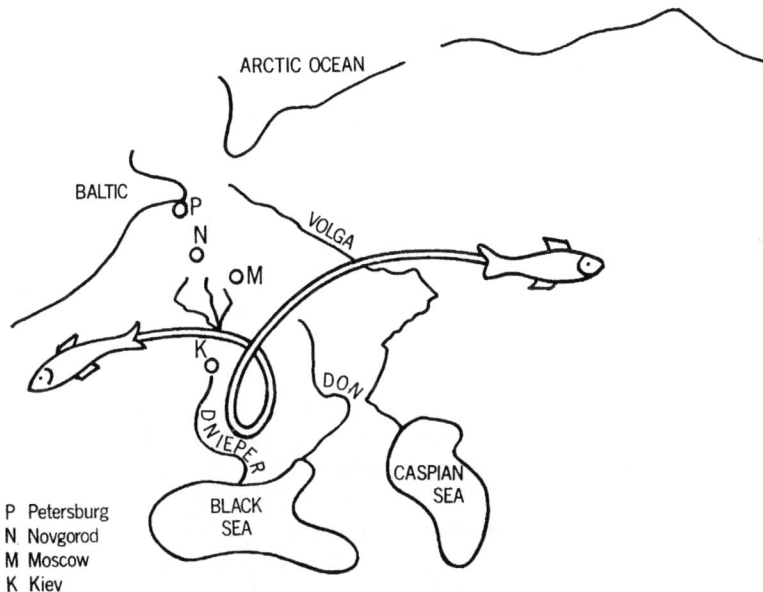

P Petersburg
N Novgorod
M Moscow
K Kiev

For a long time Siberia could not be secured by any official treaty but the region offered work and food to emigrants. The advancing Russians were hunters aiming to reach the heart of Asia through the great forests. In this way the Russian soul glided, in ceaseless yet scarcely noticeable movement, far into the east, through the immeasurable forests and over lakes and rivers. The first resistance, by Mongolian Buddhists, came only when Lake Baikal and the

Amur basin in the Chinese orbit of power had been reached, but the movement continued to the Jenissei and Lena rivers and into the extreme north-east of Asia. Finally the ' fish ' moved by way of Alaska down the Pacific coast to California. For Siberia there followed two centuries of well-planned expeditions.

Looking westward, Peter the Great made St. Petersburg his capital and called the city ' the window towards Europe '. He transferred the Slavonic-Greek-Latin academy from Moscow to the new capital and set up a school of navigation under the direction of an Englishman. Agricultural labourers, who had enjoyed various degrees of freedom, became serfs. Peter now called himself Tsar of all Russians.

His grand-daughter Catherine the Great, whose mother had been a German princess, conducted international politics in the grand manner. Her ambition was to expand Russia even further east and west, as well as southwards. Her troops conquered the Crimean Peninsula and her navy destroyed the Turkish fleet opposite Kios. As part of the terms of the ensuing armistice, Russia gained the right of passage through the Sea of Marmora and the Dardanelles.

Along with Austria, Catherine shared three times in the partition of Poland. Her ideas of reform were taken from Montesquieu and Beccaria. Accordingly she achieved the opposite of her intentions. It was her aim to weaken the power of the aristocracy which through opposition to everything foreign merely grew stronger. Later she had English advisers and supported the aristocracy, thereby increasing the demand of the serfs for freedom.

The brief rebellion that followed collapsed and Catherine finally gave up all attempt at ' Enlightenment '—even persecuting her ' enlightened ' subjects. But she could no longer ward off alien influences.

Politically a great power comparable to Ancient Rome, this Russia, based on the Asiatic model of absolute rule combined with the ideal of westernization, was un-Russian.

In 1823 mass deportations of political suspects to Siberia began. Voluntary emigrants were now joined by columns of prisoners, including criminals, but composed principally of men accused of political offences, most of whom had been sentenced without trial by the Minister of the Interior or even on the strength of an accusation by their village authorities. Men and women, the old and the sick, went on foot to the east, chained and with their heads partly shorn. Those charged with the more serious offences had to drag five-pound weights on their feet. Almost a third of the columns consisted of mothers and children accompanying their husbands and fathers. All prisoner transports followed the same path, from Perm in Russia to Tobolsk in Asia.

At the Russian frontier stood a stone; no frontier stone in the world can have seen more suffering; none has been passed by so many men and women with broken hearts. It was usual for the exiles to rest a short while at this place and call a last farewell to their homeland.

The Russian peasant, even as a convict, was devoted to his soil; heart-rending scenes took place at this frontier post. Many wept; some abandoned themselves completely to their grief. Some knelt down and pressed their faces against the beloved earth, others kissed the cold stone. When they had to move on, exiles and criminals alike made the sign of the Cross before passing the frontier dragging their chains.

146

Many exiles died in the prisons and hospitals of Siberia, others were allowed to return, others, again, settled there. Many of the political prisoners fled abroad *via* the east, and reached Europe. But with their stay in Siberia the real Russian tradition had been lost to them and their experiences in Asia intensified their hatred of Tsarism to a religious fanaticism.

While Russia's folk soul listened eastward and westward, the earth of European Russia dreamed on in a dull brooding state. With the endless steppes, the vast forests and swamps, the boundless grasslands and black soil whose cultivation was a slow and arduous process, physical Russia is like a formless body of ancient time.

Her mighty rivers have no outlet into oceans but evaporate in inland seas. The Volga, winding like a ribbon from western Russia to the south-east, ends in the Caspian Sea, the Don flows into the Sea of Azov which in one place is linked to the Black Sea.

The Black Sea receives the Dnieper and here too the mighty waters evaporate. The Black Sea is connected by the Bosphorus to another inland sea, the Mediterranean. The Baltic has likewise no link with the ocean apart from the Kattegat, and the North Sea beyond the Arctic Circle is frozen for most of the year. The Russian earth with its watercourses is therefore sufficient unto itself. It is heavy and laden with destiny; it is waiting. This brooding atmosphere was described by Merezhkovsky in speaking of the world of Chekhov's art:

> No historic age, no peoples—as if amid the vastness of eternity there was nothing but the end of the nineteenth century and nothing in the world but Russia. Gifted with an extraordinarily keen eye and ear for everything Russian and contemporary, he is almost blind and deaf to anything of another people or age. He saw Russia more clearly than anybody else, but he overlooked the world.*

This is the mood of a people that is not yet truly born and lives dreamily in its mother's womb.

But the Russian earth is not only dreamy and self-absorbed as created by nature; it is also filled with light. Deep in the Slav soul is the conviction that the earth is not only matter but is a being that has taken the form of matter and needs help to become spiritualized. The earth is holy and must be treated with love. Everything is holy that men have created in connection with this earth. And of all the Russian Christians who honour it, St. Sergius was the representative.

The Russian-human qualities of calm patience, generosity and child-like confidence achieved complete balance in him. Though respected by princes he remained a peasant and shared the joys and sorrows of other peasants. He could master spade and axe alike. He had powerful hands, a practical intelligence and great perseverance. For those who sought his presence he found ways of communal life free from all oppression. He could guide men because his devotion to them was deep and lasting and his immediate followers lived in monasteries not held by rules but by mutual understanding and common tasks. Seeing his goal clearly, he was never in haste: he did not break existing ties, but waited till harmonious solutions were

---

* Dmetri Sergeievich Merezhkovsky (1865–1941).

147

possible. Inwardly he was strong like a rock, and yet humble and gentle. Into the Russian people he planted the ideal of freedom in community. This ideal was rooted in his faith in the Trinity which is a union and yet a diversity.

His entire life, centred on the Eucharist in which Heaven and Earth are united, was an altar offering made for the future of mankind. Through his example, reverence for the Sacrament could take root in the souls of the Russian people with extraordinary strength. Nicolas Zernov wrote thus in his book on *St. Sergius, Builder of Russia*:*

> In the Eucharist, the three-fold Godhead calls upon the diversity of men to experience harmonious love and freedom . . . The struggle between the powers of light and the powers of darkness rages around the Sacred Meal. Its significance goes beyond the human race and has world-wide effects. In it, man is called upon to offer the Godhead in the name of the whole of creation the entire gifts of the Earth, which he has transformed through his own work. The Eucharist is therefore the prophecy of transfiguration, the transfiguration of the entire cosmos, the promise that its redemption will be achieved through man's co-operation with the three-fold Godhead . . .

Our own time, its outlook governed by natural science, has as yet little understanding for this Christianity of the future. But in the Asian East, the spirituality of St. Sergius is known. The Russian painter Nicholas Roerich, who went to live in the Himalayas, tells how the Indian seers honour St. Sergius as a Bodhisattva: as one of those who beheld the features of Christ.**

In the words of St. Sergius lies the mood of the Holy Grail. The Russian soul has the mission to realize the experience of the Holy Grail as the message of an all-embracing universal Church of the future. What had been and is being prepared by some individual men in Europe up to the present century can then sink into many as the experience of Whitsun, and flame through united souls.

Christ is spirit. The fact that He once existed in human form unites Him with material phenomena. His impulse works only in the soul. But the ecclesiastical institutions of the world are there to unite men, so that they can lift up their souls into the spiritual world.

The Russian people are the Christ people. The listening for mighty events lying between the childhood stage of this people and its maturity placed souls before the need to choose their future path. The Russians believed in man's power to distinguish between good and evil. They were neither naïve nor sentimental. Every Sunday, they assembled in their village churches and listened to the constantly repeated words of the Sermon on the Mount. Whether they were themselves good or evil, they had no doubt that these were revelations of the truth. They were generous enough to forgive those that had trespassed against them and they were humble.

Above all they believed in the shared responsibility of all for all. Even the Russians of Moscow, who could have no faith in human justice, had confidence in divine guidance. It was not important for them to possess political rights or economic freedom. As Christians, they could all hear and follow the voice of God.

---

* Nicholas Zernov, Tr. A. Delafield, 1939.
** Nicholas Roerich (1874–1947). *The Golden Blade*, 1975.

The peasants could even preserve their human dignity in the times of serfdom: the tradition of self-government in rural communities was preserved throughout the centuries of social degradation and oppression. Despite the oppressive political system, the feeling that Russians are equal before one another was never lost among the people. Though the Tsars could dispose ruthlessly of life and property, as the bearers of the divine image they too were members of the same family. The Russians were coarse, a prey to their passions, and often corrupted by the use of force. Cruelty and harshness undermined the existence of millions, but all this was unable to extinguish their longing for holiness*.

There were always those among them who through a life of chosen renunciation were enabled to become in old age teachers of the people. Through the presence of such men the power of Christ could work ceaselessly. To be a *Starets*, as such a teacher was called, is a dignity no Church can bestow for it flows entirely from the spiritual authority of the individual, which must be self-revealed.

One of the greatest of these men was St. Seraphim. His story is simple and earnest. By the time he was ten—in 1769—he had learned to read so fast that he became seriously ill. The Queen of Heaven then appeared to him and restored him to health. Later, with other young men, he went on a pilgrimage to the Church of St. Sophia in Kiev. At nineteen he entered the forest hermitage at Sarov where he spent eight years of his noviciate with two old men. He learned to bake bread for the Sacrament and he worked in the forest with a carpenter. Again he fell seriously ill, and again the Divine Sophia came to him. She appeared between John and Peter, to whom she said: ' He is one of us.' In 1786 he became a monk and received the name Seraphim.

At the age of thirty-five, abandoning his worldly goods he went into a retreat lasting thirty years. In his hut in the forest he was attacked by robbers and severely wounded and as he lay there, seriously ill, the Holy Sophia, again with John and Peter, appeared to him, saying: ' He is one of us.' He recovered, but could no longer raise his body upright. When the two old monks had died he began an eighteen-years' silence. He thus learned spiritual listening and later, when asked why he had not spoken for so long, he answered: ' Silence is the mystery of the future, but our words are the tools of this world.'

In 1825 he became the ' elder ', the Starets. He had the gift of healing, the insight of the seer, the fire of the mystic and the humility of the instrument of the Godhead. Now he opened the door of his cell to all men: rich and poor, criminals and the pious came to him early and late and found guidance and recovery.

One of his pupils, Nicholas Motolov, the son of a landowner, described an episode in the life of the Starets, who demonstrated to him the nature of the Holy Spirit.

> ' Man's true aim,' so he said, ' is to acquire the Holy Spirit. His grace is the light that illumines men.'
> ' How can I know that I am in Him ? '
> ' I have told you already . . . I have told you how men dwell in Him and how they must recognize this fact. What more do you need ? '

---

* Read *The Gulag Archipelago*, by Alexander Solzhenitsyn. Collins (Fontana), 1974. Editor.

. . . The pupil had made every effort to understand the answers of his teacher . . .
He sat on a tree stump in the forest, facing St. Seraphim. It was November and it had
begun to snow. He persisted with his questions: 'I must understand this more clearly.'

Then the Starets grasped him firmly by the shoulder and said: 'Son, we are both
together in the spirit of God. Why are you not looking at me?'

'I cannot look, father, because fiery flames are coming from your eyes. Your face is
brighter than the sun and my eyes hurt.'

'Do not be afraid, my son. You too have become as bright as I. You too are now in the
fulness of the spirit of God, or you would not see me as I am.'

Then he bowed over him and said: 'Thank God for His infinite mercy. You saw that
I did not even make the sign of the Cross. Only in my heart did I ask God, "Lord, allow
him to behold with his bodily eyes the descent of the Holy Spirit whom Thou givest to
Thy servants when Thou appearest in the light of Thy glory." Look, the grace of God
came like a loving mother, through the grace of the Mother of god herself. Come, son,
look into my eyes.'

The pupil looked at him and was filled with even greater reverence. He saw the face
of the man to whom he spoke lit up as if in the heart of the Sun. He saw the movement
of the lips, the changing expression of the eyes, and he heard the voice; but he saw neither
hands nor body, only the radiant light that shone from him, casting its brilliant reflection
over the snowy forest.

'How do you feel now?' asked Father Seraphim.

'I feel a calm and peace my soul has never known before.'

'This is the peace of which Christ says: "Peace I leave with you; my peace I give
unto you . . ."'

St. Seraphim worked for the eternal birth of the spirit in the soul of every humble believer,
preparing throughout his life the Whitsun of humanity. In the twentieth century we are
perhaps not able to appreciate the full significance of such activity. But in coming centuries
men will look back with gratitude and reverence on those who prepared the Slav peoples for
their later maturity.

From the eighteenth century onwards more and more Russians went to live in Western
Europe, but owing to the nature of their folk soul they were not yet ready for western ways of
thinking. The West reached the age of natural science step by step; from the Middle Ages,
through the Renaissance and the Reformation. Men were well prepared for the struggle
between tradition and 'enlightenment'.

To the Slavs, intellectualism came over-night and the effect was overwhelming. Everything
became doubtful to the Russian intellectual—he himself, other people; the Heaven that
became empty and no longer comforted him as it had done in the past, the Earth that appeared
abandoned, from which he nevertheless expected a new paradise. He stood in the conflict
between God and man, between predestination and free decision, between apparent chaos
and a deeper order. Enlightenment alone if carried to a conclusion gave no meaning to human
existence but led to atheism and killed all the certainty the soul had felt in the past. Western
people, particularly the English, could stand this situation; but Russians who abandoned

themselves to it uncritically lost their piety and peace. And yet in their hearts the longing for man's cosmic dignity was unextinguished.

It was a misfortune for the Russians that they did not listen to Goethe who in his innermost nature stood on the same ground of deep spirituality as the Russian folk soul, and that they allowed themselves to be blinded by superficialities and abstractions which are not the true spiritual Europe.

They were disappointed and despair and bitterness gained hold of their souls; yet they wished to spread Enlightenment in Russia, hoping thus to destroy Tsarism and the established Church. To gain all, they wanted to destroy all. Even God had to be rejected for the sake of human freedom. Bakunin wrote in a manuscript of 1879, *God and the State*, ' If God exists, man is a slave. But man can and must be free: therefore God does not exist . . . As a jealous lover of human freedom, which I consider fundamental to everything we adore and worship in humanity, I reverse Voltaire's words and say: " If God existed, He would have to be abolished." '

Respect for man stands on a weak foundation when reverence for the divine world ceases. Man's self-doubt was the heaviest of all trials for the Russian. Gorky wrote:

What is he, this human being? Do you understand him? He takes you by the collar and crushes you under his thumb nail like a flea. Perhaps you will then feel sorry for him: yes, then you can reveal to him his stupidity. He will put you on the rack for your trouble and will tear all your veins out, an inch per hour. Yes! Mercy! Disgusting! Cruel, but true.

This cry came from the helplessness of the Russian soul in ordeals of life where the thinking of the Enlightenment could not be united with a Christian outlook.

High and serene, remote from all human aberration, shines the memory of the divine image of spiritual man and a spiritual humanity. Despite all chaotic tendencies the Russian arch-angel inspired Slav souls with the mood of such a realization. Soloviev could see this in its purity: ' The appearance of the new spiritual man in Christ is the central event of world history. The end or aim of this history is a spiritual humanity.'

This word stands for all time in the annals of the world. It is for ever true. But to humanity it must first become true, and only humanity can make it so. The Father Will has spoken. The Will of the Son has achieved it. Human Will must listen and fulfil. It is free. Russia is both white and black; she is the bright Russia of St. Seraphim, and the Russia ruled by demons.

In the nineteenth century, the light-filled Russia was resting in itself, living in the humble souls of simple people: pilgrims, illiterates, monks, sectarians, small traders, factory workers, artisans and peasants who spent their days in heavy toil and endured sickness and sorrow without complaint, convinced that all would be for the best in the end. In pain and privation they saw no evil to be avoided; indeed, they often suffered and died joyfully in the certain conviction of Divine love.

That the Russian soul should turn inwards, it was endowed with a generosity that will contribute greatly to new forms of community in the future. Generous participation in every-thing human rings through every one of the long works of the great Russian authors.

Dostoievsky listened lovingly to the inmost heart of criminals, idiots and saints. Souls were all that mattered to him and he looked for one solution only: man—in whom God is ever-present, in us and around us. All his stories portray a mood of emptiness and absence—the waiting for the abundance of the presence of God. Human dignity always faced him, even out of the possibility of guilt. 'Why should sin exist? God gave man freedom, the absolute power to choose between good and evil: this is the basis of the true dignity of the human soul.'

The great Tolstoy also listened to the simple and the humble who bear love and generosity of soul as a general mood. What he observed he compared with the pure image of the Son of Man. He could see the dangers threatening and longed to place a mantle round the shoulders of the Christ people in protection against intellectualism and fanaticism: he wanted time for development. Tolstoy sacrificed the conventional aristocratic outlook in which he had been brought up in order to become a peasant himself and share with other peasants a life in the succession of Christ. This enabled him to write his tales of peasant life which are of a beauty and profundity rarely attained in the literature of any language.

The Fishes of the Zodiac indicate the home of divine spirits who willed in the beginning to create man as a being of great diversity. The first archetypal image of the human form was nevertheless only a reflection of those higher powers and lacked independent will; and out of this lifeless image in the course of aeons man evolved, gifted with life, soul and spirit.

But present-day humanity is still far from the goal set by the spiritual world; for there are two tendencies in the cosmic Fishes, a dark backward longing, harbouring the memory of the ancient archetypal image of physical man, and an urge forward to a spiritual man as the ideal of complete humanity.

Thus two ways exist for development. If the first is followed the ancient image will harden and a race of dependent men, automatons without individuality, bereft of soul and spirit will arise. The other path is that of the Russian archangel who implanted the longing for cosmic dignity that can unfold only in love and freedom, by the permeation and illumining of the body with the life of the spirit.

The present time is filled with the sound of battle between Michael and the Dragon. A consciousness already trained in clear thinking can fight the deadening effects of materialism. Only those who created it and lived with it, understanding it in all its consequences, can really tame it. The Russian soul, then lacking the necessary intellectual weapons, should have kept out of the struggle but did not do so, and has had to suffer these consequences.

Despair of the state of modern society and doubt in the meaning of earthly life gained hold of thousands—even Lenin and Stalin—while exalted aims, as the earliest revolutionaries experienced them, burned now as torment in the Russian heart. Mocking thoughts were every-where. 'Look at the hollowness, the egotism! This can only bring chaos. Men cannot rise to a true dignity, so let us force them to brotherhood and equality, in the ideal state*.'

Into this despair the modern world concept struck its icy rays: 'There is no God, the Earth is a grain of sand in the infinite solitude of the universe: man is less than dust—the world of stars is a machine and the individual but a cog in the smallest wheel.'

What had been thought in the West was carried out in Russia to the bitter end in practical life. The Russian can be both angel and devil. A man of the West is able to hold a

---

* Read *Solzhenitsyn*, by David Burg and George Feifer. Hodder and Stoughton, 1972. Editor.

materialistic philosophy and still go to church on Sundays, for his thinking and willing are kept apart by feeling. In the Russian everything becomes at once passionate deed.

The logical aim of the thinking that led to communism is a humanity without individualities, incapable of catastrophe—which is an awakener—dull, peaceful and contented. The glowing idealism behind it is directed by demons. The robot, submitting automatically, would be the fulfilment of diabolical plans, released because ancient impulses have been dragged into the present. In Russia, an additional factor was the uncontrolled power of the blood, accompanying the still immature people through history. Hatred asserted itself; first in the individual against Tsarism and oppression, then in the demons, against humanity.

Yet the Russian soul injured and misunderstood, is waiting, in need of human beings, longing for responsible men who will recognize its exalted nature; for it is those in authority who are most in danger of falling a prey to errors.

In time to come, when a new cultural epoch is the task of the whole of humanity, souls will look back in history to our day and earlier centuries, seeking historical symptoms of the impulse of the Fishes. Dark chaotic memories will cloud the spirit's gaze on the childhood phase of Russia's soul, as the awakened Slav people come upon the evil of the past and take its burden upon themselves; but beyond the superficial Russia of Byzantinism, Tsarism, the age of Enlightenment and of atheism, their destiny will shine to them from the primordial realm of the cosmic Fishes.

They will not create new thoughts, for that is the task of our time; from the purified substance of former striving the soul's raiment will be woven; they will become vessels, to receive the flames of the spirit from the heights. Vladimir Soloviev knew the secret of transformation and renewal and tells it in his fairy tale, *The Secret of Progress.*

' Do you know the tale?' he begins.

Everyone should know it. He described a hunter who had lost his way in the dark forest. An old, old woman begged him to carry her across a river. ' You cannot find the path there alone,' she said, 'but I shall guide you for I come from there myself.' She was ugly and repulsive. He hesitated to take the old woman, but then had pity and thought: ' She must be more than a hundred years old. What burdens she has had to carry in her life—I in my turn will have to make some effort for her.' He took her on his shoulders, but felt as laden as if he had been carrying a coffin. He waded into the river and gradually his burden seemed no longer quite so heavy. It even lightened with every step. Something he had never experienced before began to happen to him. He walked on and did not look round—but when he arrived at the other shore, he saw that the old woman had turned into a beautiful maiden.

This tale was written for Soloviev's time, the end of the nineteenth century. It will have its full significance when the Slav peoples are ready to cross the river to ages of greater spiritualization. The tale ends with the words: ' The saviour saves himself.' This is the secret of progress; there is no other, nor will there ever be one.

The coat-of-arms of Imperial Russia displays the red double eagle of the Byzantine Empire. But the heraldic symbolism of Russia must be understood differently from that of other great states of Europe. In the latter, the outer figures, the ' supporters ', characterize the nature of the folk soul and the inner heraldic pictures refer to the people's history. This is not so with Russia, where the double-headed eagle carries the small coats-of-arms of the absorbed peoples on its wings; these refer to historical events, to Byzantium and the people connected with it. But in the centre, in the very heart of the eagle, is the picture of Michael, and this image belongs to the spirit of Russia. His victory over the Dragon is an ideal in the Russian soul and some day this will be clearly revealed. Russia will then be ' Holy Russia.'

Fig. 2. *The Coat-of-Arms of Imperial Russia.*

Fig. 3. *Ancient Coat-of-Arms of Kiev.*

The soul of Russia still shows itself only in the mystical feeling of a people who for hundreds of years have knelt before the icons of their altars. The strength of Russia will reveal, through the transformed Sense of Hearing, the secrets of mankind's evolution. To understand what the heart knows, one must listen in complete stillness, uttering nothing oneself, waiting for what is revealed. The new culture will ' hear ' what today is overwhelmed by the noise of the modern world; will once more experience what Pythagoras called the ' Music of the Spheres.'

This is indicated in the ancient coat-of-arms of Kiev. A childlike angel with great wings holds in its left hand a shield that protects the heart, in the right, a sword of flame. This is the Russia of the future.

The Russian archangel, bearer of this future, prepares in self-surrender to receive it; heeding everything that comes, not hostile. The soul of Russia, spiritualized by a thousand years of infinite sorrow, awaits its time.

154

The Balkans

GREECE, BULGARIA, ROMANIA:
SERBIA AND MONTENEGRO
(FEDERAL UNITS OF YUGOSLAVIA):
ALBANIA, TURKEY

ABOVE PRE-CHRISTIAN HELLAS shone the heavenly Ram which, during the flowering of Greek culture, rose in spring with the morning sun on the eastern horizon. The Ram is the leader of the Zodiac and the other star images follow; and through this link, ancient Greece became the forerunner of all the later European cultures.

The relationship with these forces is indicated in mythology in the story of Helle and Frixos. It is told that Helle, travelling with her brother to Colchis, carried upon the golden fleece of a ram, fell into the sea over what we know as the Hellespont. She was the soul of Greece, who united her people with the Ram forces. The name Hellenes comes down from her.

Those in Greece who were led into spiritual life at carefully guarded Mystery centres worshipped the Golden Fleece in love and reverent devotion. The Golden Fleece was the human soul itself, still permeated with the light and wisdom of creation.

Although this inner mythical perception came to an end, the love of wisdom—*philos-sophia*—remained in Hellas. Out of what had previously been initiation experience, the Greek soul could bring forth philosophy, and conceive the content of outer phenomena in thought and word.

Through Homer, the rhythmic word became the educator of the people. In Sparta, choristic lyric, the word spoken in choir, was later evolved, and when Athens became the centre of Greek culture, Greek tragedy and comedy could grow out of the power of language. At the time of Christ, Greek became the vehicle of the message of the Eternal Word, of the Lamb of God: ' In the beginning was the Word, and the Word was with God, and the Word was God. The same was in the beginning with God. All things were made by him: and without him was not any thing made that was made.' This was first written in the Greek language.

In modern times the peoples of south-eastern Europe, the Greeks and the Slavs, are orientated towards the Ram impulses, and to words—as distinct from imagery—through the development of the Sense of Words, of Speech. That these different peoples should be related to the same cosmic forces may at first seem doubtful; there seem to be few links, for Greece experienced her great flowering in the distant past while the Slavs will not reach theirs until the remote future. They may differ outwardly in many respects but that does not preclude a common relationship with the cosmic Ram.

Man himself differs greatly between old age, youth and childhood, and yet is a unity. And just as former experiences and future aims can work in him simultaneously, so ancient memories and future hopes resound through the folk soul of the peoples of south-eastern Europe.

A religious link between Greece and the other Balkan countries was the Orthodox Church whose ritual, unlike that of the Church of Rome, was carried upon the spoken word. Rome's contribution to Christianity has in the course of time acquired the character of imagery, arousing awareness and delight of the eyes. The Sacrament of Transubstantiation was performed in full sight of the congregation; but the words remained alien to the people for they were spoken in Latin, a language unintelligible to most. The more important aspect was the visible action round the altar.

In contrast, the rite of the Eastern Church remained invisible, hidden from the congregation by a screen. Only the door, through which no-one passed but the celebrating priest, linked the worshippers with the sanctuary. In devotion before the reality of the Transubstantiation, hearts united with all that was spoken. People would stand for hours surrendered to the content of their own language, strengthening their souls through the Holy Word.*

The Slav language became that of the Church as early as the ninth century, when Cyrillus and Methodius translated the Bible into the Old Bulgarian tongue. As Methodius had invented his own written characters, called *Glagiolica*, the distribution of Christian documents was ensured. Moreover Chrabru, a Bulgarian monk from Mount Athos, wrote a brief work, shortly after the schism leading to separation from Rome, and in it he laid down the pronunciation of the different letters. ' These are Slav letters,' he wrote, ' and this is how they have to be written and pronounced.'

In transmitting an understanding for the sound of language to coming generations, he worked in the spirit of the two Slav Apostles, of whom he said: ' There are still those among us who saw them.' His book, copied again and again, was an intimate companion to the whole development of Slavonic culture.

For the southern Slavs and the Greeks, moving towards centuries of oppression under Turkish rule, there arose a common spiritual home with which they could all feel united although it was remote from outer events. This centre was on Athos. The Holy Mount—Hagionuros—rises as a majestic pyramid from the Aegean at the extreme end of the isthmus

---

* Rudolf Steiner, *The Driving Force of Spiritual Powers in World History*. (Lecture p. 5.) Tr. by Dorothy Osmond, Toronto, pubn, 1972. Distribution by Rudolf Steiner Press, London.

of Chalkidike. At the highest point is the chapel of the Transfiguration: ' Here, the light from Mount Tabor seemed to shine anew.'

The first documentary evidence of a religious community at Athos dates from 842: almost at the same time, the independence of Germany, France and Italy was being prepared through the Strasbourg Oaths. Athos, also, served the emerging Europe.

A legend tells of the words of the divine Virgin: ' I begged for the mountain, and it was given to me.' It is said that after the Resurrection she wanted to carry its message to Cyprus but was shipwrecked at Athos. As she set foot on land the statues of the gods cried out and fell on their knees. She blessed all beings and went out to sea again.

The first monasteries on Mount Athos, all built before 1000, were dedicated to her: two to the annunciation of her birth, and two to her death. The monks of Athos venerated her as the Woman clothed with the Sun, of whom St. John speaks in the twelfth chapter of the *Apocalypse*. Athos was the desert that could offer her shelter. She was Panageria, the world-embracing Sophia of the stars: ' He has made thy soul wiser than the heavens,' said a Theotokion.

To the Eastern Church, she was the meaning and end of all creation. She was the wisdom of the world of the stars, and at the same time the wisdom that underlies all created things, the Holy Spirit. Through her the created world attains its transfiguration for her own body is completely transfigured. Mount Athos had been given her by her Son, Who was accompanied by angels, and Whom the soul can receive.

Fig. 4. *Mount Athos.* Isthmus of Chalkidike, Greece. Site of an independent republic of twenty monasteries. *By courtesy of Routledge and Kegan Paul Ltd. from their book ATHOS AND ITS MONASTERIES.*

The monks on Mount Athos were conscious of the working of the Godhead within man and the community. To them, the holiest of all festivals was Easter. In the innumerable monasteries and smaller sanctuaries on the mountain—up to a thousand have been counted—not a single picture of the Resurrection can be found. It was experienced inwardly as the message

157

of salvation through the word alone: 'Christ is risen!' These words resounded on Easter morning, first in the churches, then passed from mouth to mouth spreading a mood of bliss all round: 'Christ is risen!' Throughout the time between Easter and Whitsun men would greet each other: 'Christ is risen!'

Of the twenty fortified monasteries on Mount Athos, seventeen were Greek, one Bulgarian, one Serbian and one Russian. In the course of the stormy times they passed through they developed into a vigorous monastic republic.

In the twelfth century some of the monks set out for the court of the Serbian prince, Stephan Nemanja, whose young son was destined for a special mission. Although dearly loved by his father, the boy did not feel at home at court. Under the pretext of a hunting expedition he escaped and went to Athos, where he became a monk and was given the name Sava. His father later joined him, leaving the government in the hands of his eldest son.

The new ruler had himself crowned by Pope Innocent III. On that occasion he had to promise that his whole people would become Roman Catholic. In secret, however, he sent his brother Sava to the Patriarch of Constantinople who, exiled from the now Latin Empire, was living at Nicaea. There the synod appointed Sava the first Eastern bishop of Serbia; and Sava then, with a crown sent him by the Byzantine Emperor, performed for his brother a second coronation.

St. Sava created nine bishoprics; and all their monasteries were placed under the Rule of St. Basil according to which Mount Athos had been governed. He encouraged education and was adopted in modern times as patron saint of all Serbian schools and universities. The convent of Hilendar on Mount Athos, founded by his father, became to the Serbs the centre of their learning and theology. Sava was the bearer and preserver of the Slav character; and through the memory of his work his people could survive Turkish rule.

The Osman Turks knew this. After the rising of 1595, they burned his relics and dispersed his ashes to destroy the very source of Serbian strength. But he was ever-present to his people in time of distress; did he not appear on the battlefield of Kumanova in 1912, dressed in white?

The cosmic Ram demands for the future a new spirituality and preserves an attitude of expectancy. And so the young Slav soul looked towards the acquisition of faculties containing the seed of future development.

In the tenth century, a Christianity arose in Bulgaria that needed neither outer tradition nor churches and monasteries, but rested entirely on the twin pillars of inner knowledge and sacrificial deed. Already, five centuries earlier, colonists had brought the teachings of Mani from Asia Minor to Bulgarian Thrace where, despite ceaseless persecution, this wisdom was cultivated in secret. But now it was no longer the secret knowledge of the sages of the Pindus mountains. The Grail impulse had brought to life forces in Europe to which Manichaeanism was no alien heresy; it could now unfold in Bulgaria.

Mani, the great Christian teacher who was killed in Persia in 276, taught that the Spirits of Darkness strove against the kingdom of Light, though without prevailing against its splendour. They were to be punished but the kingdom of Light contained only good. The Spirits of Light then took some of their own goodness and mixed it as leaven with the substance of evil. The resulting turmoil brought Death into the world, giving the Darkness the possibility to devour itself.

The human race was the archetypal man originating in the kingdom of Light who was to intermingle with the kingdom of Darkness to transform it. Not punishment but the penetration of evil with good was to bring redemption. To become ready for this world task the soul has to discard all the inheritance of tradition and rely only on the divine light of the spirit, growing gradually able to have faith in its own depths. The Slav Manichaeans therefore led severely simple lives and were gentle and taciturn. They acknowledged equality between the lay state and the clerical, and between man and woman.

The movement became known in history under the name of Bogumil, who appears to have been at its head. Bogumil means 'beloved of God, friend of God'; and under this wise guidance Bulgaria became a flourishing kingdom which embraced Macedonia, Epirus, Wallachia and parts of Hungary and Transylvania. The Bulgarian Tsar Peter, son of the powerful Simeon I, was a Manichaean and was venerated by the people as a saint. Four Macedonian Fathers who lived in the wilderness revealed themselves as Manichaeans and these 'Apostles' became the leaders of the entire population. By the time the country's outward power collapsed, Manichaeanism was pulsating through Serbia, Montenegro and the Herzegovina—all encompassed within the southern Slav soul.

The Byzantine Church was more representative of the resting aspect of the Ram and tended, accordingly, to guard the treasury of ancient clairvoyance as tradition. The Manichaean outlook was therefore utterly alien and the Church fought the Bogumils with everything in its power. In Pindus, prisoners were blinded and murdered. Persecution continued for many years. The alleged heresies of the Bogumils were listed, and in the resolutions of synods heretics were solemnly excommunicated at each point. Monks, priests, bishops and patriarchs took part in the struggle.

Treatises written against the Bogumils as late as the thirteenth and fourteenth centuries are evidence of the continued existence of the sect. But the suppression was carried out with such thoroughness that only a single document of the Bogumils could be established beyond doubt. This is the *Liber Sancti Johanni*, a conversation in which St. John asks about, and Jesus explains the original conditions of the cosmos.

The Bogumils collected and spread Slav apocryphal and gnostic writings which they passed on unaltered. Certain manuscripts of Croat, Serbian, Bulgarian or Russian origin, suggesting Manichaean authorship, have been attributed to a mysterious personality, the priest Jeremija, often identified with Bogumil. One such writing tells that Jesus, at the age of ten, found the head of Adam; that He tilled the soil on the way to Bethlehem; that Probus the Emperor's son took Him with him as an assistant tax gatherer and that Jesus bathed with him and called him brother. It was emphasized that to regard other men as brothers was praiseworthy.

Many of the songs, myths, and particularly legends of the southern Slavs draw on the *Apocrypha* for their content, no less than on Bogumil traditions. In the years of Turkish rule the constant recitation of Christian ways of thought was to prove a great source of strength. Although the movement eventually disappeared, competent scholars have proved that Manichaean-Bogumil traditions have lived on in southern Slav and Romanian literature.

In the fourteenth century the Turks invaded south-eastern Europe and bitter times came upon the Slavs. The Turks, the terror of Europe, had until shortly before been a peaceful nomadic tribe in central Asia. In 1235, under their leader Suleiman, they moved to Armenia. Their sudden mysterious rise seems connected with the failure of the Crusades.

When a great spiritual enterprise collapses prematurely, a void arises to be filled by base forces. The Crusades could have led to a fruitful synthesis of European Christianity and the wisdom of the East. The Turkish invasions, however, were an attempt to link decadent central-Asian spirituality with the purely external virtues of the West.

The failure of the Crusades was sealed in 1291 by the fall of Acre. In 1259 Osman I had been born. He it was who turned the peaceful nomadic Turks into ruthless warriors; he called himself Lord of Bithynia and his soldiers Osmanli, the Sons of Osman. His son Orkhan became ruler of the Turkish state; in 1355 he crossed the Dardanelles with eighty warriors and occupied Gallipoli. After its capture in the following year, victorious campaigns against the West began. Suleiman, the first Turkish ruler to set foot on European soil, was buried on the shores of the Hellespont.

A century later—in May, 1453—Constantinople fell into the hands of the Turks. The Church of the Holy Sophia was turned into a Turkish mosque.

The Hagia Sophia was the oldest place of Christian worship dedicated to the Divine wisdom. The church was planned by Constantine the Great at the foundation of the city in 328. At the Emperor's order the Trojan symbol of Divine wisdom, the Palladium, was buried within the city walls so that Constantinople should become its servant. The name Hagia Sophia was given in the fifth century. (Plate 35.)

After the fire of 532 in which it was destroyed along with that quarter of the city, the Emperor Justinian immediately began a reconstruction. His official chronicler records that the newly rebuilt church was a work of infinite beauty; so bright that it seemed as if the vast interior was not lit by the sun from outside, but created its light from within. The dome appeared without visible support as if suspended by a golden chain from the sky.

In 1455, two years after this sanctuary had been lost to the Christian world, Fra Angelico, creator of some of the loveliest paintings of the Queen of Heaven, died in Italy. In 1452 Leonardo da Vinci, the first outstanding natural scientist, whose inventions have the quality of prophecy, had been born. Doors were closing to experiences of the soul that had their basis in the past. The light that once shone from the East was to become dim, so that from depth of soul and through the transformation of the age of natural science, the West should send a still more pure spirituality to the East in the future.

The ancient light of Eastern wisdom was a gift of the guidance of the world. The light of wisdom of the future must arise within man and through man. The doors of the Hagia Sophia were to re-open to Christians only when the time for a new, direct knowledge of the Divine Sophia could begin.

The Turkish army gained control of the entire Balkans. Serbia, Mores and Attica were first overcome; Wallachia had to surrender, Bosnia was captured and the Albanian army scattered. The Turkish cavalry swept across Europe as far as Styria and Carinthia. Mohammed II had the courage of a lion. Caffa, the Genoese colony in the Crimea, the northern coasts of the Pontine swamps and Otrento in Italy, fell successively into his hands. The great Sultan died in 1481 on the eve of a new eastern campaign.

Under Suleiman II, who reigned for forty-six years, the Osman Empire attained its greatest power and splendour. It was the Golden Age for poets and scholars: Suleiman himself, under his poet's pseudonym ' Muhbibi ', wrote a *divan*. Indeed many of the rulers of the wild Turkish warriors had been poets. When the last of these kings died, in 1807, the liberation began of the peoples of south-eastern Europe who had gone through years of servitude and degradation.

In Greece, the Byzantine Church was more or less left alone, although the conquerors demanded heavy tribute and collected it with savage methods. The peasants, in poverty and fear, took to the mountains. Often they became robbers, calling themselves Clephti, ' those released from tyranny '. Their deeds were sung in innumerable ballads. The closer the time of liberation approached, the more of an honour it became to be a Clepht.

In Serbia also, under the first shock of Turkish rule, the Christian population fled to the mountains. Many of them found welcome in Bosnia, in the Herzegovina, Croatia, Dalmatia and later also in Hungary. Those who stayed behind in Serbia suffered for centuries under two oppressive systems: the Turks, and the Greek Orthodox Church which tried to absorb the Serbian Church. Churches and monasteries became poor and deserted.

In lonely, almost inaccessible places of refuge in the mountains and forests, tiny centres of worship were built, often partly or even completely under the ground. There the words of the hidden ritual were heard in reverence and devotion. The native language remained as a culture-preserving force.

The Bulgars, suffering in the same way, fled to the Balkan mountains finding safety and shelter in deep forests and ravines. ' Balkan ' is the name of all the mountains of the peninsula south of the sombre Danube. Every one of them has its own sonorous and beautiful name, along with legends and memories. The Bulgars lived there in seclusion in close contact with nature with whom they shared their joys and sorrows. They numbered many thousands and their songs were their comforts and companions.

To all southern Slavs, the Bulgarian writer Paissy, born in 1722, lit the perpetual flame of growing self-awareness. In youth he became a monk on Mount Athos: in middle age, after extensive travels, he wrote his Slav-Bulgarian history. His mode of expression was sometimes archaic and heavy, sometimes lively and popular, but always suited to the events he described.

Using old-Slavonic, Russian, Serbian and Bulgarian expressions, he told of the greatness of the Bulgars who had once been representative of all the southern-Slav peoples. In an age of utter aridity Paissy threw the firebrand of the word into the receptive Slavonic souls. His work, and commentaries upon it, passed from hand to hand. In 1824 his Bulgarian primer was published and declared basic in the newly founded Bulgarian schools.

To understand the history of the Bulgars, Serbs and indeed all the southern Slavs, one must try to feel what it meant to any European people to live under an alien rule and alien language, dominated by a people with whom there was no intermingling. They were deprived of written books and there was no positive influence beyond the endlessly repeated tales, legends and proverbs or the personally copied word that could echo within the soul. But through the Sense of Speech the folk soul, active in the cosmic realm of the Ram, could work undisturbed in the different linguistic groups. It needed only a few men of genius to raise the latent wealth and guide it into future channels. They came, and with them others able to develop the given impulse.

Among all these peoples as well as among the Greeks, great philologers appeared and collected the literary remains of their countries. They drew the awareness of their compatriots towards the language that had been spoken on their soil in defiance of all obstacles through the centuries of darkness. Every one of these devoted scholars believed in his ability to root out all alien influence from his own tongue and do full justice to the spoken word. And each one knew that his people would only become independent if the common language that had held them together in suffering were to become the foundation of their future state organism.

In Bulgaria's liberation the discovery of ancient songs and proverbs was of the utmost importance as these were the immediate expression of the folk soul. Many were gathered by Dimitar Miladinoff, the son of a potter, and a primary-school teacher in various Macedonian towns. He was denounced as a dangerous revolutionary by the Metropolitan of Ochrida, Mileti, and thrown into prison. His younger brother who hastened to Constantinople to obtain his release was also imprisoned. A legend arose that they had been freed and had met outside the gates of the prison, where they had fallen into each other's arms and died in their embrace.

Another collection of simple songs that spoke to the Bulgarian heart was made by Petko Slaveikov. Professor Kraesteff, who edited Slaveikov's work, wrote that even when he looked through these songs for the hundredth time, he still found in them part of his own soul and that of his people. ' I can recall few moments of my life,' he told, ' in which I felt the profound happiness I feel now, when I read this little book, nor have I ever, so it seems to me, experienced the union with the folk soul in such ecstasy.'

Slaveikov had made a collection of 17,441 proverbs which appeared in print shortly before his death. Although most of his own poetic writings had been burned by the Turks, they had contributed to the people's liberation. After the Russo-Turkish war, at the Berlin Congress in 1878, Bulgaria was recognized as a principality. In 1886 the Bulgars became independent: but like the other Slav peoples, they later fell victim to Russian communism.

A Bulgarian coat of arms, said to have been adopted some time between 1615 and 1676 by Alexce Michailovich, shows a lamb carrying a banner. It is an expression of the impulse of the

Fig. 5. *Ancient Coat-of-Arms of Bulgaria.*

cosmic Ram that enabled the Balkan peoples to break through, after long oppression, to a new sense of responsibility. As Bulgaria, then a powerful kingdom, had once been the leader and representative of all the southern Slavs, so the Bulgarian coat-of-arms is a common symbol.

Vuk Stephanovic Karadzic, a linguistic genius, was born in 1789. Through him the Serbs and Croats received a uniform language, deeply rooted in the vernacular, and yet quite renewed in parts. He settled in Vienna where he made the acquaintance of Kopiker, a Slovene scholar who became the founder of the Vienna Slavonic school, and who was looking for a Serb or Croat to write down folk songs for him and tell him more about the Serbian language. He became Vuk's teacher, collaborator and protector.

Vuk collected Serbian folk songs and gathered material for a dictionary, issued in 1818 along with an entirely new grammar devoted to the dialect of southern Herzegovina, then still preserved in purity. He replaced etymological spelling by phonetic. His grammar was written according to the language ' . . . of those Serbs who live in the villages, far from the towns'.

Despite serious attacks he gathered on his journeys further folk songs, legends, fairy tales and proverbs whose style and language he improved. With Danicic, a professor at Belgrade university, he translated the Bible and wrote *The History of the Serbo-Croat Language to the end of the Eighteenth Century.*

From a philological-philosophical point of view, Danicic supported Vuk's reforms. The poet Branko Radicevic, who aroused the enthusiasm of students with his *Songs*, acknowledged Vuk as his teacher and adopted the language of the people for his work.

The most outstanding Croat and Serbian scholars now jointly declared that the two peoples had but one language and that one dialect, that of the south, should predominate. Though the Croats retained Latin characters, they had the phonetic system of spelling preferred among other peoples.

The liberation of Serbia came at the same time as these profound changes. In 1867, three years after the death of Vuk Stefanovic, the Turks withdrew from their last Serbian strongpoints.

Romania is the ancient Dacia, which was romanized by the Emperor Trajan in the second century A.D. In its history, the country came to be known as Wallachia and Moldavia, which in the ninth century formed a common state with Bulgaria. Manichaeanism left lasting effects. Through legends and tales, a knowledge of the part of evil in the course of progress continued among the Romanian peasants. The Wallachians had a strong connection also with Mount Athos where small Romanian communities had been living since the ninth century. During the Turkish rule a monk from Mount Athos, Nikodemus, went to Romania where he founded the two small monasteries of Voditz and Tismana which have survived into modern times.

Romania experienced with particular intensity her intimate relationship to the other southern Slav peoples. Her language and orthography show Bulgarian influence and the scribes of the earliest known manuscripts came from Serbia; and the first printer to settle in Wallachia was Nikodemus, the monk from Athos.

The exclusive guidance of the Eastern Church lasted till 1700 when, under Polish influence, the Metropolitan of Alba-Jula with over a thousand priests joined the Catholic Church, thereby to some extent breaking the link with Slav tradition.

In the eighteenth century Romanian historians discovered Roman characteristics in their language. Grammarians quickly became interested. The most outstanding among them was Thimotheus Cipariu whose work contributed greatly to Romania's eventual liberation.*

---

* Read John Fletcher, *The Painted Churches of Romania*, New Knowledge Books.

During the Hungarian revolution of 1848, he published a manifesto at Hermannstadt in which he demanded Romania's complete independence, and a Romanian gathering was planned at Blasendorf. Despite a ban imposed by the Hungarians, 40,000 people appeared at the given hour and place, which was known thereafter as the ' Field of Liberty '.

Every year on the same date students and other young people assembled on the market square. They marched through the town in torchlight procession, flying the Romanian flag, to Cipariu's cottage where everybody joined in the national anthem. Cipariu opened his window and replied quite calmly, as if it were not he personally who was being honoured, but the Romanian folk soul to which he had devoted his entire life. He had himself learned fifteen languages with the sole desire of developing further the individuality of his people. He died in 1878.

At Cattara, on the Dalmatian coast of Montenegro, St. Sava had founded a monastery dedicated to St. Michael. In 1389, when Serbia fell under Turkish rule, several Montenegran tribes took to the forests of the ' Black Mountain ' whose rocks were covered with black mosses. They fought constantly against the Turks who could never gain complete control of the country. In 1516 the government was taken over by an ecclesiastical dignitary.

In 1830, Peter Petrovich, the last episcopal ruler of Montenegro, became Head of State. He collected the songs of the people and also wrote songs of his own which in time became folk songs. Through his efforts and those of his successors Montenegro achieved independence in the Peace of Berlin. The country later became part of Yugoslavia.

Until they attained independence, the Albanians were the least known among the peoples of south-eastern Europe. Their language was not spoken or even understood anywhere else, nor did they possess a literature. Albania was moreover the last state to become independent, for the fire of the word was missing. Yet this, although reserved and unreceptive to alien influence, was the bearer of the folk soul. When the Turks banned the use of their language in schools, the Albanians chose to remain illiterate. Devoted to their own idiom, they stood firm until they became a republic in 1925.

The southern Slavs achieved their liberation without any outstanding difficulties. The time was ripe and outer events more or less followed historical necessity. It was as with growing children—having learned to speak they repeat their wishes until they are fulfilled. Not force, but diplomatic discussions at peace congresses established southern Slav independence.

The story of Greece was different. She was the leader, indeed the forerunner, in the fight against foreign rule and here too, national consciousness was fired by language. As if suddenly aroused, and stirred to action by ancestral deeds, Greece opened her struggle, her self-awareness increasing with the exhausting severity of its course.

The beginning was clandestine and illegal; it glimmered through underground literature and popular song. Constantine Rhigas, a native of Thessalonica, was a herald of things to come. He wrote an inspiring national song, went to Vienna and became the publisher of a Greek newspaper. The folk songs he wrote were like a cry from the depth of the soul of the Greek people. They were copied secretly all over Greece and passed on orally.

In 1796 Rhigas founded an organization called ' Hetaerle ', which assumed an almost religious character and as a secret society, spread rapidly. He included Serbs and Bulgars in his striving, hoping to fire their enthusiasm sufficiently to make them share in the struggle. But through a chain of misfortunes he was handed over to the Turks by the Austrian government and the purchase of his release was too long delayed.

' I have seen enough', he said, shortly before his death, ' and the time of harvest is coming when my people will gather sweet fruit.' A few years later his organization became the ' Hetairia Philike ', which continued to grow with increasing speed. After 1815, the ' Philomuses ' worked along similar though more scientific lines.

Twelve years before Rhigas, in 1748, Adamantios Koreas was born in Smyrna. He was to become the most famous Hellenist and philologist of his country. The ideal of the dignity of his fatherland, once the representative of a great civilization, filled him completely; all the numerous writings he published abroad were to him only a means towards a Greek Renaissance.

To make the culture of classic Greece intelligible to his people, he bridged with sure judgment the linguistic abyss that separated modern Greece from antiquity. He banished all foreign expressions, particularly those of Turkish origin, replacing them by Greek words taken from the language of classic authors and giving them a modern ending or inflection. Uncorrupted forms that had been lost, he re-introduced. He thus founded a vernacular suitable for all, based on the ennobled yet universally spoken word.

When awareness of language had been made the focal point of national life and the dead language of the past consciously brought to life again, the Greeks decided to change their name. They had been called Romanaei; now they called themselves Hellenes. Memories of the greatness of their past began to assume reality in their hearts. The sea captains of Psara and Hydra, who still swore by the Mother of God, renamed their ships after the heroes of ancient Greece.

The signal for the rising against the Turkish oppressors came in 1821 and the revolt, begun by peasants and the Clephti, spread rapidly. In the Peloponnese, Archbishop Germanos raised the banner of rebellion; other leaders of the Church followed. Patras was captured and a proclamation was issued in the city: ' Peace to the Christians, respect for all consulates, death to the Turks '. Athens fell, except for the small area round the Acropolis. Thebes also joined the rebels. When Mahmoud II realized the seriousness of the situation, he called all Moslems to arms. Counter-blows followed, and for Greece the struggle turned more and more into a seemingly hopeless and interminable war.

Meanwhile the European conscience had been aroused by her courage and resolution, and attention was drawn to this gallant country, the cradle of the later cultures. Greek language became an impulse carried by Irish monks in the Middle Ages; and through Erasmus of Rotterdam it became an integral part of the European learning. After the Renaissance Greek was taught in every university. It belonged to all—a source for the understanding of a common past. Suddenly, a wave of sympathy swept across Europe.

Volunteers came forward, money was collected to ransom prisoners and societies were founded to alleviate distress. Rashid Pasha exclaimed in horror: ' We are no longer fighting the Greeks, but all Europe! '

Public opinion grew so strong that statesmen were forced into action. Applying military pressure, England, France and Russia finally achieved the liberation of Greece which became official through the Protocol of London of 1830. In the new state the reformed language worked out by Adamantios Koreas was introduced in schools and for the press, while the vernacular continued in everyday use.

Turkey, after many, often very painful experiences on European soil, passed through a profound transformation. In Europe she retained only a narrow land-strip including the Hellespont and Constantinople. The Hagia Sophia continued in Moslem hands. Serenely the dome still enclosed the sanctuary once dedicated to the Divine Sophia who seemed buried and forgotten. But when Turkey ceased to oppress other peoples, a new breeze began to blow for her too. The Turks founded a new state: in 1923 the Ottoman Empire ceased to exist, for under the wise leadership of Kemal Pasha the country had become a republic.

Spiritual life was now divorced from the power of the state. Educational and scientific institutions, including theological colleges, were placed under the authority of the Commissariat of Public Education. Problems of dogma and religion in general became the concern of the Department of Religious Affairs and the Caliphate, which had hitherto chained religion to the state, was abolished. The Turkish language was modernised, and freed from Arabic and Persian influence. The new civil code, the basis of many further changes, was taken almost word for word from the Swiss code.

The religious influence of Islam having thus been removed from the realm of state, women were not merely given the vote in 1934, they also gained full political and social equality. Titles were abolished and Kemal Pasha called himself simply Kemal Atatürk.

Economic life also underwent re-orientation and was freed from state links. For the first Balkan Conference in 1931, delegates from Yugoslavia, Bulgaria, Romania, Albania and Greece came to Istanbul to discuss with Turkey the joint economic problems of the whole peninsula. An International Chamber of Commerce was founded, based on Istanbul.

Kemal Atatürk was in earnest in developing the positive aspect of European influence in his country. Turkey became Europe's protector on the east. To the best of her ability she closed the gate that could give access to spiritually unjustified forces from Asia.

Kemal accomplished yet another deed. An inner urge led him to open the Hagia Sophia to all humanity: he felt that the hour demanded this step. Since then innumerable people, of every faith and country, have visited the Hagia Sophia and have been deeply moved by its tranquillity and beauty and the radiance of its colour.

Since the middle of the twentieth century the first corner of the Venus pentagon has pointed to the Ram. Deep in the innermost sanctuary of the soul of the south-eastern peoples lives the will to cultivate true devotion in a world of scepticism. Through reverence, the force of sacrifice arises that can disarm illusion and fear.

The archangel of south-eastern Europe looks into the future. He incorporated impulses of language into the process of transformation towards his distant goal and, on the path, awakened his peoples. But their development to the formation of states is only the first figuration of possibilities whose attainment will take ages of hard striving.

What Manichaeanism began in educating the Slav soul to a readiness for sacrifice, and what was preserved as a selfless and devoted Christianity through centuries of isolation, will arise in the individual human being with a strength and purity as yet beyond our imagination. Then the Word will no longer work as a power confined to a certain nation. Peoples only prepare the path: the spoken word, strengthened through all it has transmitted in the course of time from man to man, will one day, as healer and awakener, transform evil through love.

Plate 33. *Vladimir Soloviev.* (1853–1900.) Russian philosopher, critic and poet.

Plate 34. *St. Basil's Cathedral, Moscow.* Built 1554–1560 in the reign of Ivan the Terrible. The Christmas festival, before the Revolution.

From the drawing by F. de Haenen, in 'Russia' by G. Dobson. A. and C. Black Ltd., London.

Plate 35. *Church of the Holy Sophia.* Hagia Sophia. 537 A.D. Constantinople (Istanbul). Founded by Constantine in 360 A.D., destroyed in 532 A.D. The rebuilding by Justinian was completed in 537 A.D. It stands on the highest point of the first of the seven hills on which Constantinople was built.

By courtesy of the Hirmer Verlag, Munich.

Plate 36. *The Madonna of Czestochowa, Poland.* One of those special icons, with a history of miraculous power.

By courtesy of the Monument Museum and Pontifical Gallery, the Vatican, Rome.

Plate 37. *The Swiss Oath of Independence*. By Stuckelberg.
Situated in Tell's Chapel, Lake of Lucerne. In 1291
tradition tells that the three men in the centre were led
to swear this oath by William Tell.

By courtesy of Herrn Joseph Nideröst.

Plate 38. *Karlstein Castle*. Near Prague, Bohemia (Czechoslovakia). Built by the last Initiate Emperor of Germany, Charles IV. (Fourteenth century.) A temple of the Grail was enclosed within the building.

By courtesy of the late Dr Karl König.

Plate 39. *The Old Goetheanum, Dornach, Switzerland.* Designed by Rudolf Steiner. Built in wood. Destroyed by fire in 1922.

Plate 40. *The New Goetheanum, Dornach, Switzerland.* Rebuilt in concrete, from a model by Rudolf Steiner.

By courtesy of Emil Gmelin. Photograph Atelier, Dornach.

Plate 41. *General Mannerheim.* From a painting by Eero Järnefelt, representing Mannerheim at the time of the Finnish 'Citizens' War of 1891.

By courtesy of the Finnish Embassy.

Plate 42. *The Veiled Isis*. By Eleanor Merry. The veil is an allusion to the secrecy of the Mysteries. Only a seer or initiate could lift the veil.

Poland

*As MANY OF POLAND's greatest writers indicate, an understanding of western Slav history can be gained only by penetrating to the realm of the soul, and interpretation of this aspect of the national character will not come easily. In a lecture of 1843 given in Paris in the *Collège de France*, the Polish poet Mickiewicz said:

> One cannot approach the idea of this country by merely reading the works of historians who, without exception, look at everything through the spectacles of Western prejudice: nor shall we get a much better picture from written laws, for these are filled with formulae borrowed from the West: the only way to an understanding is through the tales and anecdotes of the people, or through the lives of outstanding individuals.

In a later lecture he added:

> This race is not yet conscious of its destiny. It demands help in this respect, and this can only come from the West.

The Polish folk spirit weaves in the realm of the cosmic Bull, whose hidden aspect is Isis, the mother of the universe. In Egypt, Isis was usually shown with the horns of a bull, indicating the source of her revelations. Exalted beings guarded there the memory of the human soul's passage from its dwelling in God to individual life; from dream-like feeling to clear thinking. The forces from the Bull region aid the development of a Sense of Thought, with which Poland has a particular connection. As humanity gradually withdrew from the common

divine ground, what had once belonged to the world soul entered separate soul existence. An ancient priesthood made the sign of the Bull the expression of these events; and if slightly varied, it will still reveal its original meaning. From the universal circle a smaller circle develops, pressing towards the periphery. It is not completely separate—it still overlaps the

---

* References given in this chapter are to translations listed in the British Museum Catalogue and are not necessarily those from which the present translations were made.

area of the other. This represents the transition from cosmic universality to the separate consciousness we find on the Earth.

The Poles felt very close to the universal mother, who was venerated as their protectress. In the Polish litany she was not merely called the Queen of Angels but the Queen of the Polish Crown. During the reign of the young Queen Jadwiga, the picture of the Holy Mother was brought from Ruthenia to Czestochowa in Poland and as late as 1957 millions of Poles still flocked there in search of strength. (Plate 36.) The Virgin, so it is felt, has miraculously saved the country many times: in 1653 for example, during Czestochowa's heroic resistance against the Swedish invaders, and in August 1920 against the vast communist armies. There is another miraculous Madonna picture in the Ostrabama cathedral at Vilna. Marshal Pilsudski died with a small copy of this on his breast. The earliest Polish song was a hymn to the Madonna; the *Bogarodzica*. Poland's armies used to go into battle with this hymn on their lips. Even in 1683 when King John Sobieski (John III) descended from the Kahlenberg upon the Turkish armies surrounding Vienna, his troops were singing the *Bogarodzica*.

The first Polish royal house was that of the Piasten, who had been peasant princes in the ninth century. Their last representative was Casimir III, who ascended the throne in 1333. Of all the kings of Poland he was the only one to be called the ' the Great'. His reign was almost entirely free from military conquest. All his striving was directed towards cultural, political and social advance. In 1364 he created the University of Cracow: his political reforms included the first complete statute of rights in Europe. He founded cities, and furthered the well-being of every class and people of his domain. Jews and Armenians, who were persecuted elsewhere, he protected. He also gave up practically the whole of Silesia and concluded a treaty of peace with the Teutonic Order.

On his death the crown passed to another branch of his line and in 1384, Jadwiga, the youngest daughter of Ludwig of Germany, ascended the throne of Poland. Although only ten years old, she was already betrothed to a German prince. She was the only woman to be elected, not merely queen consort, but monarch with full regal powers. In 1386 she was forced to marry Prince Jagiello of Lithuania whom she did not love.

Jagiello ruled over the last pagan country left in Europe. In Lithuania, Sun, Moon and stars were venerated, and the holy fire burned constantly in every home and every temple. A corner was reserved in every house for the snake, to whom a bowl of milk was offered at each meal, for she was the protecting spirit. The Teutonic Order, the Greek Church, Franciscan monks and Manichaeans—all had attempted Lithuania's conversion to Christianity, but with little success. However, when Prince Jagiello was baptized, married and crowned, he promised to lead his entire people to baptism and to unite all Lithuanians and Ruthenians with Poland. He returned to his country for a short time to make certain that every oak in the sacred groves was felled. In agreeing to her marriage Jadwiga had made a sacrifice; Jagiello now similarly made a sacrifice in giving up the ancient cult of his people.

Their joint renunciation marked the beginning of Poland's great peaceful expansion. During Jagiello's absence, Jadwiga, still almost a child, rode with the Polish nobles to the south-east and re-united the provinces of that region with her country. Whoever met her on the way acclaimed her as sovereign. She redistributed ancient privileges, abolished oppressive taxes, and spread peace everywhere.

Soon Poland was the hope of all the peoples between the Baltic and the Black Sea. The Princes of Moldavia, the Ruler of Bessarabia and the Bishop of Kiev all pledged their loyalty. The uniting power of the folk soul was active: Poland's generous and expansive being could embrace and protect all these different peoples. In 1399, at the age of twenty-five, Jadwiga died.

In 1413, twice seven years after her death, the entire Polish nobility combined with the nobles of the Lithuanian Empire. The Declaration of Horodlo, a unique document, contains the words:

> In the name of the Lord, Amen. May this deed and this document be preserved for all eternity. It is known that no man will be bound if he is not carried by the mystery of love, commits no evil and radiates good. Through love, laws are made, kingdoms are governed, cities caused to flourish and the well-being of the state is increased to the utmost. Therefore we prelates, nobles and governors of the Kingdom of Poland, all in the name of all, and each in the name of each, wish that all signatories now and in future take heed of this act. So that we should dwell in the shade of the wing of love, and so that we can live under the rule of love for the fulfilment of our religious aspirations, we have combined, united and intermingled. We combine and unite ourselves, our genealogies, our purposes and also our weapons with the nobles and Boyars of Lithuania, so that from this day they may possess, use and enjoy them as we enjoy what we received from our forebears, out of true love and brotherly harmony.

To this exceptionally strong sense of community that united the Poles and also drew in other peoples, a counterbalance had to arise. Late in the fifteenth century, from a religious background, came a gentle young man preparing a revolution for the human mind.

Nicolas Copernicus studied medicine in Padua and canon law at Ferrara, where he obtained his doctor's degree. In Padua he was a pupil of the great astronomer, Domenica Maria di Novarra, who let him share in his own researches and observations. In 1493 a book appeared, *Del Sole*, in which Alexander Achillini defended the teachings of Aristotle and Ptolemy, and the neo-Platonist Marsilius Ficinus upheld Pythagorean views. It is thought that Copernicus knew this work and also the *Epitome in Almagestum* (1497) by Pürbach and Regiomontanus, a critical study of the Ptolemaic system, based on empirical evidence. He could compare these writings with his own studies.

The impulses for his world-picture were already active about 1500, but, fearing contradiction, he did not publish his work. In 1514 he distributed a small volume *De Hypothesibus Motuum Coelestium*, giving a *résumé* of his views, and in the following years he evolved his lifework.

A cleric himself, he drew no further conclusions from his theories. He agreed with Aristotle —whom Christian scholars called a fore-runner of Christ—that no complicated thought should be resorted to in explaining the universe where a simple one is adequate. In placing the sun at the centre of his system, Copernicus had interpreted the structure of the universe with the simplest possible thought, making earlier, more complicated systems superfluous. He dedicated his great work, *De Revolutionibus Orbium Coelestium*, to the Pope. But the first copy of it was put into his hands only on his deathbed, in May 1543. He had not changed only the astronomical picture of the world. Man's earthly home, hitherto immovable, was racing around a sun now fixed in space and only appearing to move.

The old security had to go: and individuals had to learn to live in separation of soul. From this need arose the *Sejm*, the great college mentioned as early as 1493.

The *Sejm* resembled a Lower House of Parliament, though not in the modern sense. Local parliaments or Diets were held by the lesser landed nobles whose privilege it was, also, to bear arms. The last Constitution of the Old Kingdom makes clear that it was intended to raise the whole people to nobility in the course of time. Service to the community was a dedication and the Poles experienced the *Sejm* as a temple where the delegates performed priestly functions. Even in the Constitution of reform of 3 May 1791, it was described as the Temple of the Legislature.

According to Mickiewicz the history of Poland is the succession of actions of different Sejmiks, meeting separately or in groups, often differing in their opinions, though rarely enemies. They acted without any clearly defined goal, but to the people they stood as a moral centre.

The *Sejm* made no laws and had not executive power. But it could discuss and decide the question of war. Several times proposals to incorporate cities and peoples were rejected, since there appeared to the Poles to be no valid reason for taking them from their owners. The function of the *Sejm* ceased when the moral issue was decided.

Financial matters were administered in a similar way. When the *Sejm* had assessed voluntary contributions, rich men could usually be found to pay in advance; they would then obtain receipts and return home, there to be repaid by their fellow-citizens.

In the exercise of justice, when the *Sejm* had made its decision on a case, the law messenger appealed to all men of good will to carry it out. It even happened that men living abroad surrendered to their judges for execution. On their return they were not arrested but were given time to prepare for death. No-one misused the concession, for a noble who evaded the court's jurisdiction would have been considered without honour.

But when a case was involved and obscure and public opinion could not distinguish where truth lay, new ways had to be sought to reach joint understanding. In Poland a free man could not rid himself of all responsibility by invoking the resolutions of the *Sejm* or smaller councils. Every law had to be weighed and acknowledged before an individual could take action according to his conviction: but in this way, out of his own free will, he became judge soldier and executive organ, and his duties lasted as long as he was of good will.

What then, asks Mickiewicz, was the aim of all these institutions? He answers: ' It was this: to develop the spirit in man, to keep him ceaselessly awake, to make him feel his dignity, realize at all times his duties . . . Nowhere else in the world has the individual been granted freedom to a similar degree.' But the aim of the Polish state was far from realization.

All Europe was moving in an opposite direction; becoming materialistic, scholastic, formalistic and metaphysical. In this rich and manifold life, Europe saw only confusion. The Polish Constitution demanded enormous efforts from the citizen. ' The history of Poland is proof that her people were advancing to the creation of a society of spiritual freedom and good will.'

No decision was acceptable in the *Sejm* unless reached unanimously in free agreement. At first, the formula in use was: ' Accursed be he who would act otherwise.' If the vote was not unanimous the *Sejm* was dissolved and its decisions declared invalid. This principle was firmly observed. But in 1652 the *Liberum veto* was introduced, whereby every participant had the right and power, by a mere statement of protest, to end a session of the *Sejm*. An entirely new one had then to be elected before legislation could continue. Minorities were not slow to make use of this weapon and in time the *Liberum veto* lent itself to all kinds of abuse. Representatives of foreign powers could by means of bribery find it a useful instrument.

To the Poles, the individual conscience within the greater organism was paramount. Politics in the general sense were alien to them. In the outside world, ' Polish Parliament ' became an expression of contempt for assemblies that could not arrive at decisions. The Poles could not see that they were destroying their community from within.

The distance between their ideals and actual conditions was vast indeed. Even the election of the king became an instrument of harm. Theoretically any one out of a million people entitled to vote could become king. Until 1572—before Jagiello's line became extinct—this possibility had not arisen. Afterwards it was a source of terrible disruption. Whenever the throne fell vacant, not only Poles but members of other royal houses tried to acquire the crown. Though the Poles fought official corruption and bribery for a long time, they could not hold out forever in the age of dynastic diplomacy inaugurated by Richelieu. Their position among the Slavs is not unlike that of Faust in Central Europe. They exhausted themselves in the highest striving without being able to bring their social impulses fully down to Earth.

Poland's first Partition was in 1772. The division was suggested by Austria and Prussia to stem the Russian threat to Poland, which appeared to be merely the first step of a Russian advance into Central Europe. The Poles had to concede a quarter of their territory. In the Constitution they received, the *Liberum veto* was preserved. In a second Partition the Polish people were left with only a third of their country. After the third, in 1795, Poland's name disappeared from the map of Europe.

After this outward dying process, however, came a spiritual revival. When the last rebellion, of 1830–31, had been defeated with terrible severity, the mission of the Polish soul had already entered a new phase. The three sections of the people, torn apart and distributed among different neighbouring states, were now like three separate soul organs whose gifts and experiences were enriched by the nations into whom they had been received.

In the Russian part, Polish thinking encountered the imaginative spirituality that is preserved within the Russian soul. Through Austria, Poles came face to face with political skill which can become a harmonizing factor among different peoples. Germany provided a link with the ceaseless activity that surveys and orders the economic life. Thus throughout nearly a hundred and fifty years the Polish people, looking towards the future yet a stranger to the present, was prepared for distant tasks in three different ways.

To individual Poles the partition of their country was grievous; to the folk soul, it was a necessary step demanded by world destiny. In the course of evolution the separation of the human soul from the world soul is not permanent, but forms an intermediate condition, a means whereby in future the cosmic soul may shine more brightly in the individual.

173

But this cannot happen while the three forces of thinking, feeling and willing stream together impeding one another. Man must learn to control and guide them separately to bring them into complete balance. When this advance has been made, humanity will rise to a higher stage. Seen from this aspect, Poland's triple partition appears as a hallowed sacrifice, brought for humanity.

In these mysterious connections lies one of the reasons why, after the country had been divided, outstanding personalities should speak with religious intensity of Poland's messianic mission. The could see clearly that their people had, through its history, become a forerunner.

They called themselves Messianists; their number included four philosophers, Cieszkowski, Trentowski, Liebelt and Hoene-Wronski, and four outstanding poets and writers, Slowacki, Mickiewicz, Norwid and the mystic Towianski. All of them contributed to Poland's task— the development of the Sense of Thought.

The poets among them transformed their insights into hymns. Julius Slowacki wrote in his *Genesis out of the Spirit*:*

Thou has placed me, O Lord, on the cliffs of the ocean that I may recall the beginnings of my spirit.

I felt myself in the past as immortal, as God's son, creator of the visible, as one of those who offer Thee freely their love on garlands of golden suns and stars. For my spirit was in the Word before the beginning of creation . . . and it was in Thee and I was in the Word.

And we spirits of the Word demanded form for ourselves, and Thou didst make us, O Lord, visible, allowing that we may bring forth out of our own will and our love, the first form, so that we could appear before Thee . . . Here, where the voice of chaos striving for form resounds in the roar of the waves, where spirits on the path I once had to follow are ascending the Jacob's ladder . . . allow me, O Lord, to stammer my past work and to read it in forms that are inscriptions of my past.

Already in the rocks, O Lord, was bedded the spirit, a statue of perfect beauty, still sleeping. I call before thy sight, O Lord, these crystals, formerly the first bodies of our spirit, today abandoned by movement of every kind, yet living, crowned by clouds and lightning . . .

The longing to be a vehicle for the spirit on the path of progress, the desire to remain within matter, the striving for consolidation and comfort of form were and are as yet the only sin of the spirits, my brothers, Thy sons!

The Messianists experienced the threefold nature of all present and future existence. They spoke of it as ' Triality '—three-ness.

Trentowski pointed to three sources of knowledge. The first is experience, which moves within the realm of substance. It acknowledges the body of the universe, though not soul and spirit. It is limited, and leads to disintegration. The other pole of knowledge is reason.

---

* *Oeuvres Complètes,* 1870.

Looking within, constructive and free, it is the source of all movement in the universe, though it loses sight of substance. The third source is the simultaneous perception of both poles, which gives all-embracing certainty. It is the only true path to a universal knowledge, for it unites outer individual experience with constructive reason: it is free and restricts at the same time.

Trentowski called this source of truth ' perception ', because the simultaneous perception of outer phenomena and their underlying laws was to him as clear as ordinary sense impressions to others. He experienced thinking as a spiritual sense organ.

In his work on the foundation of a universal philosophy,* he wrote in 1837:

> Perceptive philosophy alone is Christian, and as soon as it is properly worked out, must contribute greatly to a true understanding and indeed to the triumph of the Christian religion. . . . . Truth presupposes triality as the final aim of philosophy and can therefore only call that science philosophy, which is trialistic and teaches triality. Triality is, in the last resort, the light in which two earlier lights, namely freedom and limitation, become one, and through which alone reality, this constellation on the sky of philosophy, can shine.

The contemplation of the world in its threefold nature involves serious responsibility, for we may enter the temple of truth and knowledge only in a bright garment; that is, if we make ourselves independent of all the deceit and falsehood we have experienced in others and in ourselves.

To Trentowski, active thinking was a universally reliable though individualized instrument for the perception of cosmic thought. Thus he could say in the introduction to his book that thinking is the general property of the spirit; that he who has spirit can agree in many thoughts with others, also spirit-endowed.

> One and the same thought appears in one individual as a shooting star, in another as a comet, in the third as a fixed star. The universal spirit individualizes itself in different persons and is revealed in every one of them.
>
> Nature is the infinite, living, moving, beautifully constituted magic round of positive thinking. In her our eye meets no frontiers: in her all our senses plunge into a bottomless abyss: in her even sun-like heavenly spheres are but small sparks that become invisible in the boundless distances of Creation. This infinite vastness of nature can yet find sufficient space in a little human brain, where it become a single thought, a single word. God spoke: Let there be Nature, and there was Nature. Man speaks the word ' nature ', and from his line flows infinity, eternity and the constant presence of this majestic universal mother! Truly, the human head is a universe, which rests on the body of a god-like Atlas and encloses infinity . . .

In parts of his book Trentowski seems to look at evolution with the eye of the Godhead.

---

* *Grundlage der Universellen Philosophie*, Carlsruhe and Freiburg, 1837.

The being that becomes man, he says, and through manhood achieves self-awareness, is able to perceive all it wills. For it is the highest form of the divine; and being truth, can understand truth in its very nature. The barrier set by humanity does not exist, for that is but a product of sleepiness, a miserable comfort for voluntary ignorance.

Thus as man begins and concludes the science of nature, so will he do with the science of the spirit. Every scientific beginning must be anthropological for only man can invent science; and to the primal and immediate science, he brings nothing but an ego, a consciousness and a feeling of the self; his being. 'The only real beginning for man is man for he best knows himself and beholds in the summit of his being the whole of nature in one.'

Trentowski penetrated with his thinking to the experience of the cosmic Isis:

> If we look through the sombre Isis veil of the night into the glories of a thousand suns, or admire the power of the elements, the beauty of a rose, the anatomy of a moth, we admire the perfection of Creation itself;—thus we behold God: . . . but if we learn astronomy, calculate the distances of the Sun from other suns or contemplate their movement, we think of the power behind these things, and when we find that this power is identical with our soul and the whole sun-universe identical with ourselves, we perceive God.

Another Messianist, August Cieszkowski who studied at Berlin University in 1831, devoted himself to dialectical philosophy. Training his thinking on Hegelian logic, he reached the bold insight that Hegel's philosophy could only be further evolved through its own methods: and that thinking, consistently applied, could grasp mysteries that Hegel could not approach. He saw in world development the expression of a balance between thinking, feeling and willing, progressively unfolding and gradually becoming manifest.

With past, present and future included in a study of this kind, the totality of historic change reveals a threefoldness that corresponds to the threefold aspect of the soul. Antiquity with its monumental creations in the realm of art took its strength from feeling. The 'Second Epoch', which began with Christianity and has lasted into modern times, was the age of the development of thinking, which attained its highest fulfilment in Hegel. The great moving power behind these events was the ego.

Until the nineteenth century thinking was Epimethean, mainly devoted to things already created, and it therefore resembled a re-thinking. But this is not its only potentiality. It can become a Prometheus-thinking; actively, from will forces, extending into the future. The will is the key to the spiritual epoch of the future; in addition to feeling and thinking, humanity will evolve a pure will.

August Cieszkowski tried to show that an understanding of the organic totality of human metamorphosis cannot be reached without recognition of the future as an integral part of history. The view that the future cannot be known is a self-imposed limitation. Kant had believed the absolute to be unattainable: later, philosophy broke through his self-imposed reservation. Similarly the fallacy that great outlines of the future cannot be recognized, must be overcome. Here lies the destiny of the philosophy of history, which thus becomes the Sophia of history.

He wrote:*

---

* *Prolegomena zur Historiosophie.* Berlin, 1938.

The future can be determined in three ways: through feeling, through thinking and through the will. The first produces seers and prophets; the second is the reflected, the theocratic, the conscious, the necessary; it produces the philosophers of history . . . Here we perceive no longer as if metaphorically, but distinctly. The third determination is the truly practical, the applied, the achieved, the spontaneous, the intended, the free; therefore it embraces the whole sphere of action—and creates those who bring about the fulfilment of history . . . The first is peculiar to antiquity . . . where humanity lived as if through the instincts: the second belongs to our own age, for we have no longer prophets since the coming of Christianity. But we have thinking spirits because truth has come into the world through Christianity, while Antiquity could not advance beyond beauty in its various manifestations . . . The third determination belongs to the future. It will be the objective realization of perceived truth; this is the good, the practical in which the theoretical is already contained.

Cieszkowski saw the solution of social contradictions in the demands men make of the future: and herein, the advance of the world spirit itself whose aim for humanity is the achievement of fully conscious deeds. Real creations, at first unconscious deeds, become the conscious deeds of humanity, which are institutions.

Thus the world spirit, through the activation of beauty, truth and goodness, unfolds itself in the articulated totality of real institutions. In the total character of the world spirit, beauty will become active in feeling, the love of truth in knowledge, the good in the will. Thus the life of humanity has to partake of these three highest predicates of the absolute as the highest fulfilment of the world spirit.

When August Cieszkowski showed his work to his father, a Polish count and great art collector, the old man was deeply impressed. He immediately ordered his carriage and drove with his son to church to give thanks to Heaven for sending him this son. During the service August Cieszkowski stood absorbed in the Lord's Prayer. Quite suddenly the history of the world became still clearer to him and what had remained obscure during his writing now shone with extraordinary directness through his thoughts. He could see the Lord's Prayer as the signpost for the evolution of the ' Third Epoch ' of humanity.

Later, he visited St. Mark's in Venice, where he concentrated his thinking on the problem of the nature of the Holy Spirit. An awareness of the link between events of history and the Trinity then lit up his soul. In the first beginnings of history he saw the working of the Father, in the second phase the working of the Son, and in the third the time of the Holy Spirit. Cieszkowski found in the three words, freedom, equality and fraternity, the basic principles of all social organization. But he also examined their justified limitations and realized that their misapplication could plunge society into the abyss.

Not all the Messianists were able to practise restraint. Many Poles approached the realm of the spirit before achieving the necessary self-control: the result was a mystic power cult. Their shortcomings were the darker side of a greatness for which they were not sufficiently mature.

The Bull is a shining constellation, spread out on the sky. In the Middle Ages it was often shown with a powerful Bull's head, great horns and prancing forelegs. In nature the bull is clumsy and enormously strong. It is the image of power and authority. In man, if the bull forces cannot live selflessly in spiritual activity, thus kept in balance, they cloud judgment and seek outer realization even where that is out of place.

Josef Maria Hoene-Wronski was a thinker who strove with great passion for the establishment of a sphere of spiritual authority. He wanted a small *élite* to acquire universal knowledge to dominate and control the rest of humanity. He was a mathematician and as a philosopher a follower of Kant. He possessed brilliant insight and could see the dangers of a fu ure dominated by materialism.

The possible negative consequences of increasing human freedom filled him with fear and led him to the conviction that the freedom of the spirit had to be curbed by the state. Men were to have perfection and knowledge forced on them. In a work* dedicated to the Emperors of Russia and Austria, the King of Prussia and Napoleon III, he demanded the setting up of the absolute authority of the state to ensure the unrestricted investigation of the truth.

With the same end in view he suggested the complete subjection of every people to the power of the state. Government, based on the principle of the law of truth, should have the power to suppress all opposition. What Napoleon I had achieved in the subjection of peoples through military authority was to be repeated in the realm of the spirit.

The necessity of a providential influence had to be made known in Europe, if the civilized world (particularly France and the West) was to be spared catastrophe—otherwise inevitable. ' Therefore,' he argued in a Postscript of January, 1852, ' it is essential to set up the universal political authority of Napoleon to prove to the world the mysterious authority providence now offers . . .'

Blinded by his admiration of power, Hoene-Wronski's Faustian nature could fall prey to Mephistopheles. His very spirituality made him a fighter against man's progress towards individual responsibility. The darker side of the Bull impulse gained control of him. His writings are said to have been publicly burned in Paris.

Andreas Towianski followed the same trend, his attitude likewise governed by his admiration for Napoleon I. Powerful inner experiences led him to believe that Napoleon wanted his work to be continued by him though on different—Christian—lines. He believed himself a saviour in Napoleon's name. As a mystic he relied on emotion, not measuring his abilities against the sober facts of the age. Because he was of the highest personal integrity he could arouse the enthusiasm of many of his compatriots. Though deeply respected by some of the leading figures of his time, he was eventually expelled from France: he died in Switzerland where he had found refuge.

Even Adam Mickiewicz was for a time influenced by Towianski. Here too, Mephistopheles gained hold of Faust. Filled with sorrow, the poet Zygmunt Krasinski, who carried the purified Polish spirit within him and who could say of himself that he knew the thoughts of others before they pronounced them, wrote in a letter after a visit to Mickiewicz:

---

* *Conférences Européennes pour populariser l'actuelle réforme absolue du savoir humain.* Metz, 1851.

Here the spirit is considered some kind of material, such as steam, galvanism or electricity, as some force of nature out of whose characteristics and potentialities power and wonder can be gained. Through holiness, it is possible to work on what is called spirit in such a way that the thing spoken of by this name becomes lightning to be used. But the error of this attitude lies in the way the master treats spirits like soldiers. He rules them with a moral cane, until they have learned a strategy called holiness, with whose help a battle can be fought. But the real Polish character respects the spirit and sees in it the sacred freedom rather than the power, not using the spirit, but leading and guiding it to its own eternal aims . . .

At the age of twenty-one Krasinski had written a drama, *The Undivine Comedy*, in which he described Poland's decline, not as it happened in his own time but as it might well have been described in the twentieth century. He himself experienced the constant presence of the ever-striving spirit:

Soul and body are but the wings on which the spirit passes in constant movement beyond the limitations of time and space. When they are used up they fall away, but the spirit does not die; human beings call this death. The spirit discards what is worn out and takes up what is fresh; thus clothed, it awakens to a new day; this is called birth. But my spirit flies again on new wings it has formed, towards higher regions. On and on it moves, towards the Lord, discarding its own bodies and its own souls like drooping leaves and absorbing the strength that is passing from them.*

He knew that the fate of the whole world depends on man's steadfastness and perseverance. Like all the Messianists, he experienced Poland's sufferings not as a national and personal event, but as a symbol of the journey through pain and temptation towards greater humanity. In a poem of a dream,** he describes how the ' great Seer ' led a youth to the sight of evil, which in the last resort must yield.

There is no death, only a series of terrible pictures of it. The Lord has never conceived death, for He is forever and everywhere life. Only those are rejected by life who have become corrupted; he who knowingly becomes evil inflicts his own death. For him there will be no resurrection to life in death. He who would rise again must be transformed— every one of these transformations appears for a time as that which we call death. This is the test of the grave. It contains a wealth of sorrow, tears, mockery and deceit. Every individual human being and whole peoples and races of humanity, and the cosmos, all must pass through this test—those who cannot withstand it must perish.

Krasinski described a meeting with the powers of temptation: ' Let your heart be filled with lion courage,' said the Seer, ' for you will now see before your eyes how illusion takes form! '

---

* *Psaumes de l'Avenir*, 1880.
** *Ein Traumgesicht*, Leipzig, 1875.

When the youth experiences pain and sorrow at his vision, the Seer comforts him with the one word, 'Think!' He must learn to bear evil in his thinking. He sees that money-changers sit on the throne of the world and that the world is a sinister stock market that destroys men. Finally he is brought before the sight of extreme suffering. The Seer says: ' Do not turn away, but look with open eyes, however it may repel you.' To overcome pain, one must fully experience pain within.

The dark form of a giant then steps among the dying. With a whip in one hand, and the other held out to those tortured to the point of death, he calls:

> Renounce the past and the future, renounce God and fatherland—acknowledge me as past and future, as God and fatherland: as I have had you nailed to the cross so I will also take you from the cross. I will call my legions and they shall take you down and I shall make you into a happy people . . .

From stormy waters the answer resounds, ' No '. The air has barely echoed the innumerable voices when two milky ways stream forth, forming a vast cross, whereon a stretched-out figure with arms extending over the world is moving towards the earth. His forehead rises beyond the sky; on his head he bears a crown of thorns formed of silent lightning. Three wounds shine on his hands and feet, and ceaselessly blood flows from them in the form of a rainbow, every rainbow dissolving and dispersing. Thus, crucified and creating, the figure descends further, filling space with sunlike light until the milky ways that support it are transformed into two bands of light, embracing everything from north to south and from east to west. The stars in their endless accumulation become a starry robe across the sky, enfolding the figure on the cross. Eyes look down from heavenly heights: a voice speaks.

> So far your world has known only hell and purgatory; but the spirit of the Lord has taken His dwelling in your breast. You are like great depths, hiding radiant secrets. Let these be made manifest through deeds of love, and let them fill the space before you, above you and around you . . .
>
> But bear in mind that no other path will lead you, no blind accident, no force, no conceit, and no lie spoken by pride. Woe to the times when ungodly power would thirst for the treasures of God. For the Lord, your Creator, holds so high the freedom He has given you that you are free to fight even against Him, and to prevail in evil. But after such a victory, He departs from the victors, who are left behind with only an eternal void, never to be filled; endless nothing, eternal death. Watch ye, therefore, over the fate of your planet!

The West can understand what was thought and suffered in Poland. As yet the Poles could not think to their conclusion the ideas that were enkindled, nor make them into clear concepts. What they achieved therefore did not yet bear fruit, though it was already a basis for the future.

One of the missions of the Polish spirit, which seeks to develop the personal out of the universal, is the creation of an increasingly living link between the Slavs and the peoples of the West. This can be achieved through the bridge of a thinking that gradually advances to new vision.

The Polish folk soul longs for its people to receive the light that flows from the eternal sources of renewal. Western man too, seeks access to these sources. Slowly the ground can thus be prepared for the great culture of the humanity of the future, though it may need a thousand years or more for its realization.

Austria and Switzerland

WHEREVER DIVERSITY unfolds in the universe it has its source in those realms of the spirit where the constellation of the Twins looks down upon Earth in winter nights. The entire Earth evolution carries this Twin character: humanity was separated from the Godhead, the cosmos was divided into Sun and planets, the kingdoms of nature were split apart, and peoples and individuals were segregated one from another. This separation is the basis for the growth of personality; but when one demand is accomplished, the next asserts itself.

In a lecture already referred to,* Rudolf Steiner pointed to the development of a sense organ that mediates direct perception of the ego of another human being. This differs in origin from the perception of one's own ego, and the forces for its evolution come from the region of the zodiacal Twins. Some old star maps show the Twins walking hand in hand across the sky, as a prophetic image of the fulfilled Earth mission leading to a higher re-union.

The development of Austria and Switzerland is linked with this Sense of the Ego, although in the course of their history they have evolved opposite characteristics. A comparison with the Twins of Greek mythology, Castor and Pollux, may help an understanding of their differences. Pollux was immortal but he had to experience Hades, the nether world. Castor devoted himself to peaceful tasks but he was mortal and like a human being he had to pass through death. One of them had to achieve the highest aims, the other had to master the problems of everyday life. Although both countries were able by dint of perseverance to guide peoples of different nationalities and languages towards peaceful co-operation, Austria had a royal and universal impulse that led to a close link with the universal Catholic Church; the Swiss Confederation was from its very beginnings the deed of simple people and has survived to the present day through the down-to-earth decision of men who claim nothing except the responsibility for their own destiny.

There are parallel trends in earlier times. In the ninth century, the Ostmark (the eastern margravate) which later became the Austrian March, and the territory of the Swiss Confederation belonged to the empire of Charlemagne. In the course of time leading families emerged in both countries, in Austria the House of Babenberg, in Switzerland the Zähring dynasty. Both held princely rank and authority in the twelfth century.

Next to the Zährings, the Hapsburgs, whose family seat was in Switzerland, achieved increasing power. When the Zähring line became extinct, the last obstacle to the unlimited growth of Hapsburg power in Central Europe had gone. But if the focal point of their power

---

* The Twelve Senses and the Seven Life Processes in Man, by Rudolf Steiner; Dornach, 12 August, 1916.

had remained where it was, the Swiss Confederation would never have come about, nor would Austria have followed her specific development.

In the year 1273, Count Rudolf von Hapsburg was elected king of Germany. Immediately, he transferred the centre of Hapsburg power to the east of the German Empire. It was as if the spiritual powers that guide historic events had intervened so that independent centres should shine forth both in the Alps and in Vienna. After his coronation Rudolf demanded the return of his fiefs from King Ottokar of Bohemia, whose rule extended over Hungary, Styria, Carinthia, and Carniola in the present-day Yugoslavia. When Ottokar refused Rudolf moved to Vienna. Ottokar died in the Battle of the Marchfeld, and Rudolf distributed Austria, Carinthia and Carniola among his own sons. This marked the foundation of the authority of the Austrian Hapsburgs and set the course of Austria's further development.

When the main interest of the Hapsburgs had been diverted from their Swiss possessions, the Confederation was founded. The impulse originated in the region of the three cantons of Uri, Schwyz and Unterwalden which, deeply embedded in the Alps, extended as far as the Gotthard. In 1291, three men of these regions met on a mountain meadow and swore: 'Each for all, all for each'. (Plate 37.) Tradition tells that these three men were led to swear this oath by Wilhelm Tell whose independence became a lasting example to the newly emerging country. Compelled by the Austrian *Landvogt* Gessler to shoot an apple from the head of his son on account of his own refusal to do homage to the badge of Austrian rule, he aimed accurately. He could do so through perfect control over eyes and hands. With the second arrow, he shot the *Landvogt* through the heart.

The tale of an apple shot from the head of a child occurs also in the legends of other nations: but elsewhere it is mythology. In Switzerland it became the historic event that determined the direction the Confederation was to take.

Wilhelm Tell has received lasting veneration. According to a document of 1387, when there were still people who had known those who had met him face to face, two pilgrimages took place each year on the day of his deed, one to his house and one to the chapel raised in his memory.

Tell showed his people how to attain a desired end, remaining true to oneself and trusting one's own ability. The individual Swiss kept faith with these ideals. Whatever he strove for he carried through. He developed the part of his personality that gave him confidence in himself through the fulfilment of his everyday duties. He was earnest, and earth-bound like his powerful mountains. The decision to self-determination which was present in all united the Confederation into a whole.

Eighteen years after the swearing of the oath, the Emperor Henry VII confirmed the independence of the three cantons. But the Swiss had to assert their freedom again and again. In the Battle of Morgarten in 1315 they defeated Leopold I. By 1386, Lucerne, Zürich, Glarus, Zug and Berne had joined the renewed Confederation.

But in that year Duke Leopold III of Austria faced the Swiss at Sempach with vastly superior forces. Tradition tells that Austrian spears stood against them like a solid wall. From among the Swiss a hero, Arnold von Winkelried, sacrificed his life for the rest. 'Take care of my wife and child', he shouted and threw himself against the enemy. With great strength he grasped the spears before him and directed them against his own heart. 'With God, conscious of freedom', runs the Winkelried song. Through the narrow passage beyond him stormed the assembled Swiss and put the confused Austrians to flight. Swiss military prowess grew; its greatest triumphs came when the armies of the Burgundian King Charles the Bold had to yield in 1476 and again the following year. But the vast booty brought passionate strife to the Swiss and it appeared at one time as if the Confederation might be destroyed from within. It was saved through the selflessness of a man of great wisdom.

Nikolaus von der Flüe was born in a peasant hut at the foot of the mountains. He was prosperous and loved the soil that he worked on from sunrise to sunset. He was the father of ten children. Respected by all, he held several offices although he refused to become a land bailiff. He came into contact very early with the Friends of God in Alsace and would have liked to join them but he felt that his place was in Switzerland.

When he was fifty years old, he left everything he had loved, his wife, his children and his farm. Near the wild river Ranft he built a shelter of bark and branches. In the following year people provided him with a simple cell. Through self-denial he was able to cleanse his soul and achieve great clarity. His fame as a seer spread throughout the country, and those in search of help found him a source of strength and hope. In addition, he had the gift of healing.

All efforts to solve internal strife amongst the Swiss had failed. On the 21st December, 1481, there seemed to be no alternative but the sword. Then the parish priest of Stanz went to see the hermit; and Nikolaus von der Flüe himself walked to Stanz during the night, through ice and snow. In a long, coarse garment, bare-headed and barefoot, he entered the council chamber. When he appeared, all quarrelling died down and at the sound of his words peace and conciliation returned to every heart. Within the hour everything was settled.

Nikolaus spoke with the certainty of one who knows: 'I will not only advise you in good deeds but will also insist on them, for I know without doubt that this is God's will.' His proposals were sound and practical; they became decisive for the future of the Confederation. Among them were the abolition of the independent authority of the cities, full equality for each canton, the union of the eight cantons into one confederacy and the acceptance of French-speaking Fribourg; thus realizing for the first time the concept of a state with various languages.

The memory of Nikolaus von der Flüe, Arnold von Winkelried and Wilhelm Tell accompanied the Swiss as their most treasured possession until science cast doubts on the greater part of the tradition. But as the expression of national impulses, it is true, and cannot be divorced from the development of the Confederation. These three great individualities had the spiritual power of selfless sacrifice. What they experienced and carried out can assure the continuance of Switzerland even in the twentieth century, for all of them valued freedom more highly than life and family.

Austria's last attempt to suppress Switzerland was made by Maximilian I. Unsuccessful, the Emperor saw himself forced to grant the now powerful Confederacy—which included thirteen members with full and equal rights—independence from the German Empire in the Peace of Basle.

For the Hapsburgs this time of the separation of Switzerland from Germany was the transition towards their own emergence as a great power. The Emperor Maximilian married the heiress of the Burgundian crown and acquired the Netherlands for his dynasty; the Hungarians were driven out of Austria, and Carniola and Carinthia were wrested from the Turks. For his grandson, who later became Charles V, Maximilian gained the crown of Spain through marriage; his other grandson he betrothed to Anne of Hungary and Bohemia. Austria could thus become a bulwark against the Turks in the east.

After liberation, Switzerland passed through a short period of indecision. The Swiss first served as mercenaries under the French, whom they later drove out of Lombardy, themselves attacking Dijon. The year 1515 brought the defeat of Marignano where the flower of Swiss manhood was killed. Political ambition, the legacy of the link with the Empire, was now shattered. This was the turning-point towards their own mission: the Swiss decided to live ' forever in peace ' with all their neighbours.

Austria and Switzerland were both affected by the Napoleonic wars. Austria had fought as England's and Russia's ally against Napoleon's armies; one lost war followed another. In 1806 the south- and west-German princes formed the Rhine League and left the German Empire, to become vassals of France. A few weeks later the Hapsburg Francis II, who in 1804 had adopted the title of ' hereditary Emperor of Austria ', was forced to resign the headship of the Holy Roman Empire.*

But through this weakness Austria was given a whole century in which to develop the characteristics needed for her future mission.

Switzerland also passed through a crisis in Napoleonic times, for her institutions had become feeble in the course of the centuries and some kind of stimulus was needed from outside to infuse them with new vigour. In 1798, Switzerland was over-run by France and transformed into the strictly centralized ' Helvetic Republic '. In 1803, Napoleon changed this unified state into a federation of democratically governed cantons which were all given equal rights. To the Swiss, the *Code Napoléon* had lasting value. At the Vienna Congress in 1815, the neutrality of the Swiss was officially recognized.

---

* He continued to rule in Austria as Francis I until 1835.

Austria

WITHIN THE WORKING of the folk souls, Austria offered a kind of vacuum; for the Hapsburg spirit, although it had brought together different peoples through wars and marriages, had served egotistical aims and lacked the dignity of a real folk soul.

In consequence, other archangel impulses that had been active mainly among peoples outside the Hapsburg monarchy, could flow into the Austro-Hungarian Empire. Thus Austrian cultural life echoed the Zodiac Twin chord, which separates but also unites.

The activity of the archangels surrounds people like a heavenly robe. It is not felt directly and does not impair a sense of self-assurance, but when different elements meet in a common task, fidelity and perseverance are needed.

In Austria despite parliamentary storms the people lived together peacefully and friction did not lead beyond normal difficulties that could be endured. A warm heart and great charm deprived uneasy situations of their sting. A Vienna of gaiety and beauty could evolve under those conditions, but also a Vienna of political dispute. Insults flew as if the contestants were attacking each other with fire and sword, whereas in fact they got on very well together. It was a Vienna of Heaven and Hades, neither aspect being taken too seriously, for the real Austria was so exalted it could be loved beyond virtues and shortcomings, and loyalty to it was a matter of course.

A special consonance within Austrian diversity became manifest in the two strongest elements, the Germans and the Magyars. The great musicians have been discussed earlier in connection with Germany. Many of them, feeling drawn to Austria, settled in Vienna where they were active for the rest of their lives. Others were born in that city. Hungary brought another stream of musical development, not flowing directly from the heights into the heart, but rising from the Hungarian earth. The Hungarian earth resounds: it sounds in spirit when the soil is dug and when men's feet step across it. Out of this elemental sounding of the earth of the wide *pusztas*, the plains, grew the incomparable feeling for music of the Hungarian peasants and gypsies.

This stream came into contact with German music in Vienna. The meeting did not take effect on the head but on the feet, and is the source of the Austrian love of dancing. While discussion in eighteenth-century Germany was centred on the nature of drama—Goethe and Schiller participated in that—the Viennese discussed different forms of the dance.

The choice between a purely stylized dancing with beautiful artistic movements, or a dance in which whole stories were performed, aroused the greatest interest, and ideas about the form of the dramatic dance led to lively argument. Between the opposites, a new dance arose spontaneously; it did not come from the stage but from a deep popular need. This was the Viennese waltz with its gay and balanced three-four time, the most harmonious of all dances.

Folk dances were at one time the last reflections of planetary movements. As relics or variations of ritual ceremonies they occurred amongst every people. The movements of the waltz are also cosmic in origin, for each couple dances in fast movement around itself but at the same time makes a large circle round the entire room. The Viennese waltz follows the movement of the Earth, which rotates in the course of a day on its own axis while moving through the whole Zodiac in the course of the year. Yet the waltz was no fading child of tradition but a lively new guest, born out of the meeting of two folk souls.

The positive and independent approach to difficulties took many different forms in Austria, and through Vincent Eduard Milde, who later became Archbishop of Vienna, it brought the first sun-rays of a new art of education. The principles were based on direct inner and outer observation of human nature.

Education was in a terrible state at that time, particularly in the country. Teachers were unpaid and did not even have buildings to teach in. Until a few years before, Vienna University had been under the reactionary control of Catholic Orders. After passing into secular hands the system of supervision ordered by the state made the independent development of a teaching body, or even of school books, impossible.

Into this seemingly hopeless situation, Milde placed his teachings. In his book* he showed a method of freeing the higher individual faculties of the child; his main emphasis was on the ego and its need for extensive help against the danger of physical sickness and spiritual decline. In 1810 he dedicated his work to the Emperor Francis I.

Another helper, when the general tension became severe under Metternich's oppressive régime, was the popular dramatist, Johann Nepomuk Nestroy. Within thirteen years he wrote over seventy plays in which he told the Viennese many a home truth that they could laugh about. The outer difficulties they had to endure he depicted against their own inner weaknesses and in this way gave them strength to pass unscathed through the troubles of the age. He led them to the healthy mainsprings of their fundamentally gay disposition.

The long Hansa valley where the river March runs contained the humble cottages of small peasants, who also carried the problem of Austria within their hearts. Germans, Hungarians and Slavs lived next to each other and intermingled; and all of them had to come to terms with conditions inevitably causing conflict. Nevertheless, weakness grew into strength. It was there that the author, Jacob Julius David, spent his poverty-stricken youth. Half blind and partly deaf, he accepted his hard fate and penetrated lovingly to realms he could neither see nor hear. His stories were about people who experienced the tribulations of life in all their bitterness and could yet come to terms with destiny. His characters were invariably placed within the greater framework of world-historic events.

Human destiny is not the result of accident, but of the guidance of the true self that lives beyond all earthly limitation.

What is generally called the ego is not this pure, destiny-forming self, but the lower ego

---

* *Allgemeine Erziehungskunde*, Vienna, 1877.

which is selfish and narrow. Often the body and its desires are spoken of in the first person: 'I' am hungry. 'I' want this or that. The everyday ego stands under the compulsion of bodily impressions and the longings of the soul.

It is only the shadow of that eternal self which remains linked to the stars and, in our time, is remote from earthly consciousness throughout life. Weaving in the rhythm of the planets it prepares the course of man's Earth existence before his birth.

Often it leads through severe demands from life to life and thus offers him opportunity to gain an increasingly clear and responsible consciousness. Joy and suffering are a means for achieving our full humanity; comfort, in this connection, may be more dangerous than pain, for it can make the soul superficial and self-satisfied. Suffering is an awakener. He who bears his fate courageously without trying to evade it unites himself with his own pre-natal will which is wise, serene and calm.

Such a man was Bartholomäus von Carneri; a descendant of Dante's family through his mother, he was born a twin, in Trieste. He became a philosopher, author and politician, yet outwardly he was severely afflicted by a curvature of the spine which kept him ailing and semi-paralyzed all his life. Asked in his later years how he could have endured such an existence, he indicated his body and answered: 'Should that be stronger than I? Should it be able to deprive life of all joy and beauty for me? Would I be truly human if I could not prove the stronger? So it has begun and so it will end.'

Carneri was a follower of Darwin but he became Darwinism's greatest moral teacher, for although his philosophy was governed by natural science his own life was proof of the victory of the spirit, the power of the ego to overcome. He was a member of the Austrian parliament in the eighteen-seventies. When he spoke, Austria herself seemed to speak. He was in no way narrow in his patriotism but saw his own people living within the historical evolution of humanity. He could realize the coming darkness, but did not limit himself to criticism. Rather he tried to ensure that Austria should remain really strong. Towards the end of his career he was very concerned about the future for he knew that true perseverance must be an act of the will.

This mission of finding faith in destiny was shared by German, Italian, Hungarian and Slav Austrians. The work of the Hungarian poet, Imre Madach, was unique and monumental, as if chiselled roughly out of huge blocks of stone. He rose to a belief in the continuance of a conscious ego that can emerge actively from all blows of destiny, even from the destruction of the Earth. At the end of his book, *The Tragedy of Man*,* the Lord says to Adam: ' I say unto thee: Man, fight and have faith.'

In a letter to his first critic he wrote:

> This is the basis of all my work; whenever man emancipates himself from God and acts out of his own strength, he is building within the greatest and most sacred ideas of humanity. Although he invariably fails; although the weakness causing his failure is innate and cannot be eradicated—this in my opinion would be the essence of tragedy— and although he himself may despair of his efforts as a waste of strength, his development

---

* 1861.

has nevertheless continually advanced. Humanity does progress and, while the struggling individual may not know it, the inner weakness he cannot himself conquer is overcome by the hand of Divine providence. That is the meaning of 'Fight and have faith'.

Still another Austrian poet, the greatest of the nineteenth century, had a hard and poverty-stricken youth. Robert Hamerling came from the Waldviertel, a harsh, poor region of Lower Austria. Illness and misfortune aged him prematurely; half his life was spent on a sickbed. Yet, suffering deeply in body and soul, he once exclaimed: 'Tell me I make bad verses, or steal silver spoons or rob the poor—but not that I am a pessimist!' The ego overcomes pessimism because it cannot be touched by life's weaknesses.

The largely Slav population of Bohemia (Czechoslovakia) was related to the Poles, and like theirs its mission lay more in the realm of human thinking than of nationalistic tendencies. Three great waves of effort in the course of their history showed this to be so. The first, in the fourteenth century came through the wisdom of Charles IV, Bohemia's best-loved ruler, who belonged to the house of Luxembourg and was the elected Emperor of Germany. He was the last Initiate emperor to occupy the German throne.

In the neighbourhood of Prague he built a castle, Karlstein, to preserve the insignia of the Empire.* (Plate 38.) A temple of the Grail was enclosed within the building. He knew that all kingship had secretly to enclose within itself the spiritual stream of the Holy Grail. Karlstein is the only building whose interior architecture approximates the ideal form of the Grail temple which men once saw in vision. Charles encouraged industry and art and through him the Bohemian folk soul began to be effective in active tendency to thoughtful spirituality. The University of Prague founded by Charles in 1348 became the intellectual centre of the whole German Empire.

In the fifteenth century the soul of Bohemia inspired the powerful Hussite movement, which made an appeal to the human will by demanding an adaptation of external life to the requirements of Christian thought. John Huss, the founder, was burned at the stake as a heretic by decree of the Council of Constance. After his death his adherents in Bohemia were still more closely united and fired the entire nation with their will for reform. The efforts of the Hapsburg king, Sigismund, to destroy them, as well as crusades organized against them by the Popes, were useless.

Eventually the movement split; one branch, the Taborites, retained their original severity of discipline; the other, the Ultraquists, renounced it and were absorbed into more external activities. In 1458 a Hussite, George of Podebrady, became King of Bohemia and in 1485 Hussites were given religious equality with Catholics.

Then another spiritual movement was born from the soul of Bohemia, that of the Bohemian Brotherhood. Its founder was Peter von Celsic, a shoemaker. He condemned the swearing of oaths in Courts of Justice and advocated the passive endurance of injuries. The brethren endeavoured to live a pure life and renounced all private possessions.

As this fraternity grew in importance it began to be persecuted. Throughout the whole of Bohemia and Moravia its adherents had to flee to the hills and woods; but their convictions had made so deep an appeal to many hearts that King George Podebrady and other potentates

---

* *Karlstein: Das Rätsel um die Burg Karls IV. (Karlstein: The Riddle of Charles IV's Castle.)* by Michael Eschborn. Stuttgart, 1973.

gave them places of refuge on their estates. At a meeting in 1457, the Brothers founded their own Church and demanded many reforms in habits of life. Lucas of Prague, however, decided in 1480 to adapt the movement more to general conditions, and in sacrificing something of its rigidity it increased its influence even more, and though still persecuted time after time, was spiritually guiding the people.

Through the battle of White Mountain in 1620, the country lost its independence to Austria. Like the Poles, a hundred and fifty-two years later, the Czechs now had to surrender all outward power. As the Poles could form a bridge between the Slav element and the West, the Czechs could do the same for the Slavs and central Europe; in sacrificing their independence for this task, they played an important part in the Austrian community of nations. But in 1848, after the first Pan-Slav Congress, they became a prey to Slav nationalism and began to rebel against their fate. They grew apart in soul from the Germans of Bohemia and both peoples increasingly felt hemmed in by an oppressive atmosphere.

In 1853, during this period of tension, a man was born in Bohemia whose soul was to seem to the Czechs like an island of peace and perseverance. This was Jaroslav Vrchlicky, whose real name was Emil Frida, and his intervention took the form of opening up the sources of world literature for his compatriots.

He translated Goethe's *Faust*, Michaelangelo's *Sonnets*, Byron's *Hebraic Melodies*, Schiller's *Wilhelm Tell*, Leconte de Lisle's *Cain*, Dante's *Inferno, Purgatorio* and *Paradiso*, parts of Hafiz' *Divan*, Tasso's *Gerusalemna Deliberata*, Ariosto's *Orlando Furioso* and Echegaray's *Saint and Fool*.

In his own writing, Egypt, the Middle Ages and modern times were brought to life in an entirely new fashion. His Slavonic soul searched the great achievements of world history for the ego of mankind shining through its many facets as one light, and growing through the individual ego into the all-embracing spirit-being of the whole of humanity. In the beginning Vrchlicky met with much opposition and ridicule. But he stood on firm ground and his work became a source of strength to his country.

Along with the interest in human beings there lived in Austria a close connection with the world of nature. Mystics who looked only within could not exist there for the mysterious forces of nature were intensely experienced; often with a strong sense of humour. The existence of gnomes and goblins was a recognized reality and in the countryside were men who knew every plant and its effect on human beings. In their understanding they could link man and nature as did Fercher von Steinwand, the peasant boy from the Carinthian mountains, who raised his experience of the interweaving of different worlds into the realm of poetry.

Born as Johannes Kleinfercher near the Steinwand (wall of stone) where his parents were poor smallholders, he was fortunate in his teachers and eventually studied law at the university. Nothing was simply abstraction to him and his poetry is vigorous and rich in imagery. He lived in the cosmic aspect of the Twins, and behind the visible world the realm of creative ideas shone forth to him.

At the end of the nineteenth century, thirteen different peoples were living in Austria, brought together, as has been shown, through Hapsburg inheritance, Hapsburg expansionism, the Partition of Poland and Austrian victories over the Turks. Through their link with Austria's diversity, all shared in a modern consciousness, in the intense experience of their difference from others. Thus on a small scale they illustrated modern humanity, where each member must of necessity acknowledge his neighbour if order is to be achieved throughout the social structure.

An equally remarkable combination of variety and unity is found in the landscape. The geologist, Eduard Suess, described Vienna as a microscopic image of the constituents of the living Earth normally extended in both time and space.* He also wrote:**

> There is hardly another part of the surface of the earth that offers such extraordinary geological diversity over so small an area as Austria. Between the Moldau and the Danube, covered by forests, spread some of Europe's most extraordinary mountains. To the north these are joined by the somewhat later curve of the Carpathians.
>
> From the south-east, the Dinaric chains stretch towards the Alps, and traces of the old Rhodope mass extend through eastern Serbia towards the Save. Between these great building stones are plains filled with maritime and lacustrine deposits that show the same characteristics all along the Danube and beyond the Urals. Out of the decay, destruction and levelling suffered throughout the ages by these components, so greatly differing in age, structure and power of resistance, the relief of Austria as it is today has emerged.

Geologically, Austria-Hungary reflected the different periods through which the mineral earth came to its present form—just as the Earth itself is the microcosmic result of all-embracing Divine thoughts.

Into this universal scene, natural and human, where the true self has been striven for, Rudolf Steiner was born on 27 February, 1861. He had a link with each of the most important national groups, Germans, Slavs and Hungarians, for his parents came from the German-speaking Waldviertel, he himself was born in Kraljewic in the southern Slav region and he went to school in Neudoerfl, a Hungarian village near the Lower Austrian frontier. As a young man he studied mathematics, natural science and chemistry at Vienna University and also read works on political and economic theory. Behind the socialist claims he could see only a deliberate blindness to true realities and it seemed to him one of the tragedies of the age that the social question, which is of universal importance, was publicised by men so entirely absorbed in materialism.

From the gallery of the Austrian Parliament building, at the side of his old friend and teacher, Karl Julius Schroer, Rudolf Steiner had often followed the passionate political debates in which the characteristics of the different peoples found expression.

Both knew that folk souls stood behind national ties; to Karl Julius Schroer they were ' ideas ', to Steiner living realities that could not be confined within the political frontiers of the unified state. Spiritual life needed to unfold independently, in harmony with the aims of the folk souls and unfettered by the power of the state. Universal concepts were needed to solve the country's national, legal and economic problems.

It was while he still lived in Vienna that Steiner prepared his first major work, *The Philosophy*

---

* Eduard Suess, *The Face of the Earth*, Oxford, 1904.
** *A Geological Picture of Austria.*

*of Spiritual Activity.** In it he shows with clear logic that true freedom requires man to purify his motives and instincts. Nature makes of him merely a natural being; society, one whose actions are governed by laws; only by his own effort can he attain to freedom. Yet freedom must be attributed to the human will insofar as it realizes purely ideal intuitions; for these are not the effects of a necessity imposed from without, but are grounded in themselves. Rudolf Steiner leads man to confidence in his individual path.

In Parliament, personality clashed against personality and people against people yet none denied the other's right to exist. There was then no question of separation, but of finding ways of living together that would be acceptable to all. The Slavs were mainly concerned about political interference in their intellectual life. The Czechs inwardly rebelled against the Germans, who in turn felt threatened by the Czechs, although they shared the memory of a long historical past that had proved fruitful in many ways. The Italian areas also suffered from the control exercised by Vienna over their cultural life. The inhabitants of the south of the Tyrol were only partly German, yet even those whose mother-tongue was Italian felt linked to Central Europe in many respects.

Among the Hungarians, proud and independent as they were, the conflict had begun several decades earlier; the Empire was therefore now officially called Austria-Hungary. What embittered the Hungarians particularly was official intervention in their cultural life. They could not forget that the Austrian government had destroyed their Protestantism. But though they were indignant when Vienna introduced German as the official language in Hungary, they accepted that Austrian officials would find it very difficult to learn Hungarian and that some kind of common language was therefore needed. Their choice fell on Latin. Yet the Hungarians had nothing against the German people or the German spirit: they loved Francis Joseph's consort, the Empress Elizabeth, whose kind, all-embracing German character belonged also to Hungary, whose debt to the German spirit was considerable. German splinter groups in Transylvania, the Banat and the Danube valley had for centuries nursed the culture they had brought with them as settlers from the region around Lake Constance.

From generation to generation, German Christmas plays had thus been performed in Hungary, and this quiet, unobstrusive activity was a source of strength to the Hungarian people as well. The Germans were a healthy ferment in the realm of culture; in part they became absorbed among the Hungarians.

Although at the end of the nineteenth century, neither Czechs nor Hungarians were thinking of separating from Austria, opposition grew throughout the Austrian provinces against claims to power that made harmonious regional development impossible. It was often said that the time had come for profound changes everywhere; but in Austria the dislike of radical change was stronger than the will for renewal, and the new measures taken proved unwise.

The Austrian problems were problems of humanity. In the summer of 1917 Rudolf Steiner (who was not known in political circles) approached the leading statesmen of Austria with a proposed solution for the complex situation of Central Europe. He realized that economic and cultural life would be more and more hindered in development if they were not separated from

---

* Berlin, 1894. English translations, also as *The Philosophy of Freedom*, 1916 to 1970. See Bibliography.

the political sphere; and he gave clear warning of the destructive consequences of the prevailing tendencies.

He proposed that the State should hand over the entire economic life to an administration chosen by its own personalities, not by the government, thus allowing it independent mobility, and should renounce control of cultural life. A freedom could then develop in which minorities could feel at home. They would discern new possibilities for the future and hope would be born anew. Only by such action could Central Europe be saved to fulfil its common cultural tasks.

Not only the future of Austria was in question, but of the world as a whole. Before the first World War ended, Steiner, then living in Berlin, had worked out directives along which a threefold social system could develop. His *Memorandum* was submitted to the last Austrian emperor, Charles I; during the negotiations at Brest-Litovsk it was among the papers of the German delegates.

Had a pronouncement in favour of new healing impulses been made from the right place, the effect could have been far-reaching indeed. The peoples of the Russian East could have understood the supplanting of Tsarism by impulses that corresponded with their longing for true brotherhood.

Among the English-speaking peoples were men who could see what was at work in the nations of Central and Eastern Europe; a central-European policy based on insight into the spiritual background of social life would have been intelligible to a western view which reckoned with historical necessities. The American peace programme should have been met by another, issuing from Europe.

The threefold system offered hope of fulfilment to the three ideals of the French Revolution —Liberty, Equality and Fraternity. Because man speaks a certain language, goes to school, or represents a point of view, his life extends into the realm of the spirit where Freedom should reign. In living under the protection of the state, like his fellow-men, he partakes of the life of rights, where Equality can rule. As a producer and consumer, he is part of the economic life, which tends towards Brotherhood.

Because of the tripartite nature of human existence, thoughts on these lines are like a rock on which a healthy social order can be based. Rudolf Steiner's book, *The Threefold Commonwealth*,* was in the hands of the delegates at the Versailles conference. In innumerable lectures he had spoken of the need to turn to new impulses, strive for their realization and understand their world-wide significance. He fought for the future of humanity. If insight and the strength to make decisions failed, the whole human race would have to suffer.

But no-one in political circles was sufficiently far-sighted to take up his suggestions and so create the foundations for reconstruction. The rejection of the proposals for a threefold social order determined the later history of the twentieth century.

The Austro-Hungarian Empire perished. The people of the German-speaking part now hoped that their political destiny would resemble Switzerland's. The other small nations, independent, or joined to related peoples, considered they could only gain in the general readjustment. In reality they lost their world mission—to give form to a joint historic destiny. They seemed

---

* Rudolf Steiner Press, London.

also to have lost the protection of world-guidance. Some turned to national-socialism, others were absorbed by Communism. Instead of radiating healing forces towards the East, the Slav peoples became the helpless prey of Russian Communism. Not only Austria's fate, but the course of world events shows the tragic results of human failure.

The impassioned struggle of eastern Communism against the West, unmitigated by any threefold system, led to the invention of increasingly destructive weapons. Waves of fear roll across the world. Humanity is faced with immeasurable disaster, even total destruction. The atomizing of the world is the demoniacal counterpart of the dual impulse out of which the profusely blossoming life of the earth emerged. Creation has been accomplished; any further tearing apart means destruction, and is a violation of the limits of the old impulse, transmuted by Christ into a new unification and reconciliation in a higher sphere.

Teaching His disciples for the last time He said:

> I am the vine, ye are the branches; he that abideth in Me and I in him, the same bringeth forth much fruit: for without Me ye can do nothing. If a man abide not in Me, he is cast forth as a branch, and is withered; and men gather them, and cast them into the fire, and they are burned. If ye abide in Me, and my words abide in you, ye shall ask what ye will, and it shall be done unto you.

> (St. John, 15; 5–7.)

This is the redemption of the divisive Twin principle. Christ is the bringer of the reality of the Trinity. He Himself is the Trinity. All thinking, feeling and willing devoted to the Trinity contribute to the healing of the world. The threefold social order is therefore a Christian solution, for the peoples of the earth to live together constructively. When efforts to introduce it had failed, Rudolf Steiner said: ' The threefold social order will come. But now it will only materialize after humanity has passed through the greatest catastrophes.'

Switzerland

WHEN THE SWISS had given up their ambition for power through territorial enlargement, they came greatly to value their self-imposed restraint. Their Confederation was like a many-facetted crystal, to be guarded with devotion.

It consists of twenty-two cantons of which two are double: and there are four fully recognized languages, German, French, Italian and Grison. Each of the twenty-four parts is an organism, largely independent of the central authority, and the least innovation is discussed in public and voted on by all adult males—often in the open air.

The basic virtue underlying the Confederation was perseverance. To the Swiss, good faith and loyalty are matters of honour in public as in private life. Not for nothing were they called ' Eidgenossen ' (united by oath); and their oath of loyalty is consistently kept.

Switzerland is the only country in Europe, perhaps in the world, where a soldier may keep his weapons and ammunition after his service expires and the right seems never to be abused. Existence is based on hard work and sobriety and from this well-ordered community wider groups have emerged, among others the World Postal Union and the World Telegraphic Union.

Yet with all his communal awareness, the Swiss meets others with reserve and his trust and respect go out to the stranger only where he finds activity in the practical sphere. He himself has created exemplary living conditions and material security: but in consequence he can be profoundly disturbed when he meets a personality whose outlook is not dominated by material interest.

The experience of difference can be immediate and crushing. And where an Austrian might through his charm avert over-seriousness, the Swiss, where he admires, takes refuge in abruptness, even rudeness. For he sees that in the long run he too will have to step beyond his earthly security and attain the certainty of a higher self with the sacrifice of his individual will.

However, where he does come to love others sufficiently to acknowledge that a spiritual attitude may have ultimate practicality, he serves them with a reverence learned in the face of his majestic mountains.

One who suffered from hostility towards his artistic genius was Ferdinand Hodler. His *Retreat from Marignano* had been awarded first prize in a competition for the decoration of the Landesmuseum in Zürich. It showed the Swiss after the lost battle, in a defeat which actually marked the beginning of Switzerland; for through death and apparent humiliation at Marignano the conditions were created for the future of their country, and this fact Hodler had expressed. His designs were rejected by the Museum directors on the pretext that they would be unacceptable to public opinion. The painter was mocked and ridiculed. Not until the Swiss Parliament, the highest authority, supported him, could his designs be carried out.

In 1904 his compatriots learned with great surprise that a Swiss painter had achieved European eminence. At the international exhibition at the Vienna Secession, Hodler's pictures hung alongside those of other famous artists. Along with Amiet, he was celebrated as the most important. The greater Zodiac Twin had been able to recognize true genius; the other had now to learn by example.

As the Austrian accepts his destiny in suffering, the Swiss would like to transform weakness into strength. This tendency becomes in him the longing to give practical help. Where the Swiss meets helplessness he seeks to give protection and is willing to make great material sacrifices.

Switzerland became a country of hospitality and refuge to those persecuted elsewhere. There they could find asylum. No one was concerned with their politics, only with their will to independence and their need. Children and sick people from other countries were generously helped, and many lives were saved. The instrument of these operations was the Red Cross, the foundation of Henri Dunant of Geneva.

In 1859, when France and Sardinia took up arms against Austria, Dunant, then aged thirty-one, went to Italy to gain a true picture of conditions on the battlefield. On the scene of Solferino after the defeat of the Austrians, he saw and tended the sufferings of the wounded and dying who were left in hostile territory entirely to their fate. He decided to do all in his power that victims of future wars, regardless of rank or nationality, should not be left helpless and abandoned. He felt himself a tool of Providence and his memories of Solferino* were written as an appeal to every European nation so that rescue societies should be founded everywhere.

> Since men will also kill each other in the future without hating each other, and since the greatest glory of war consists in destroying as many human lives as possible, while every day more terrible weapons of destruction are invented with a perseverance well worthy of a better cause, and the inventors of these implements of murder are given every encouragement by the countries of Europe . . . should we not use a time of comparative calm and peace to solve a problem of our own making from a Christian and human point of view?

Dunant hoped that the care of the wounded could be entrusted to volunteers. Even as he sought rescue for all, he saw that help must come from every nation and class—although his age glorified war and national pride, and class barriers were in general still unbreached. His suggestions were found practicable by a few active, socially-minded men and his ' voluntary aid ' societies were taken up in 1864. Unceasing effort and vigilance was required, however, to establish the concept of the Red Cross as neutral and international. He carried his vision among men often unable to conceive a universal ideal; and to those who helped him the quality of his genius could present great difficulty.

---

* *Un Souvenir de Solférino*, 1862.

196

He was both vain in his mission and humble as its instrument. His burning compassion and prophetic enthusiasm, as well as a naive trust in the word of princes, could lead him far beyond normal convention and caution, and while he had them, his whole means and strength were spent on petitions, publications and exhausting journeys. Orders and honours were abundantly bestowed on him by the heads of European states, but after the disastrous collapse of ventures in Africa and his consequent resignation as Secretary in Geneva, he had to learn what it was to be soon forgotten, to live in ill-health and penury, sometimes even destitution, although he continued his labours for the Red Cross and other benign causes. He underwent periods of despair and ensuing self-recall. Once he wrote, looking back, that few had suffered as much as he from envy, unscrupulousness and the stupidity of hypocrites.

He was nearly seventy when a percipient young journalist ' rediscovered ' him in a hospital room in Heiden. After that, a warmth of gratitude and of acclaim for his true achievement, by then somewhat better understood, centred upon him. In 1901, the first Nobel Peace Prize, shared with Frederick Passy, was added to his recognitions. But his latter years were lonely.

Switzerland itself has no orders or titles. For each Swiss, high or low, feels himself to be the equal of his neighbour, and every one of them knows the extent of his own efforts and considers that enough. Dunant's last birthday was held quietly with a few faithful friends. By his own decree he was carried unattended to his grave.

Another individual who was the guiding instrument of a mighty project was Louis Favre whose name is linked with the St. Gotthard tunnel. The Gotthard is a region where nature forces of every kind meet, and for a long time it was inaccessible and full of mystery. Mountain people built the first bridge, suspended on chains, across the deep gorge of the river Reuss. At the time of the Knights of the Grail, a track was made for pack animals; only pilgrims and beasts of burden took the dangerous route. But from the thirteenth century, pack animals carried merchandise across the mountain which then saw increasing numbers of pilgrims on their way to Rome. In 1717, after the bridge had collapsed in a storm, the Kirchberg was pierced to carry a path above the abyss. At the highest point of the mountain poor travellers were offered free food and shelter, others were accommodated in a hospice.

It was in July, 1778, that the first carriage, drawn by four horses, rattled along that steep path: it had to be steadied by four strong men. It belonged to the English geologist, Greville, who took a whole week to reach Magadino in the southern valley of the mountain. Between 1812 and 1824, a new and carefully constructed road was made.

By 1863 the Swiss had realized that the Gotthard could be an asset to them if a railway were run through it, and Louis Favre, an engineer from Geneva, was commissioned to construct a tunnel, to be completed by 1878.

But from the very beginning the Gotthard resisted with all the unexpected powers at the disposal of disturbed nature—with floods, avalanches and falls of rock. When the preliminary work was at last completed the mountain was suddenly shrouded in a thick layer of snow. The ancient giant would not readily surrender its sacred peace. In the winter of 1874 the water supply for the turbines failed and a reservoir had to be built to draw on the river Tessin (Ticino). The next year, water suddenly gushed from the crevices in the rock at the southern borehole. The struggle with water lasted over a year. For the problem of air and lamps in the tunnel Favre had to instal a powerful ventilating system at each end: and his time was running short.

No concessions were allowed to Favre, such as the Italian government granted contractors and engineers when the Col de Fréjus was being pierced; and no honours, as to Ferdinand de Lesseps in Egypt. In Switzerland the administrators of the Gotthard decided to withhold payments and asked Favre to bring proof of his integrity.

Accidents reached a terrible level. Twice there were explosions in dynamite stores. The water supply from the Tessin was interrupted by an avalanche and Favre had to take new steps to feed the turbines at least partly, to keep the work going. Then came the bursting of four high-pressure reservoirs: a new one built from the remains was put into action the same year.

The yearly toll of injuries and fatalities in the quarries and installations was so heavy that court proceedings by the state were suggested. In 1878, after thirty-one more deaths had occurred, the Gotthard company wanted to stop the work, although Favre protested. Yet at last, human endurance triumphed. By Christmas, 1879, the mountain had been pierced. But Favre did not live to see it. In July he went to the northern borehole with some strangers to show them the work. At the entrance he stood gazing into the darkness of the tunnel as if listening with an inner ear to the fearful voice of the mountain. Those who were with him could hear only the raging of the Reuss. Inside, he sat down on a rock and asked for water. It was found that his heart had stopped.

The piercing of the Gotthard was of great significance for here, at the centre of the longitudinal expansion of the Alps, lay the spiritual focal point of Switzerland. Within its heights lie seven lakes, and many others more deeply hidden mirror the heavens like restful eyes. Earlier geologists considered it the place where at the beginning of time the Earth received its structure. Here, fire formations of the earliest stones and water-borne Neptunic deposits lie next to each other.

The plant world too repeats on a small scale the features it develops over the Earth: the cryptograms that struggle in these icy regions are the vegetation of the north, the fertility of the northern valleys expresses the middle zone and the tropic growth on the southern slopes where palm trees occur approximates southern conditions. Even the animals of the north and the tropics meet here, where furry creatures of the icy regions and the scorpion often live in close proximity.

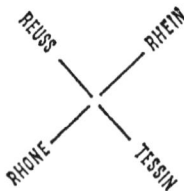

The Gotthard is the source of four important rivers which have inscribed a cross deep into the Alps. This is like a symbolic writing that can be deciphered in various ways.

In astronomy, the cross within the circle is the accepted sign for the Earth.

In the cross, opposite directions meet at a central point. With outstretched arms, man too is formed like a cross. At the centre he unites the forces of the universe.

All the alpine roads linking north and south in Switzerland were at one time dangerous. Seven of them were placed under the protection of saints to help the traveller in storm, cold and solitude. Today the passes have lost their menacing loneliness and a traveller's request for protection has come to be thought unnecessary. The Swiss have turned those prayers into prayers for their fellow-men and an admonition to self-discipline.

In their 1934 *Alpenbuch* the postal authorities ask the traveller to think strength-giving thoughts as he crosses the mountain passes: 'On the heights of the Gotthard Pass may the wanderer think of all who live on the great rivers that have their source in the Gotthard.' The Simplon is dedicated to St. James of Compostella: 'On this mountain, looking from valley to valley, we think of the mysteries and ways of all peoples.'

The great St. Bernard, whose monks and faithful dogs have for centuries sought lost travellers, appeals: 'On the heights of this pass may the wanderer think of all the homeless on earth.' The pass across St. Bernardino is entrusted to that follower of St. Francis of Assisi with the words: 'May he who seeks recovery from sickness in the valleys of Grison think, on the high mountain pass, of the saint, the sick yet blessed poor Franciscan friar, Bernardin of Siena.'

The Bernina, Julier and Majola passes were dedicated to St. Maurice who with six thousand Egyptian Christians of the Theban legion died a martyr's death in the Rhone valley. 'May the wanderer practise true courage and supreme obedience.'

Such thoughts as these indicate the mission of the Swiss: to direct their understanding to all peoples united with the heart of Europe through the four great rivers, and to the path of every nation; to feel for all who are inwardly and outwardly lonely and homeless; to hold the will to heal, and practise a loyalty to the true self that overcomes the earth-bound nature.

In this small, rocky country, whose population stands firmly on the ground, Rudolf Steiner* spent the last twelve years of his life. During his early years in Austria he had planned, with thoughts of regal power, his book about human freedom. In Germany from 1889 to 1912 he

---

* Rudolf Steiner (1861–1925).

had opened up the sources of the spirit to human striving. In Switzerland, he gave practical indications for a renewal of cultural life. His proposals for the threefold commonwealth date from these years.

From Switzerland he visited other countries. The questions he was asked at that time directly concerned practical life. In co-operation with doctors he evolved the fundamentals of a new art of healing. To orthodox medicine he added a deepened knowledge of body, soul and spirit, as well as understanding for the healing properties of plants and minerals. When he was asked about the care of retarded children, he gave answers that inspired a new art of curative education which offers profound understanding of those souls who cannot adjust themselves fully to conditions on Earth in their present lives.

In response to questions from the director of the Waldorf-Astoria cigarette factory in Stuttgart, who wanted to found a school for the children of his employees, he gave courses for teachers, initiating a new type of education which meets the innermost needs of childhood and adolescence.

Several Protestant clergymen approached Rudolf Steiner with problems of pastoral care and the celebration of the Sacraments today. When a sufficient number of people demanded advice of this kind, Rudolf Steiner gave courses to priests, which led to the foundation of the Christian Community.

Young farmers asked about the application of healing principles to agriculture. In the resulting lectures arranged by a Silesian landowner he gave all the instructions necessary to open up the soil to the forces of the cosmos, thus allowing it to gain new life forces.

He also gave a new impetus to art. For the sculptural treatment of wood and clay he created examples in which the normally invisible movement of the intermediate stages of forms in metamorphosis is made manifest. In painting, he showed how the rhythms of temporal metamorphosis can be re-created and colours adapted to the laws of the rainbow. Architecture also received new impulses through him. Modern buildings whose form is based on the cube are the image of present-day utilitarianism. In future, the more man becomes conscious of the spirit the more this type of architecture will yield to living forms. Rudolf Steiner showed the way to such development.

He also made possible a wider understanding for music whose connection with the world of stars he made evident. His new art of movement, Eurythmy, brings speech and movement, as well as music, into harmony.

In every sphere he led beyond earlier ideals and showed the way towards a healthier development. In particular he appealed to young people for decisions made consciously in the depth of the heart. Through his own life he showed what can be achieved by a human being filled with wisdom. His life was a continually renewed sacrifice to humanity, a ceaseless effort to stretch out a helping brotherly hand in every situation. Whatever he did he achieved out of love, presence of mind, and fully mastered capacities that were rooted in star wisdom.

Rudolf Steiner himself designed the Goetheanum* building. Here the science of the spirit was to find a home. Constructed entirely in wood, it was like an image of the cosmos and of

---

* The Goetheanum, Dornach (near Basel).

the development of man. The succession of columns in the great hall was an illustration through form of the basic impulses of the planets and of the peoples of Europe. The columns led the gaze to the large cupola, which was joined to a smaller dome painted with scenes of past and future as they appear in the world chronicle of Divine spirits. (Plates 39, 40.)

On the Eve of New Year, 1922–23, the Goetheanum was deliberately burned down. At midnight the flames pierced the domes and rose like a gigantic torch to the sky. The pillar intended as the representation of wisdom burned on into the morning. Two years and three months after the fire, Rudolf Steiner died.*

He had carved a large statue for the Goetheanum. This escaped the flames, not yet having been moved to its intended position; but it remained unfinished. It shows the Representative of Humanity between the two Adversaries who accompany evolution. Above Him is the tempter who would draw man away from the Earth, below Him the other, whose aim it is to keep humanity earth-bound. Standing between is Christ who brings healing balance. What He achieved mankind should one day be able to attain.

The statue of the Representative of Humanity concerns all future earth development. It can be an appeal to every human being to be wide awake, if he is striving to be fully human and to become truly free.**

---

* Rudolf Steiner before he died, designed a model for the New Goetheanum, to be built in concrete.
** The statue now stands in the new Goetheanum.

Finland

THE FINNISH FOLK SPIRIT receives its guiding impulses from the constellation of the Crab, where there is a softly-glowing, seemingly insignificant group of stars called the Beehive or Cradle. In the course of time Finland can become like a beehive, where the essence of the different stages of human development will be carefully gathered, and after being transformed, will be given back to the world.

Finland rises from the sea. Rocks at sea level one hundred and fifty years ago now stand considerably higher and are no longer touched by the waves. Where large ships once sailed, only small rowing boats can pass today. Cities formerly at the seaboard are now inland and have ports some distance away. The coast near Turku has risen by more than twenty inches in a century.

It is a country of endless forests where herds of reindeer roam, a 'land of a thousand lakes' and a thousand islands. Its geological structure is chiefly of hard crystalline granite, though there is another, younger granite which is not firm, but decays. It is coarse-grained and brownish-red, and occurs in huge blocks throughout Europe, from the west of England to Russia. These were carried by the rivers of the great Ice Cap and when the ice melted they were left behind. Wherever this Rapakivi granite is found in Finland, it gives monotony to the landscape, for it does not mix with any other type of rock.

In the second century A.D. the Finns came to regions previously inhabited only by Lapp nomads. Courageous fighters and lovers of freedom, they needed no state authority while their hunters were penetrating the northern forests and their herdsmen settled the agricultural land. By the time of their christianizing in the twelfth century, there were three main areas of settlement: the south-western plains of Suomi,* the forest region inland toward the lakes, and eastward round the shores of Lake Ladoga. Swedish Catholics arrived from the west and Greek Orthodox Russians from Novgorod; and between these mutually hostile neighbours Finland's destiny began to unfold. By the fourteenth century Swedish power had firm hold; in 1362 Finns were given rights in the election of the Swedish king and, later, seats in the General Estates. When the Reformation came it excited no passionate opposition. (At the time of the Swedish crusades, a Holy Father had recorded sadly that the Finns went back to their old beliefs as soon as the danger was over.) But one consequence, of far-reaching later importance, was that Finnish replaced Latin as the language of the Church.

In 1581 Finland was made a Grand Duchy of Sweden. Incessant Russo-Swedish conflicts

---

* Finland.

202

on her soil brought poverty, plague and famine. The worst devastation came at the opening of the eighteenth century when in the 'Northern War' Russian troops burned and ravaged their way to the Gulf of Bothnia. A further invasion took place in 1741.

Afterwards came a period of comparative peace and internal development, and during this time the idea of a separate Finland could begin to take shape. But in 1809, when wider issues were afflicting Europe, the Tsar Alexander I by agreement with Napoleon invaded and annexed Finland. He gave an undertaking, never fully implemented—and for motives that are still disputed—to respect ancient privileges and traditions; and Finland became an autonomous state within the Russian Empire.

The nineteenth century, however, was to bring Finnish national feeling to awakening, and ideas of independence were fostered by a strong literary movement integrating elements of the Finnish language and reanimating a distinctively Finnish culture. One of its leaders and pioneers, and a true representative of his folk spirit, was Elias Lönnrot; at the time of the Russian invasion, seven years old.

Scholars were beginning to take an interest in the poetry of Finland's past. In 1819 H. R. von Schröter published a series of Finnish runes. In the same year Reinhold von Becker went on a study tour in Finland: on his journeys he visited Zachris Topelius (the elder), a retired doctor who was the first outstanding collector of Finnish folk poetry. Greatly encouraged by this visit, Topelius began to publish in instalments his series, *The Finnish People's Ancient Runes and Other Songs*. Pedlars wandered to his house and sang him songs that had lived among the people for hundreds of years. Other people were invited and he thus discovered a great, unexpected treasure of memories of the distant past. But this was only a beginning.

Old songs were being collected elsewhere in Europe at the time, but while most were complete in themselves, what the Finnish folk memory had preserved was a comprehensive whole, an all-embracing epos that pulsated everywhere among the people and was transmitted by individuals only in fragments. The whole nation was its voice. Finland was the ' *Kalevala* ', the ' land of heroes '.

To understand the epic in its completeness, however, a man was needed who could hold within himself the quintessence of all the singers of old. Elias Lönnrot could absorb the different parts and could unite them: through him the original impulse came to life again.

Lönnrot, the son of a village tailor, was born in the parish of Sammatti on Haarjärvi.* He endured poverty and hunger but worked to become a doctor, and when he had finished his studies he settled in the north, in the small town of Kajaani close to the home of the Karelian folk singers. In peasant clothing he wandered from farm to farm, village to village, and lived among the people. The rune singers could still recite many long poems from memory. In 1834 he made a journey to Vuokkiniemi on Latvajärvi where he met the most outstanding of all northern rune singers, the aged peasant Arhippa. To Elias Lönnrot, Arhippa's songs were not separate runes but part of a rich legacy, handed down for generations and carefully guarded as the relics of ancient soul power and spirit vision, from which men could gather strength.

---

* *Järvi*—lake.

The spirituality of the past can only form new roots in a modern nation with the help of time rhythms. When Lönnrot published the *Kalevala*, then consisting of thirty-two runes with over 12,000 lines, in 1835, it took fifteen years to sell an edition of only five hundred copies.

Lönnrot went on collecting. Encouraged by him, David Europaeus, a young student, went to north Karelia where he met a folk singer famed as a 'great *laujala*'. He gathered songs from the White Sea to Lake Ladoga and other scholars collected in Finnish Karelia and on the Karelian Isthmus. Lönnrot studied everything brought to him, choosing for every verse and incident the most complete rendering. In 1849 he brought out a new edition of the *Kalevala*, fifty runes with a total of 22,795 lines.

In beautiful rhythmic songs, these runes tell of the fate of three great heroes, Väinämöinen, Ilmarinen and Lemminkainen. Their deeds were celebrated at every festival, for the threefold impulse whose expression they are has lived since earliest times in the Finnish people. In the days of the earliest epos, they lived along three great bays, the gulfs of Bothnia, of Riga and of Finland. The soul of Finland was still poured out over the region and her people experienced through the earth the Trinity that shone into them. But the threefold impulse came also from the heights. In the constellation of the Crab three stars form a high arch round the Beehive. To ancient clairvoyance, three rays pointed from the centre to these three stars. This trinity, a reality of the Finnish folk spirit, is echoed in the *Kalevala*.

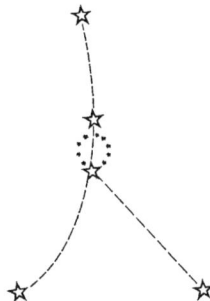

At festivals and celebrations of every kind, the *laujala* would choose an assistant. Sitting opposite, they linked hands, and with their knees touching they would bend rhythmically forward and back. The *laujala* began his song, then it was taken up by his assistant, and thus they continued in melodious monotony, always swaying, always touching. In this way, through the figures of the heroes, they and their listeners could experience the development of the soul forces of thinking, feeling and willing, as it had come about. Through the deeds of Väinämöinen, an ancient heroic being, these forces were experienced as still untamed, suffering and creating, and not yet completely within the individual soul. In the tale of Ilmarinen they could feel another formative force active in them; and Lemminkainen was a spiritual elemental power whose influence extended to the physical plane. The story of the forging of the ' *Sampo* ' with its many-coloured cover, speaks of the forming of man himself.* The last rune is that of

---

* In *Earthly and Cosmic Man* (Rudolf Steiner Publishing Co.), 1948, Rudolf Steiner describes this as the forging of the human ether-body, forged by the interworking of three soul members. Editor.

the maiden Marjatta, child of beauty, who wandering with her flocks swallowed a cranberry and afterwards in lonely rejection bore a holy child.

> . . . I shall bear a mighty hero
> And shall bear a noble offspring . . .

To become immersed in the songs was a deep urge, everywhere encouraged. The mutual rhythmic movements during the singing transmitted an experience of the Sense of Touch, which is the gift to the Finns of the constellation of the Crab.

The *Kalevala** became to them what Homer's songs had been to Greece. It grew to be the spiritual force that carried and guarded Finland's culture; and many a traveller to the north formed the conviction that he had to acquaint himself with this great epos before he could reach a real understanding of the Finns.

In natural talents the Finns are orientated towards the material world. Like other nations, they gained their independence when materialism was flourishing everywhere, but in Finland this need not bring about as it does elsewhere the drying-up of the soul: for the *Kalevala* is a quickening source of powerful spiritual images. Imaginative in colour, form and sound, glowing in the beauty, strength and wisdom of its imagery, inspiring through the strange old pictures that point to the extraordinary, it stands as a guardian behind the Finns, who have to come to terms with the tendencies of the age. Finland has shown that a material civilization may be kept in check if it is blessed and permeated by great imaginations; and when childhood and youth are steeped in the vitality of the nature spirits, of the sacred trees and ensouled animals, and enriched by reverence for heroic deeds.

In everyday life, Finland's relation to the Crab forces finds expression in the annual ' Crayfish Feast '. At the end of July when the Sun shines down from this constellation the whole nation is under its impress, and everywhere crayfish are cooked and eaten through late afternoon and early evening. Crayfish ' tastes best ' then.

The impulse of the heavenly Crab has given the Finns their love for the *sauna*, a steam bath which keeps the body pure as a temple. Before birth, when the soul is gathering the forces to form the body during its descent to Earth, it finds in the region of the Crab the image of the ribs, which will later enclose the noblest of organs, the heart. They are like piers or walls protecting the interior. The body itself is a house where soul and spirit can dwell. It is a temple. The Finnish people have always had reverence for this temple, which was cared for in a unique manner. The *sauna* baths originated in this reverence.

Sauna means bath house. From earliest times, stones were piled up under a small platform. A fire was then lit and the bathers undressed, ascended the platform and poured water over the hot stones until steam filled the room, causing everybody to sweat. Then the skin, the bearer of the Sense of Touch, was beaten with birch twigs to stimulate it further. Then the bathers jumped into a nearby lake or stream, or rolled in the snow, to cool themselves. Every Saturday throughout the year all the family, men, women, children, farm hands and friends

---

* English translation, *Kalevala. The Land of Heroes.* Everyman's Library, J. M. Dent, 1936.

would go to the bath house to beat each other with steaming birch twigs; in summer they would go every day. From the poorest Karelian smallholder to the rich landowner in Ostrobothnia, the *sauna* has the same significance. All enjoy it: poets have described it in verse, painters have depicted it on canvas, singers have sung its praise, for the *sauna* meant not only increased well-being but a greater awareness of being at home in a physical body, cleansed even inwardly through the enormous heat.

In *The Seven Brothers*, Alexis Kivi, the famous Finnish author, describes such a bath:

> The evening came, a melancholy September evening. Eero told Routio and Timo that the bath was ready, and the men's sombre mood brightened up a little. They went to the bath, and Timo threw water on the hot stove until the hot black stones popped like rifles and a cloud of hot steam filled the bath house. Everybody now lashed out with the supple leafy birch twigs, so pleasant to the skin; their furious beating could be heard far away.

Inani, one of the seven brothers, says elsewhere:

> A farm house without a bath house is useless to the farmer's wife or her help, if they have children. A steaming bath house, a barking dog, a crowing cockerel, a meowing cat— these are the signs of a good farm.

The human body is treasured highly in Finland and attention to its hygiene requires no seclusion, for there is nothing unworthy about the body in the eyes of those who honour the Finnish folk spirit.

The Crab impulse to experience the body as a temple acts also in the realm of culture. Every sanctuary of the Christian era has its prototype in the temple wherein the Holy Grail was preserved, the original building of kingship. Lars-Ivar Ringboom has studied the origin and basic form of this temple in his outstanding work, *Temple of the Grail and Paradise.**

Painstaking research upon region after region, building after building, persuaded him that it originated at the birthplace of Zarathustra. He did not dare take the leap to spiritua perception which could have yielded him still fuller truth; but this truth lives in the Finnish folk spirit that longs to guide its people from form to content, from matter to spirit.

The entire life of humanity should resemble a temple—but the dwelling needed on earth for spirit, soul and body to feel protected is a secure social edifice. There was no security in Finland at the time of her declared independence from Russia. It was 1917, and anarchy threatened. Russian garrison troops still in Finland were supporting the Red extremists of Finnish labour organizations in disruption and violence, while a secretly prepared White liberation movement remained hopeless and inactive through lack of arms. In December, General Gustav Mannerheim was called to his life's task.

He was fifty years old: and like many Finns had served in the Imperial Army, but after the

---

* Lars-Ivar Ringboom. *Graltempel und Paradies*, Stockholm, 1951.

Revolution, finding he could not raise a counter-movement in Petrograd, he returned to Finland. As a cavalry officer he had travelled in Europe and experienced the Russo-Japanese war. He then carried out a unique mission to China, partly to foster goodwill for Russian interests and partly scientific in intention. In two years he covered nine thousand miles on horseback and must sternly have proved his many-sidedness, discarding in the solitudes of Asia some of the prejudices and limitations of the age, and confirming the self-discipline that enabled him later to place his powers unreservedly at the disposal of his folk spirit. (Plate 41.)

With his sober sense of fact and his insight into the needs of the hour, Mannerheim set out to create and supply an army, and to rid the country of its hostile elements. In no way intimidated by superior enemy strength, he began the struggle in Ostrobothnia, and in under four months Suomi's White army had step by step secured north Finland and cleared the expanses to Karelia, where Finnish troops five times outnumbered had maintained an unyielding defence.

From the tundras of Lapland and the Islands of Ahvenanmaa, as Mannerheim proclaimed, to Rajajoki on the Karelian Isthmus, the Finnish lion, saved without foreign help, flew everywhere. But Helsinki and the south were liberated by Finnish troops trained in Germany; and with German intervention in spite of opposition from Mannerheim. When the Senate decided that the country should then organize its defences on German lines, he could not accept their policy and resigned.

After Germany's collapse in 1918, they turned to him again. Finland was starving. He agreed to seek support in Britain and France, acting unofficially, and while he was still in Paris, a new threat loomed from Russia and Mannerheim was asked to become Regent. For seven months, until the election of a President, he held this office. There followed an active twelve-year period of retirement, until he was summoned again in 1931 to take charge of Finland's defences. During this time the famous line of fortifications bearing his name was built across the Karelian Isthmus.

His old age has become legendary. At seventy-two he took command of Finland's defensive Winter War of 1939–40, and then for seven unparalleled years gave his strength both as soldier and as statesman for her survival as a neutral independent land. Finland made him her only Marshal. His final service was as President until ill-health forced his resignation in 1946.

War was his calling, but he came to hate war, finding it justified only as a last defence against greater evils. After his term of Regency in 1918–19, he gave his energy to welfare and education. In 1920 leading personalities met in his house to discuss an organization for Finland's youth, for he wished no less than the creation of a new community through the children. Clearly he outlined the great task, and the press at once published his appeal. He had set aside 50,000 Finnmark for the care and education of children who had lost their breadwinner through the war—regardless of which side he had fought on.

Mannerheim aimed not only to heal the wounds of war, but to have all generous-minded friends of his country work to rebuild the community and above all, to ease the fate of those whose need seemed greatest to him: those who had to suffer without fault of their own.

With the co-operation of his sister, who had trained in London at St. Thomas's Hospital, he soon had an organization with branches all over the country. One result was a rapid fall in child mortality rates. In the 'Children's Castle', maternity and child-care nurses were trained.

Mothers' guidance centres, a travelling child-care exhibition, school medical and dental services, were also introduced. At Mannerheim's personal request, farmers' clubs were founded for the education of the youth in the countryside. Importance was not only attached to gymnastics, swimming and archery, but also to treatment for children in need of special care, and for delinquents.

In 1919, in Central Europe, Rudolf Steiner published his book on the Threefold Commonwealth. That the birth of Finland should have coincided with these proposals for a new social order is a fact recorded in the spiritual annals of history. The same threefold impulse that once brought forth the Kalevala had been crystallized into practical suggestions. It could have answered the search of the Finnish folk spirit, that arose in the mid-eighteenth century, for a form of society that could become a renewed expression of the divine will. As it remained unaccepted elsewhere, it also failed to materialize in Finland.

Yet the Finns did develop their cultural life, the life of rights, and their economic life, without disregarding the needs of the region, and of the age. Cultural life really became like a beehive as the productions of the rest of the world were studied.

By the outbreak of the Second World War, more books of a high quality were being published than anywhere else, in proportion to the population. The university bookshop in Helsinki was the second largest in Europe. Public libraries existed even in the smallest villages; at the same time, most Finns were eager book buyers.

Proportionately, the Finns have more schools than any other country. They also love museums and galleries which are found in every province. Helsinki has at least a dozen. In the National Museum, instruction is given in every subject important for daily life: a healthy diet, the care of the feet, accident prevention, how to distinguish poisonous from other fungi and so on. Models of nursery schools are on display—and of cradles—and models of bath houses, wooden huts and modern buildings of every kind are available for study. Even in 1906, women could have a share in the life of the state, for Suomi, still part of the Russian Empire, was the first European country to allow them to vote.

Helsinki developed into the ' white city of the north '; all its old houses were replaced by bright stone buildings and it became one of the friendliest cities in Europe, entirely without slums. People live in small convenient flats that are built in large blocks with communal kitchens. Pleasant old people's homes and fine hospitals are open to all. The Sofianleho Orphanage is one of Europe's most modern children's homes. In the suburbs are innumerable small houses and still further out are summer camps and municipal swimming baths. The streets of Helsinki and of other cities contain many fine statues.

Finland's economic wealth is based on her forests, in the past the home of ancient magic, now the source of industry and trade. Immense sawmills process timber for export. An industry was established to make prefabricated houses, furniture, veneers of a high quality made of only the best birchwood, matches and other small objects. A series of huge paper factories, interrupted by the sawmills and power stations, rose on river banks. Modern methods of production and transport were used, and in laboratories chemists and other experts sought methods of using waste products to spare the forests as much as possible.

The materialism of the age grew into a delight in the worthy ordering of everyday life, and with serious intent and a modest confidence in themselves the Finns stepped into the stream of contemporary culture and civilization.

While the folk soul is engaged in transforming materialism, the desire has arisen to master the body to the utmost and physical agility becomes an ideal. The whole nation has been trained in athletics and for a time the Finns led the score of international prizes. The running of the famous Paavo Nurmi never displayed any effort—he seemed to touch the earth, to which all men are bound, only in passing. His mastery can be expressed with the sign often used for the constellation of Cancer, the Crab.

Enthusiasm for his achievements was so great that he joined other representatives of his people in having a statue erected to him. It stands near the entrance to the Helsinki stadium. No other nation has experienced this athletic mastery as so directly the expression of its own character.

The training of the body to be an asset instead of an obstacle is the external aspect of the mood of the Crab. In the opposing loops of the sign, a leap is necessary from one side to the other and is accomplished in athletics with the body.

But the leap can also be attempted in the realm of the spirit and then it demands a change of consciousness, to make possible an understanding that transcends matter.

The Finnish people have a word which fundamentally describes their character. *Sisu.* Its meaning is 'strong and persevering', not only in physical endurance, but through the individual's own will and decision. With *sisu* the Finns need not remain bound to the past but should be able to venture the leap across the gap, to conquer the future.

The ability to leap demands a selflessness strong enough to accompany the soul when it abandons what is outlived to enter the new lands of the spirit undamaged. Through inner purification, the abyss can be bridged between materialistic, limited thinking and spiritual perception.

In the Crab leap, an ability to love matter becomes a new capacity for loving the world spirit that is manifest in matter. The word ' matter '—compare *mater*, mother—points to the nature of the Queen of Heaven and to the divine substance of the sacrifice of the most exalted spirits of the spheres. Such new Christian insight into the nature of matter is a service to the

Finnish folk spirit. It is also the task of the whole of humanity, for since Christ united Himself with the Earth, matter is increasingly ordered and permeated by Him. Spiritualized matter becomes the temple of a distant future age, already being prepared.

When humanity is ready for the future change of consciousness, the very first phases of which we are experiencing now, then *sisu* will have triumphed in those who did not despair. After an earthly journey fraught with hindrance through thousands of years, mankind will pass from a cycle of time completed into a new phase.

PART III

Historic Responsibility

The White Horseman

TWENTIETH-CENTURY EUROPE is like a house that has to be rebuilt, when the old one, outlived, has crumbled. As with an individual life, it will depend on the makers whether or not the house can become a work of art.

It often appears as if a man fulfilling his everyday tasks had no influence on wider decisions and events, but this is by no means true. He may, as in the following tale, grow mature enough to read in the book of wisdom and to recognize the shape of the past: and if he courageously takes up its consequences to transform them, he will bring healing forces to bear upon his work.

One day a Roman senator killed his slave in anger. This was nothing very unusual at the time, one could do far worse things than that. But when he did so, a son was born into a family of devils. The father said to the boy: ' No need for *you* to learn anything— strong and handsome as you are! Lie down and sleep until I whistle.' So the lad did as he was told.

The senator died, rich in honours. Later, he came back to earth again and so spent his days that once more he became a highly respected man.

Yet again he returned to earth, and this time he worked as an architect. He was asked to raise a large building on old foundations and conscientiously he worked out his plans for it. Often, at evening, he would sit in a tall, high-backed chair and with closed eyes would think and dream about this building.

One evening as he sat in contemplation, he heard a whistle. Annoyed, and even perturbed, he looked about him. The door made a harsh sound as a strange little figure hobbled in; part child, part monster he seemed, with a hideous devil's head and thin, spindly legs.

' With your permission,' he said and bowed, ' I am going to stay.'

' What—? How dare you! ' exlaimed the architect sharply. ' You have no business here. Go away! ' But he found he was stammering with alarm.

' You called me! ' the devil leered, and began running round him.

' *I* called you? ' He tried to rise. 'You are lying—away with you! '

' You longed for my company,' the monster-child assured him.

But now the architect was pulling himself together. ' Beware of mocking me,' he warned. The devil's ugly face contorted as if he were about to cry, and yet . . . ? The architect distinctly heard a laugh. And the creature had disappeared.

Then it was that things began to go wrong with the great building. The stone ran out. Instructions were disregarded. The workmen were lazy. What could have happened, the architect wondered; for he was a capable man, the plans had been admirable and he had looked forward with his whole heart to the rising of the finished work. Worse was to come. One day a great storm swept the whole of the scaffolding and the newly raised walls away into the river.

Shocked and stricken, he sat down that evening in his tall chair, and as he closed his eyes a few anguished tears fell upon his hands. All at once he heard a sound like approaching hooves. He opened his eyes. There was moonlight beyond the window, and outside were prancing two snow-white steeds. On one sat a horseman, clad in white and holding a white banner displaying the Queen of Heaven surrounded by golden signs.

'Mount the white horse and follow me!' said the horseman—so calmly that the architect obeyed without hesitation; and the two rode off together. Far into the blue winter night they rode, swift as the wind, while everything beneath them shone and glittered in the gentle light of the moon. The trees beneath the horses looked like clouds. They came to a house with a light shining in a window, and there they dismounted and looked in.

Inside sat a man in a tall, high-backed chair. His eyes were closed, but he held a book in his hands. So silent was it they could hear every breath and the window-pane seemed utterly transparent. But suddenly the silence was shattered, as through the door hobbled a repulsive little form with a hideous devil's head and thin, spindly legs. He bowed politely and said, 'With your permission I am going to stay.'

The man opened his eyes and the watchers could perceive his horror, as attentively, he studied his visitor. 'Who are you?'' he presently asked.

'I am your son,' replied the devil-child, and began to dart around him.

The man looked at him sharply; then he laid aside his book, and swiftly catching him, said: 'Be still a moment! And let us see whether you are speaking the truth.' He took him to the mirror hanging opposite the window. Carefully he compared his own face with that of the devil and finally he said: 'Yes. You really do look like me.' And then, with a reluctant recognition, he whispered, 'But you are—a murderer!'

'*You* are!' shouted the devil.

The man released him. 'I don't understand—yet,' he admitted. 'But you may stay with me.'

'Then you must look at me!' the monster-child implored. 'I can only stay if you will look—again and again.' And all at once the hideous face seemed less contorted.

'Yes,' agreed the man. He sat down and began to read anew, and as he read his expression changed. When he looked again at the monster, compassion filled his gaze. He closed the book.

'We shall be companions,' he said, 'until you are transformed—until you bear the likeness that I myself must bear.'

The white horseman made a sign to the architect. Without a sound they mounted their horses again and set out on their long journey back. And the architect now knew: the obstacles in the way of his great building would be surmounted. It would one day come to be.

In the traditions of the Holy Grail, there were known to be twelve great transforming virtues, related to the course of the Sun as it moves in the year through the twelve Signs of the

Zodiac. A study of the character of the twelve distinct groups among the peoples of Europe reveals a connection of each group with the forces from one starry region. Britain, for example, has a special connection with the Scorpion and, as was shown, the basic quality growing in the British people is a tolerance that is revealed in their historical patience.

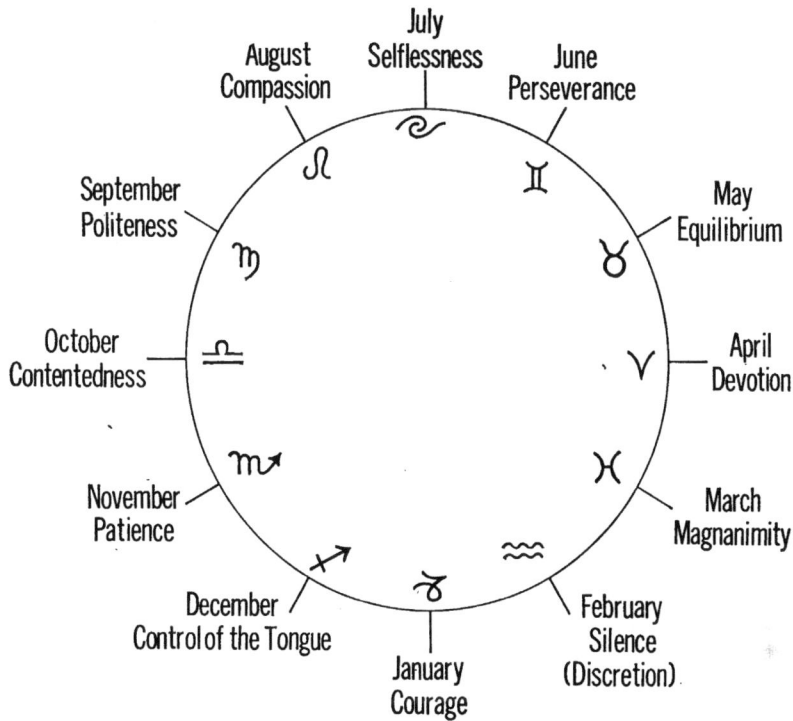

If these twelve inward steps are practised in accord with the Sun's annual passage from Sign to Sign, each one undergoes transformation to become a basis for the next one.*

Beginning with the turn of the year—December 21–January 21—courage becomes redemptive force; silence (discretion) becomes meditative strength; magnanimity turns into love; devotion to a capacity for sacrifice; equilibrium into progress; perseverance into steadfastness; selflessness leads to catharsis; compassion becomes freedom; politeness, from being outer form, becomes a tact of the heart; contentedness becomes calmness; patience leads into insight; and control of the tongue becomes a sense of truth.

Working thus within the evolution of the world, a man becomes the protector of the banner carried by the white horseman. The golden signs encircling the Queen of Heaven become his own light-bearing moral forces.

The impulses indicated by the Venus pentagon are also forces of light. At the time of Christ

---

* Compare the *Sternkalender* of 1969–70, published by the Philosophisch-Anthroposophischer Verlag, Dornach. (Editor.)

the five corners of the pentagon pointed towards the Scorpion, the Lion, the Twins, the Ram and the Goat. Since then the pentagon has completed a full round of the Zodiac and is now on a second journey. In the middle of the twentieth century the first corner pointed towards the Ram, the second to the Waterman, the third to the Scorpion, the fourth to the Virgin and the fifth to the Sign of the Crab. At the end of the millennium the pentagon will point to the ecliptic Signs* as follows:

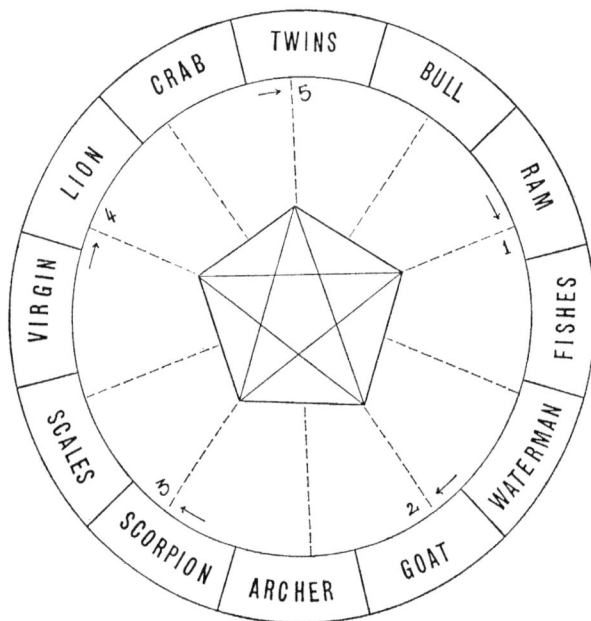

The forces of this outwardly intangible pentagon can accompany with their constant presence the efforts of individuals and of humanity.

Venus, the pentagram star, is an element of absolute harmony. When a human being unites with it consciously through his inner attitude and clarity of thinking, he will do two things: he will follow his path of inner development, sure of his aim and content to wait: at every point he will feel connected with all the stages of the way—just as the lines of the pentagram link together all five points without interruption. He will also find the right connection with the beings outside him, indeed he will feel them within himself, whether they belong to the human kingdom or to the other realms and spheres of the universe.

---

* Not the fixed star constellations. (W. O. Sucher).
The corners here would correspond as follows with the diagram by W. O. Sucher on page 38.

1 = I and VI
2 = VII and II
3 = III and VIII
4 = IX and IV
5 = V and X

Plate 43. *Coronation of the Virgin*. By Taddeo Gaddi (1300–1366).

By courtesy of the National Gallery, London.

Plate 44. *Madonna*. School of Crivelli Carlo Crivelli, (*circa* 1430–1493).

Plate 45. *Madonna with the Strawberries*. Old School from Upper Rhine (*circa* 1420). She passes a rose to her Child, sits where snowdrops, lilies of the valley and strawberries, grow. She holds the book of wisdom.

By courtesy of the Museum, Solothurn Kunst-Abteilung.

Plate 46. *Coronation of the Virgin.* By Raphael (1503). In heavenly heights above the Virgin's tomb, around which are the Twelve Apostles, Christ places the crown upon the Virgin's head. Roses and lilies fill the empty tomb.

By courtesy of the Vatican, Rome.

Plate 47. *Madonna with the Veil*. By Raphael. The Virgin with her left arm embraces the young John the Baptist for whom she is lifting the veil that covers her sleeping child. The face of St. John is radiant with vision—he can see more than the painting depicts.

By courtesy of the Louvre Museum, Paris.

Freedom and the Parsifal Path

EVERYTHING ACHIEVED IN EUROPE as noble spirituality contributes to the development of future human faculties. So far the greatest achievement has been 'freedom', although what is now understood as freedom is but a pale shadow of what it may become.

We think ourselves free if we can do as we like; but this is often mere arbitrariness which only increases the tyranny of our own weaknesses. Freedom requires not just an emergence from the compulsions of our lower nature, and independence of the judgment of others, but also emancipation from a blind faith in Divine guidance that seeks no deeper understanding. The free individual does not act like a frightened child before the powers of creation, but as their brother.

Freedom is something so exalted and serene that to gain it man must learn to experience without wavering the whole tragedy and bliss of the universe. He must distinguish between good and evil. It was for this that the cosmic worlds were gradually shrouded in darkness, with the result that not only the perception of spiritual beings was lost, but also the power to recognize demonic worlds whose vast legions of negative spiritual forces seek to divert humanity from its goal.

These powers hope to sever the Earth from the spiritual world and conquer it for themselves; when they are not observed in full consciousness and transformed, they can work without restraint. Man with his growing, though irresponsibly used independence falls more and more under their influence. He comes to deny the streams of life of the Divine creative power and endeavours to replace these with inventions of his own. He will gain material control of the planets; he will try to intervene in the cosmic order with machines. To the causes of the ensuing catastrophes he will be completely blind within his soul and, through his own fault, will vegetate in demonic surroundings, a slave of the powers fighting against Christ. He will live in lies and illusions and think himself free.

An inattentive humanity, overcome by egotism and without understanding, may easily succumb to this danger.

Across the centuries, however, the mysteries of the Holy Grail now shed their helping light. When the veiling of the world of stars had become a fact to advancing humanity, not only was the structure of a future Europe being laid; it was known at Grail centres that the capacity for a Christian understanding of man and the cosmos might be completely lost, and so the path that can lead to a new communion between Heaven and Earth was at the same time being prepared.

Where faculties have to be developed, someone must be there who is willing to take upon himself the burden of a painful beginning, and able to perform a deed for the first time. The personality who achieved this during the ninth century was Parsifal. As an individual he was a great leader, but on assuming his Parsifal life he renounced all the advantages his wisdom and greatness could have brought him. He took upon himself the darkening consciousness that had to struggle through the valley of godlessness. As men today usually grow up without knowing of spiritual adventures, Parsifal grew up ignorant of the chivalry and knighthood of his time. And as modern man meets the marvels of life without asking their significance, Parsifal was led to the Grail Castle without investigating its mysteries.

Wolfram von Eschenbach described the deeds of his Parzival in the imagery of contemporary knighthood. In an age unaware of the wisdom of the stars, he described the path of one who, experiencing the powers of the planets within himself, met and overcame evil.

After death every soul passes through the realization of its own weaknesses: as it ascends to planetary spheres, it finds memories of earthly failures and only after painful purification can it enter higher worlds. Parzival underwent such suffering on Earth in quite as real a manner. His path led him to the experience of guilt, shame and rebellion, which the modern world finds in its history. And thus he brought within the compass of human freedom on Earth not only the supersensible journey in the world beyond death, but actually the course of human destiny. He prepared the new ascent.

The path is one of gradual inner transformation, as a man passes from sphere to sphere. When Parzival had left and forgotten her, his mother died from sorrow. His own sorrow when he learned of this was a penance imposed upon him from the region of the Moon.

An understanding communion with others has healing character, but in the Grail castle Parzival failed to ask the question of compassion, and found himself, through his own lack, rejected by King Arthur's Round Table. Excluded from the circle of friendship, he passed through the purification of the sphere of Venus. In his despair he longed to reach the Grail by force; and in this he shared the situation of a later humanity which tries to win its salvation by outer success. He cursed the Godhead. This led him to trials of consciousness in the realm of Mercury, where the soul's hostility to love and wisdom is overcome in pain.

When Parzival's quest has led him away from the Round Table, Wolfram's story turns for a time to the adventures of Gawan. The paths of these two heroes are different, and yet their destinies are secretly and inseparably interwoven.* Behind the figure of Gawan stands the Parzival who was then striving with his ordinary human faculties for the purification of his soul. As Parzival, he received his first insight into the cosmic background of the Holy Grail when, on Good Friday, guided by his Grail horse, he came to the cave of the hermit, Trevrizent. He thereon entered the sphere of the spiritual Sun and could survey the path he had already traversed. He became conscious of the extent of his failures.

Again it is Gawan's turn. He has to master the ancient Mars world that rules in Klingsor's kingdom. Klingsor is the power that fights the Grail, and Gawan-Parzival contributed to the transformation of that world. He overcame the illusions that cloud a true perception of man and nature. Then Parzival approached Jupiter's living sphere of wisdom and could gather a wreath from the radiant tree of King Gramoflanz, as Gawan also had to do.

---

* Compare W. J. Stein: *Das neunte Jahrhundert*, 1928.

218

The two must now fight one another; and thus Parzival overcame his own Gawan ego. In the next struggle, through the wreath of virtues he had won, he proved stronger than King Gramoflanz himself, and could now be received into the bright future-worlds of Jupiter.

The hardest of all fights was still to come. All the obstacles arising in man's bodily constitution as a result of past transgressions appeared to him in his black-and-white brother, Fierefiz, who is still unrecognized. Parzival had to master the realm of the will within himself. The sword that he had wrested from an earlier adversary is broken in this fight; but his life is given back to him, for his heathen brother will not strike a disarmed enemy. And so they reach one another. When Parzival's name appears on the holy vessel summoning him to lordship of the Grail, he must take a companion, and Fierefiz goes with him. Divine spirits have recognized Parzival as an independent force. He was given authority in the Sun cosmos to share their responsibility. He had recovered the dignity of man and found serenity of spirit: but his sorrows must become infinitely greater as he sees not only the goal of humanity but also the dangers that are threatening the future of the world.

For over a thousand years the Grail mysteries ran secretly through Europe's history. They may have influenced Bulgaria in the Middle Ages. Certainly, in the eleventh, twelfth and thirteenth centuries they flourished among the Cathars and the Templars, the two Orders so ruthlessly destroyed. The last refuge of the Cathars, Montségur, fell in 1244, and there was then a danger that the shining thread leading into the future would be broken. During that time of persecution, the Grail story was preserved and spread by the minnesingers and the troubadours.

Within the perilous spiritual darkness, a mysterious personality known in closed circles as Christian Rosenkreuz took up the guiding thread once more. He transformed the image of the Grail into that of a black cross, from which shine seven red roses. The Rosicrucians, working in complete silence, were nevertheless very active. Tycho Brahe (born in 1546) probably belonged to the circle. With instruments invented by himself he found the positions of a thousand fixed stars and traced the movements of the planets—thus paving the way for the modern approach to the world of stars. In 1604, three years after Tycho's death, Valentin Andreae, a seventeen-year-old student, wrote in an an inspired state *The Chymical Marriage of Christian Rosenkreuz*.* The approaching scientific study of the stars was complemented by the Rosicrucian knowledge of initiation.

Even in recent times, there have always been individuals in whom Grail and Rosicrucian impulses were variously active. And from the twentieth century onwards the fruit of the Parsifal path can ripen in souls seeking purification. Their personal striving then becomes a sacrificial deed for the world. A second great experience is the bearing of inner solitude. No-one who decides to take this journey is spared loneliness; for every step demands the independent effort of the ego, as Parsifal showed in his life.

To our present-day consciousness looking everywhere for quick results, impulses that appeared twelve hundred years ago and deeds of that time seem to fade away in a meaningless past. But if cosmic rhythms are considered it becomes evident that the immediate future shows

---

* See *A Commentary on The Chymical Wedding of Christian Rosenkreutz*, by M. Bennell and I. Wyatt. Hawkwood College, Stroud. *A Christian Rosenkreutz Anthology*, compiled by Paul M. Allen. Rudolf Steiner Publications, New York.

striking connection with the life of Parsifal. A Venus pentagon cycle leads from that period to the end of the millennium.

As at the end of a solar year of 365 days the Sun shines from the same groups of stars as twelve months earlier, so the meetings of Earth and Venus, having passed round almost the entire Zodiac since the ninth century, are now approaching the places they had during Parsifal's life. The star rhythms are the expression of divine thoughts. The Venus rhythm indicates that the end of a cycle is near and that seeds sown in that earlier time can now put forth their shoots.

There are many well-founded and justified interpretations of the Parsifal path. The following outline shows it in its cosmic aspect. The description that can be given in our time is a first beginning and an indication. Upon this way, a man can learn to know himself as the reflection of the universe. Since he is born out of the world of stars, the planetary spheres and the fixed star circle live within his organism as a transformed image.

But through his deeds of former lives and through the stream of heredity with which he linked himself in birth, he bears a fallen cosmos within him. He has become a self-willed, inwardly darkened being, whose awareness of his cosmic origins has been lost. Even the thought of carrying a fallen cosmos within is meaningless to him, and he can scarcely sense any longer what this fact means to the life of the Earth and to all social future.

Yet he now has opportunity through his own efforts to permeate his being with the spirit so that it can reflect the universe and the aims of the cosmos.

When Christ still dwelt out in the universe, the spheres of the stars were the vessel that He filled. His Being radiated from the Sun throughout the Zodiac, penetrating the activity of the individual planets and ordering the relationship between Earth, Moon and Sun. Then, upon Golgotha, He united Himself with the Earth. Those who love the Earth can therefore become more and more the vessel He now would fill.

But a great gap divides our everyday personality from that which the Hierarchies can accept as a human being. Man therefore needs unfailing courage and perseverance, for the events in which he shares are as powerful and dramatic as the reality of the cosmos itself. The hitherto unrecognized is perceived, what was normally rejected is lived through, what would otherwise be unbearable is endured. He who takes the path acts on his own responsibility. He must take care that experiences of his spiritual progress do not divert him from any outer duty. They must be guarded in silence and self-control within the hidden sanctuary of the soul. The brighter his awareness becomes in the course of spiritual experience, the more the world of demons will attack him in its fury, placing obstacles, distress and temptations in his way. He must learn to pray in a new manner. The love of the Logos, the Divine Son whom he serves, will then accompany him.

In experiencing the Moon sphere, he learns that forces active there have led him to birth and that others make possible the growth of his daily bread. The body is experienced as the image of the Godhead, not as man's immediate property. This may seem strange to everyday consciousness: but it is the basis of a heightened morality. In this sphere, the ingratitude of modern mankind towards the mother forces of creation demands atonement.

The escape from material illusion teaches a man how greatly is he indebted to the other inhabitants of the Earth, to the animals, the plants and even the minerals, which he uses for his own selfish purposes. Above all he realizes the wrongs he has done to his fellow men and he thirsts for forgiveness. It becomes irresistibly clear to him that he can only be forgiven if he forgives those who have wronged him. Forgiveness is not only a well-intentioned forgetting, but a deed: the positive realization that the guilt of others is linked with one's own guilt. Forgiving is a decision to share the sin of others and thus to heal it and this leads in turn to an increased readiness to take part in a new way in relationships between different peoples.

The question that Parsifal fails to ask about the suffering of Amfortas and the nature of the Grail here assumes social significance: inability to heal the wounds of nations is the result of such failure.

At the next stage, the trial becomes harder. What has guided and protected a man so far now leaves him. He perceives that the age he lives in hovers at the brink of an abyss. He looks on his own race with shame and sorrow because it has forgotten that its dignity depends entirely on its share in the ascent of man. For comfort he may try to dwell on his own success, but this is a form of temptation. Even the part of his striving that he considered selfless may be rejected by the world of Divine selflessness.

When pride and conceit have fallen like ashes from the soul, the human spirit is received into the spirit realm of the Sun. What seemed important in everyday life is now wiped out and nothing is around him but darkness, filled with longing for the Christ Sun. But the Ego of Christ, the Higher Ego of humanity, is no longer on the Sun, and only what man has absorbed of Him in earthly life can become his guide. Today, this is very little.

Man stands in a void, himself empty, under attack by adversary powers who would gain him for themselves. But if he remains awake in the certainty that the Godhead can redeem him from evil when the time is ripe, then the void within will gradually fill with the waves of the great universe which bear in mighty chorus the message of strength, wisdom and love.

The outer world is now replaced by those Divine thoughts that gave the material world its form and existence. The spirit learns to understand that the creation is the *Name* of the God-head and that he hallows this Name by understanding the cosmic origins of nature. He is in the sphere of Mars, and by wakefulness and inner struggle, transforms his own rebellious soul element into spirit strength and a will to peace.

If he can do this he is received into the life world of Jupiter wisdom. The spiritual ear opens to the sound of the distant future and in devotion he speaks the words: Thy Kingdom come. Through this prayer the human spirit is woven into the evolution of the future and yet remains entirely itself. It begins to feel the New Jerusalem which more exalted spirits are engaged in building.

In the Saturn sphere, a man beholds his own past lives, and knows how he helped to create the present and that his future will be the consequence of decisions now taken. Light and Darkness are unveiled before his spirit, and he can choose between them. In this most sacred and fateful hour, the adversaries try with greater force than ever to tempt him into demonic dependence with promises of power, splendour and happiness; the radiant Divine spirits themselves await him who sees the cosmic battleground and who fights in freedom for their aims.

As the Parsifal path appears, written in star language into spirit worlds, a man recognizes his own eternal name, which is also his mission. He is able to watch his bodily existence so objectively that without disturbing his everyday duties he can consciously raise his soul to spiritual worlds of the cosmos and there become a force in world history.

Nothing and no-one will be able to hinder his decisions. He knows how to wait: a thousand years are for him as a day and a night—and every hour an affirmation of the Ego's powers of resurrection. He is free.

The great archetype of this journey is found between death and rebirth. The ' Midnight Hour ' in the Saturn sphere is followed by descent into a new incarnation. On the Parsifal journey, also, the road back begins after the powerful experiences on Saturn. The way is reversed. On Saturn the soul is filled with love for the Earth. In Jupiter, it has the experience of the Grail chalice, or of a rose that flowers from the coming tribulations of life. On Mars it perceives the reality of Earth as a parable of the spirit.

Man is now filled entirely with loyalty to the Earth. He is devoted in his daily life to all beings, even the smallest and most insignificant receive his loving attention. He is kind towards the weak; not rejecting evil, because he knows from experience that transformation is possible. He is sober in his thinking, orderly in his actions, punctual and reliable, for this is what he demands of himself. No activity is too humble to be carried out with loving concentration.

His profound modesty, his complete acceptance of destiny and his equanimity may distinguish him from other men. Silently he guards within his selfless heart the vessel of Eternal Light that comforts the souls of men and sustains the worlds of the stars.

Sophia of the Stars

MEN IN THEIR ERSTWHILE dreamy consciousness, still sustained within the godhead, were enfolded by the mantle of the great World Mother; her names were many and they differed according to the region of the cosmos where the temple sages could experience her. As Demeter, she was the Mother, the primordial earth-essence; as Artemis and Diana, the Moon goddess; as Aphrodite she worked in the Venus sphere of the planets; as Astarte she was the Virgin of the Stars, permeating the universe. In Christian esoteric teaching she was known as Sophia, the source of cosmic wisdom.

The ancient Egyptian priests experienced her presence in the goddess Isis, when they performed their sacred temple rites of healing. They revered her as a pupil of the great Hermes, acting from the domain of Mercury. She was a daughter of Saturn and her sphere extended to Sirius. Isis was often represented as mother, with the child Horus in her arms. Her temple at Saïs had inscribed on its portal the words: ' I am the All. I am the Past, the Present and the Future: no mortal has yet lifted my veil.'* Plutarch records a mystery saying from Saïs added to this temple inscription: ' And the fruit to which I have given birth has become Sun.' (Plate 42.)

Isis was perceived in many changing manifestations in the course of time. In the farthest past, she was Nut, the queen of the universe, who encircled the world with stars. Later, she became the heavenly cow, with moonshaped horns upon her head, enclosing the Sun; later again, in human shape, she still carried the Sun between the horns.

In Europe also, Sophia was experienced in varying ways and under many names. To the northern Germanic peoples, she was Frigg, world mother and queen of the gods. In the ancient Celtic world to which most of Central and Western Europe belonged, she was active as the goddess Briganzia, and elsewhere as Brigan and Brig. Ireland's Druid initiates also knew her as a goddess, Bridghe, whose tree was the tree of initiation; the ash was sacred to her on Earth as the tree of life. She was the ever-helping healer. At Chartres, Sophia was worshipped as the Virgin with the Child, who had carried the Spirit of the Sun through cosmic worlds to Earth.

After the life of Christ, St. John could write of her in the *Apocalypse* as the world mother, and saw her destiny as a great sign in the sky: the woman clothed with the sun, the moon beneath her feet and on her head a crown of twelve stars. She was threatened by a dragon who swept a third of the stars from the heavens and cast them on the earth. Her child was removed to God. Michael and his angels fought with the dragon, who was banished to the

---

* *Ancient Myths. Their Meaning and Connection with Evolution.* By Rudolf Steiner. Steiner Book Centre, Toronto, 1971. (Distrib., Rudolf Steiner Press, London).

earth. Then the dragon pursued the woman anew and she was given two wings like those of an eagle so that she could fly to the wilderness where she would be nourished.* Direct human experience of the Divine was about to withdraw.

In early Christian centuries the Gnostics could still remember the descent of the ' Pistis Sophia ' through planetary spheres. But by the fifth century, in the west, Bridghe was withdrawing from the Irish seers, and began thereafter to accompany the Celts as St. Bridget. She was still felt as a protecting and a healing force; and all beauty under the heavens and under the sea was hers. As late as the tenth century, Fulbertus of Chartres sang his praise of the queen of heaven as the Star of the Sea, and even in the thirteenth, Brunetto Latini experienced her as the Goddess Natura, who granted spiritual vision to him, as Bridghe and Persephone had bestowed it in the past. She remained for a time as Urania, ' the heavenly one ', the Muse of Astronomy.

When the gateway to a living experience of the cosmos had all but closed, a cosmic memory of the starry Isis arose again in the soul of Europe. As if through a miracle unfolding in the human heart, she appeared in the paintings of perceptive artists in different countries as the Queen of Heaven. But between that remote age when the starry mantle of Nut sheltered the world and the beginning of modern times, the Earth had passed its turning point. The Sun Spirit, whose image shone from the head of Isis, had died on the Cross of Golgotha as a human being, to become henceforward the Spirit of the Earth. The mother of the world of the stars was His mother. And whereas formerly the presence of the Heavenly Virgin had been experienced only in the darkness of closed temples, now it was no longer sealed from the outer senses. She could become a revealed mystery.

On innumerable paintings of the fourteenth and fifteenth centuries she appeared in Europe before human eyes. It may be that Christ, clothed in light robes like her own, places a crown upon her head. (Plate 43.) Or as the crowned Sophia, she may hold the book of cosmic wisdom in her hands. On another picture, the Sun encircles her head, the sky is covered with stars and one of them is on her mantle. (Plate 44.) Elsewhere, the crown is composed of stars and rays, or the Moon rests under her feet. From her head, in very many paintings, shines the radiance of a new Sun.

Sometimes the Heavenly Virgin appears as an altar figure, who passes a rose to her child, sits where snowdrops, lilies of the valley and strawberries grow, and has a white and red rosebush with birds behind her. She holds the book of wisdom. (Plate 45.) The spiritual cosmos is hidden behind the representations of the world of nature, but the memory of the changing, advancing star-Isis, preserved in Europe's soul, created a visible record for future generations.

Such pictures could be painted while European humanity still believed the Earth to be the centre of the solar universe. It could be realized without difficulty that the Earth was of importance to divine beings, and that the most serene spirits could unite with it for the sake of the future. An inner awareness of Sun and stars as servants of Earth evolution was the life-substance of the soul.

---

* *Revelation of St. John*, XII.

224

Through the Copernican system which replaced the Ptolemaic, the ensouled cosmos disappeared for the progressing sections of humanity. In the heliocentric world picture, the planetary spheres, hitherto the dwellings of divine beings, were empty. The planets were only mechanically moving, material globes. But if the Earth is no longer the centre of cosmic events, the belief that the Logos descended to it becomes questionable: and when the planetary world is governed only by the law of gravity, Isis and man's spiritual link with the stars have lost all meaning.

What had at first been hypothesis to Copernicus—whose editor described his work on planetary movement as one hypothesis among others—was then adapted to astronomical events. Although it was condemned by the Church and on the Index until 1832, the book had revolutionary effect. Upholders of the heliocentric system were persecuted and even burned; but within a comparatively short time, the new ideas had taken hold.

About the time that Copernicus was in Italy, forming his conception of the universe, one of the last pictures of the *Coronation of the Virgin* was painted there. It came from Raphael's hand, in 1503. In heavenly heights above her tomb, around which are the Twelve Apostles, Christ places the crown upon the Virgin's head. Roses and lilies fill the empty tomb. This was an ending. (Plate 46.) A few years later, Raphael painted the *Madonna with the Veil*. Here everything is changed. She has been completely absorbed into nature. Her flowing veil assumes the shape of a heart. She still wears a crown but it has become dark and greyish blue, like a leaden crown of suffering. With her left arm she embraces the young John the Baptist for whom she is lifting the veil that covers her sleeping Child. The face of St. John is radiant with vision—he can see more than the painting depicts. Isis Sophia, the divine wisdom, reveals to him the mystery of the Eternal Son, the heart of future Earth existence. She alone can lift the veil of knowledge. (Plate 47.)

In the twentieth century we see the effects of the loss of star wisdom; the normal human being has attained a high degree of independence—beyond the reach, in the past, of all but the hardiest souls. For materialism is often accompanied by a strength hitherto unknown: it needs deeply rooted courage to be a materialist and to aim to master all the problems of life with one's own resources. The new gift of human responsibility has been attained by many. The human ego can stand alone.

Beginning with his personal experiences, modern man can find the full realities of life. He has experienced the purely material phase in our time, the purely spiritual in past millennia. He must find the balancing insight not to pursue either way one-sidedly. Consistent thinking can now trace matter back to spirit, and reveal the spirit in its material manifestations; it can accept the visible and the invisible as components of a manifold reality, to which the stars belong macro-cosmically and man micro-cosmically. Thus a basis has been created making possible again a search for the Sophia of the Stars; for the finding of a man's own ego leads to the World Ego and its Soul.

The search for Isis now concerns all humanity and those who approach her may rise to new tasks through the wisdom of the stars. From being a receiver, man may become a giver to the Beings who are the expression of the cosmic worlds. A once faithful acceptance of divine guidance

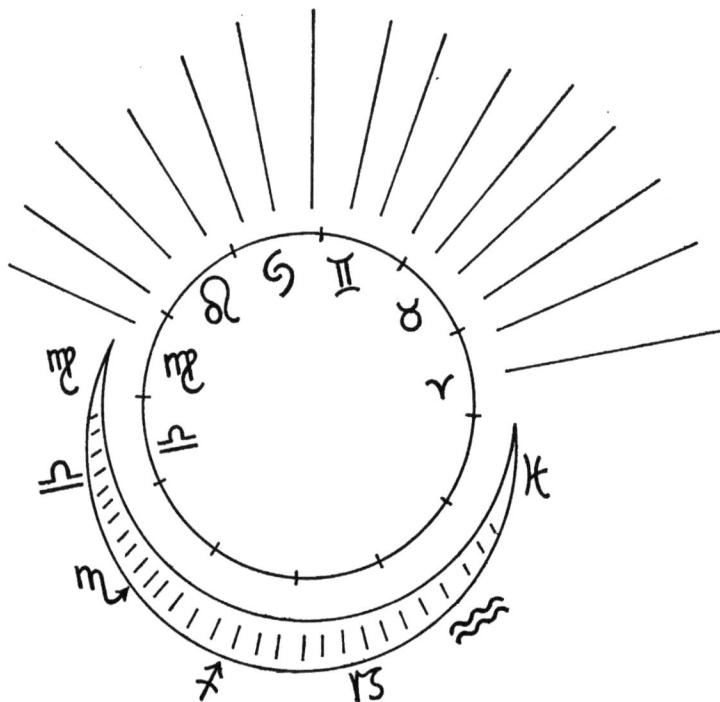

becomes active participation in the future; and thus also the astronomy buried in the tomb of materialism may be redeemed and ensouled, that Isis may shine through it again.

The ancient name for Europe is 'Erebus'—darkness. Europe was the 'Land of Death', for here the light of the old exalted wisdom died, and through Europe spiritual darkness fell over all humanity. But out of it, a new way to the Light has come: since Golgotha, death has become a transformation and a new beginning. Europe's hard destiny can be a fount of life and experience for many, the unique sustenance for a future humanity. The peoples of Europe have only to find the courage to recognize in their individual dramas the new revelations that can redeem the past.

---

* Willi O. Sucher describes the above diagram as follows:

The radiating Sun resting in the crescent of the Moon has always been the symbol of the Holy Grail: the Holy Host which, according to the legend, was brought down from heaven every Good Friday by a dove and laid in the cup of the Grail. In the Zodiac, the seven constellations from the Ram to the Scales are representative of the seven principles of the Cosmic Christ; comparable to man's physical body, life body, astral body, 'I' as soul kernel, Spirit-self, Life-spirit, and Spirit Man, but at a much higher spiritual level. (Rudolf Steiner explains these terms in his *Theosophy*, Rudolf Steiner Press, London.) Christ in His highest principle is the Lord of the Kyriotetes; that is expressed in the Ram, the Lamb of God, or Mystic Lamb. (*Gospel of St. John*, 1, 35–36.) The vessel, the man who is called upon to receive the Christ into his being, is represented by the seven constellations from the Fishes to the Virgin. Starting from the Fishes, they stand for his seven principles, as given above.

226

Bibliography

Note: The Bibliography gives a list of works—by authors linked with European culture—to which special reference has been made. The works of foreign authors, if translated, are mentioned in their English editions. Some historical sources are also given.

Adams, W. H. D. *The Maid of Orleans*. London, 1889.

Bacon, Francis, of Verulam. *The Works of F. Bacon*, collected and edited by James Spedding. London, 1857–74.

Bacon, Roger. *The Opus Majus of Roger Bacon*. Transl. by R. Belle Burke. 2 vols. Philadelphia, 1928.

Bakunin, M. *God and the State*. London, 1894.

Bateson, Mary. 'Mediaeval England' (1066–1350). *Story of the Nations*. London, 1903.

Bedier, Charles. (Translator.) *Le Roman de Tristan et Iseut*. 1900.

Bennell, M. and Wyatt, I. *A Commentary on the Chymical Wedding of Christian Rosenkreutz*. Michael Press, Stroud, 1964.

Berg, R. *Der heilige Mauricius und die thäbaische Legion*. Halle, 1895.

Bett, H. *Johannes Scotus Erigena*. A Study. Cambridge, 1925.

Blake, William. *Europe: A Prophecy*. 1804.

    Jerusalem. London. 1804–20.

Boehme, Jacob. *The Supersensual Life*. Ed. by H. R. Allenson. London, 1908.

    The Way to Christ. Ed. by J. M. Watkins. London, 1911.

Bond, Francis. *Dedications and Patron Saints of English Churches*. London, 1914.

Boyesen, Hjalmar H. 'History of Norway'. *Story of the Nations*. London, 1900.

Bridget of Sweden. *The Revelations of St. Bridget, Princess of Sweden*. London, 1873.

Buckle, Henry Thomas. *History of Civilization in England*. 2 vols. London, 1857.

Burckhardt, J. *Geschichte der Renaissance in Italien*. 1878.

Butler, A. *Lives of the Saints*. 12 vols. London, 1926–38.

Camera, Matteo. *Memorie storico-diplomatiche* . . . 2 vols. Salerno, 1876–81.

Camoens, Luis de. *The Lusiad of Camoens*. Transl. by R. Duff. London 1880.

Campanella, Tommaso. *La Città del Sole* . . . (City of the Sun.) Ed. by E. Solmi. Modena, 1904.

Carème, Marie Antonin. *French Cookery;* comprising *L'Art de la Cuisine Française, Le Pâtissier Royal, Le Cuisinier Parisien*. Transl. by W. Hall. 1836.

    Le Pâtissier Pittoresque. 1842.

Cervantes Saavedra, Miguel de. *Don Quixote*. New York and London, 1923.

Charpentier, Louis. *The Mysteries of Chartres Cathedral.* London, 1966.

Chaucer, Geoffrey. *The Canterbury Tales.* Ed. by A. W. Pollard. 2 vols. 1894.

Chrestien de Troyes. *The Romance of Sir Percival of Galles.* (In English verses from the Anglo-Norman original.) Camden Society, 1844.

Cieszkowski, A. *Prolegomena zur Historiosophie.* Berlin, 1938.

Colnet de Ravel, Charles de. *L'Art de diner en ville.* Paris, 1861.

Copernicus, N. *De Hypothesibus Motuum Coelestium.* (1514). *De Revolutionibus Orbium Coelestium.* (1543). *Preface and Book I* transl. by J. F. Dobson. London, 1955.

Dante Alighieri. *Divina Commedia.* Transl. H. F. Cary. London and New York, 1903. Transl. by D. L. Sayers. Penguin Books, 1949–62.

Darwin, C. *On the Origin of Species by Means of Natural Selection.* O.U.P., London, 1951.

Davies, N. *Education for Life. A Danish Pioneer.* London, 1931.

Descartes, R. *Les Passions de l'âme.* Texte presenté . . . par P. Mesnard. Paris, 1937. *The Philosophical Works of Descartes.* Transl. by E. S. Haldane. Cambridge, 1931.

Dostoievsky, T. M. *The Brothers Karamazov.* Transl. by C. Garnett. Everyman's Library, 1927.

Droysen, Ernst. *Der Tempel des Heiligen Gral.* 1872.

Dunant, H. *A Memory of Solferino.* (1862). London, 1947.

Edda. *The Elder or Poetic Edda.* Transl. by Olive Bray. 1908.

Elmes, J. *Sir Christopher Wren and his Times.* London, 1852.

Erdmann, J. E. *History of Philosophy.* Ed. W. S. Hough. 3 vols. Library of Philosophy, 1890.

Erigena, Joannes Scotus. *De Divisione naturae libri quinque.* Oxonii, 1681. *Expositiones super Hierarchias Coelestes Sancti Dionysii.* 1871. *Ueber die Eintheilung der Natur* . . . uebersetzt . . . von L. Noack. Philosophische Bibliothek, 1868. Migne, J. P. *Patrologiae Latina.* Vol. 122. Paris, 1850.

Eschborn, Michael. *Karlstein: Das Rätsel um die Burg Karls IV.* Stuttgart, 1973.

Eschenbach, Wolfram von. *Parzival.* Transl. by H. M. Mustard and C. E. Passage. New York, 1961.

Fichte, J. G. *Addresses to the German Nation.* Transl. by R. P. Jones. Chicago and London, 1922. *Science of Knowledge.* Transl. by A. Kroeger. 1868. *The Vocation of Man.* Transl. by W. Smith. The Catholic Series, 1848.

Fletcher, John. *The Painted Churches of Romania.* New Knowledge Books, 1971. (Editor.) *Russia: Past, Present and Future.* An anthology based on the work of Rudolf Steiner. New Knowledge Books, 1968.

Flor et Blancheflor. *The Tale of Fleur and Blanchefleur.* Transl. by Leighton. 1922.

Francis, Saint of Assisi. *Il Canto del Sole. The Hymn of the Sun.* Italian and English. Swan Press, 1927.

Freeman, Edward A. *The History of the Norman Conquest of England.* Oxford, 1867–79. 'Sicily'. *The Story of the Nations.* 1892.

Fueter, Eduard. *World History, 1815–1920.* Transl. by Sidney Bradshaw Fay. London, 1923.

Gibbon, E. *History of the Decline and Fall of the Roman Empire.* 1776–88. Everyman's Library, 1954.

Gladstone, William Ewart. *Bulgarian Horrors and the Question of the East.* London, 1876.

Gobineau, J. A. de. *The Renaissance*. Transl. by Paul V. Cohn. London, 1927.

Goethe, J. W. von. *Faust*. Transl. by A. G. Latham. 1908.

    The Fairy Tale of the Green Snake and the Beautiful Lily. Transl. by Thomas Carlyle. 1877.

Green, John Richard. *A Short History of the English People*. London, 1934.

Grimod, de la Reynière, A. B. L. *Calendrier Gastronomique*. 1843.

Haskins, C. H. *The Normans in European History*. London, New York, 1916.

Havard, H. *The Heart of Holland*. Transl. by C. Hoey. London, 1880.

Hawkins, Gerald S. *Stonehenge Decoded*. London, 1965.

Hegel, G. W. F. *Hegel's Science of Logic*. Transl. by W. H. Johnston. London, 1929.

Heidenreich, A. 'The Externsteine'. Christian Community Journal. June, 1935.

Herder, J. G. von. *Outlines of a Philosophy of the History of Man*. Transl. by T. Churchill. London, 1800.

Hoene-Wronski, J. *Conférences Européennes pour populariser l'actuelle réforme absolue du savoir humain*. Metz, 1851.

Hooke, Robert. *Micrographia*. 1665.

    Extracts from Hooke's Micrographia. Oxford, 1926.

Huebner, Johann. *Genealogische Tabellen*. Leipzig, 1737.

Ihne, Wilhelm. *Roemische Geschichte*. Vol. 1. Leipzig, 1868–90.

Jeantin, (—). *Les Chroniques de l'Ardennes et des Woepres*. Paris, 1851.

    Historie du Comté et des pays Haut-Wallons. 2 vols. Paris, 1859.

Jewett, Sarah Orne. 'The Normans'. *Story of the Nations*. 1891.

Jocelyn, John. *Meditations on the Signs of the Zodiac*. New York, 1970.

Kant, I. *Critique of Pure Reason*. Everyman's Library, 1934.

Karadzic, Vuk S. *Volksleider der Serben*. Transl. by Talvj. Halle and Leipzig, 1835.

Kivi, Alexis. *Seven Brothers*. Transl. by A. Matson. London, 1929.

Kolisko, Eugen. *Reincarnation and Other Essays*. London, 1940.

    Three Fundamental Problems of the Anthroposophical Knowledge of Man. Kolisko Archive: Brookthorpe, 1943.

    'Sir Christopher Wren'; 'Jeanne d'Arc'; in The Modern Mystic, Vol. II, 1938–39.

    'Thomas à Becket'; 'Sir Thomas More'; 'Oliver Cromwell'; 'Benjamin Franklin'; in The Modern Mystic, Vol. III, 1939–40.

Kolisko, L. *Gold and the Sun*. Kolisko Archive: Stroud. 1947.

    The Moon and the Growth of Plants. 1936.

    Sternenwirken in Erdenstoffen. Stroud, 1953.

Krasinski, N. A. Z. *Psaumes de l'Avenir*. *Oeuvres Choisies*. Transl. by C. de Noire-Isle. 1880.

    Ein Traumgesicht. Uebersetzung aus dem Polnischen. Leipzig, 1875.

    The Un-divine Comedy. Transl. by H. E. Kennedy and Sofia Umińska. London, 1924.

Legrange, Charles. *Mathématique de l'Histoire*. Bruxelles, 1900.

Lane-Poole, R. *The Early Correspondence of John of Salisbury*. London, 1924.

    (Editor.) *Joannis Sarisberiensis*. 1927.

Lane-Poole, S. 'Turkey'. *Story of the Nations*. London, 1922.

La Place, Pierre S. *Exposition du Système du Monde.* Paris, 1796.
    The System of the World. Transl. by J. Pond. London, 1809.

Latini, Brunetto. *Li livres dou tresor.* University of California Press, 1948.

Lawless, Emily. 'Ireland'. *Story of the Nations.* 1912.

Lawrence-Archer, J. H. *The Orders of Chivalry.* London, 1887.

Lessing, G. D. *The Education of the Human Race.* Transl. by F. W. Robertson. Reprinted from Anthroposophy. London and New York, 1927.

Lokys, G. *Die Kämpfe der Araber mit den Karolingern . . .* Heidelberg, 1902.

Lönnrot, Elias. *The Kalevala. Land of Heroes.* Translated by W. F. Kirby. 2 Vols. Everyman's Library, 1936.

Loyola, St. Ignatius of. *The Testament of Ignatius Loyola.* Transl. by E. M. Rix. 1900.

Lucas, C. T. L. *Ueber den Krieg der Wartburg. Abhandlungen der Könige.* Deutschen Gessellchaft zu Königsberg, 1838.

Machiavelli, N. *The Works of Nicholas Machiavel.* Transl. by E. Farnworth, London, 1775.

Malory, Sir Thomas, *Le Morte d'Arthur.* 2 vols. Everyman's Library. 1953.

Maltwood, K. E. *Glastonbury's Temple of the Stars.* London, 1964.

Mannerheim, Karl G. *The Memoirs of Marshal Mannerheim.* Transl. by Count Eric Lewenhaupt. 1953.

Marx, Karl H. *Das Kapital.* Transl. by S. Moore and E. Aveling and edited by F. Engels. London, 1896.

Masson, Gustav. 'Mediaeval France'. *Story of the Nations.* 1888.

McLauchlan, T. *The Early Scotch Church . . . from the First to the Twelfth Century.* Edinburgh, 1865.

Mendel, Gregor J. *Experiments in Plant Hybridisation.* Harvard University Press, 1925.

Merry, E. C. *The Ascent of Man.* New Knowledge Books. 1963.
    (Translator and illustrator.) *The Dream Song of Olaf Asteson.* New Knowledge Books, 1961.
The Flaming Door. New Knowledge Books, 1962.

de la Mettrie, Julien. *Man as a Machine.* Transl. by G. Smith. London, 1750.

Michel, John. *The View over Atlantis.* Distrib. by Garnstone Press for Sago Press. London, 1969.

Michelet, Jules. *Jeanne d'Arc.* Collection Nelson. Paris, 1934.

Mickiewicz, A. *Gems of Polish Poetry.* Transl. by F. H. Fortey. Warsaw, 1923.

Milde, V. E. *Allgemeine Erziehungskunde.* Vienna, 1877.

Miller, W. 'The Balkans, Roumania, Bulgaria, Serbia and Montenegro.' *Story of the Nations.* 1896.

Molière, J. B. *Plays from Molière.* By English dramatists. London, 1891.

Monet de Lamarck, J. P. B. A. de. *Zoological Philosophy.* Transl. by Hugh Elliot. London, 1914.

Montaigne, Michel de. *The Essays of Michael, Lord of Montaigne.* The World's Classics, 1901.

Montesquieu, Ch. de Secondat, baron de. *The Spirit of Laws.* (1748). Transl. by T. Nugent. London, 1823.

Montmélian, B. de. *St. Maurice et la légion thébéenne.* 2 vols. Paris, 1888.

Morfill, W. R. 'Poland'. *Story of the Nations.* 1893.
    'Russia'. *Story of the Nations.* 1890.

Nweton, Isaac. *Memoirs of the Life, Writings and Discoveries of Sir Isaac Newton.* Sir David
   Brewster. 2 vols. Edinburgh, 1855.
   Optics, or a Treatise of Reflexions, Refractions, Inflexions and Colours of Light. London, 1931.
   Sir Isaac Newton's Mathematical Principles of Natural Philosophy and his System of the World.
   University of California Press, 1934.
Novalis, (Friedrich von Hardenberg.) *Hymnen an die Nacht: Christenheit oder Europa.* Leipzig,
   1912.
   Schriften. Jena, 1907.
Oefele, Edmund von. *Geschichte der Grafen von Andechs.* Meran, 1877.
Ovidius Naso, P. *The Metamorphoses . . .* Transl. by H. King. London, 1871.
Perels, Ernst. *Papst Nikolaus I und Anastasius Bibliothecarius.* Berlin, 1920.
Picton, James Allanson. *Oliver Cromwell: The Man and his Mission.* London, 1882.
Poppelbaum, H. *Truth and Error in Astrology.* New Knowledge Books. 1954.
Poupardin, René. 'Louis the Pious.' 'The Carolingian Kingdoms.' *The Cambridge Medieval
   History.* Vol. 3. 1911.
Quicherat, J. *Procès de condamnation et de réhabilitation de Jeanne d'Arc.* 4 vols. Paris, 1841–49.
Rabelais, F. *The Histories of Gargantua and Pantagruel.* Transl. by J. M. Cohen. London, 1955.
Ringboom, Lars-Ivar. *Graltempel und Paradies.* Stockholm, 1951.
Routh, E. M. G. *Sir Thomas More and his Friends.* London, 1934.
Rowe, G. L. *Towards a Rational Democracy.* Threefold Commonwealth Research Group. Pam-
   phlet no. 1. London, 1938.
Sand, George. *Countess of Rudolstadt.* Transl. by F. H. Potter. 2 vols. New York, 1891.
Sarrazin, Gabriel. *Les grands poètes romantiques de la Pologne.* Mickiewicz; Slowacki; Krasinski.
   Paris, 1906.
Scharfenberg, Albrecht von. *Die juengere Titurel.* 1835.
Schelling, F. W. von. *Of Human Freedom.* Transl. by James Gutman. Chicago, 1936.
Schiller, F. von. *Demetrius.* Nach den Handschriften des Goethe- und Schiller Archivs.
   Weimar, 1885.
   Letters upon the Aesthetic Education of Man. Transl. by R. Snell. London, 1954.
   Poems and Plays. Edited by H. Morley. London, 1889.
Schmidt, C. G. A. *Histoire et doctrine de la Secte des Cathares ou Albigeois.* 2 vols. Paris, 1849.
Schneider, Camille. *Eduard Schurés Begegnungen mit Rudolf Steiner.* Basel, 1933.
Schuré, Edouard. *The Great Initiates.* Transl. by F. Rothwell. London, 1929.
   Les Prophètes de la Renaissance. Dante; Léonard de Vinci; Raphael; Michel-Ange; Le
   Corrège. Paris, 1920.
   In R. Steiner: *The Way of Initiation,* Biographical Notes. London, 1908.
Seitz, Ferdinand. *Die Irminsul im Felsenrelief der Externsteine.* Pähl, 1953.
   Rätsel um die Externsteine. Pähl, 1958.
Shakespeare, William. *Works.* Ed. by Sir A. Quiller-Couch and J. Dover Wilson. University
   Press, Cambridge, 1921.
Siebmacher, J. *J. Siebmacher's grosses und vollstaendiges Wappenbuch.* Regensburg, 1857. 1876.
Simson, B. (Editor.) *Jahrbuecher der deutschen Geschichte.* 'Ludwig der Fromme'. Münich, 1862.

Sincai, Gheorghie. *Chronica Românilor.* . . . Bucuresci, 1886.

Slaveikow, P. *The Shade of the Balkans* . . . Bulgarian folk songs and proverbs compiled by Pencho Slaveikow . . . Transl. and ed. by Henry Bernard. London, 1904.

Slowacki, J. *Oeuvres Complètes.* (Genesis out of the Spirit.) Transl. by W. Gasztowtt. Paris, 1870.

Snow, Terence B. *St. Gregory the Great.* London, 1924.

Soloviev, V. S. *The Antichrist.* Reprinted by the Christian Community Press from *War and Christianity*, London, 1915. *God, Man and the Church.* Transl. by Donald Attwater. 1938. *The Justification of the Good: An Essay on Moral Philosophy.* Transl. by N. A. Duddington. Constable's Russian Library, 1915.

Springer, A. *Handbuch der Kunstgeschichte.* 6 vols. Leipzig, 1923–29.

Stanley, Arthur P. *Historical Memorials of Canterbury.* Everyman's Library, 1906.

Stefánsson, Jón. 'Denmark and Sweden with Iceland and Finland'. *The Story of the Nations.* 1916.

Stein, Nora. *Aus Michaels Wirken.* Eine Legende- und Bildersammlung. Betrachtung über Michaels Wirken im Lichte der anthroposophischen Geisteswissenschaft von Ita Wegman. Stuttgart, 1929.

Stein, W. J. *The British: Their Psychology and Destiny.* New Knowledge Books, 1958.
The Earth as a Basis of World Economy. Present Age Journal (Special Number). 1937.
Die Weltgeschichte im Lichte des heiligen Gral. Band 1: Das Neunte Jahrhundert. Stuttgart, 1966.

Steiner, Rudolf. *Ancient Myths. Their Meaning and Connection with Evolution.* Toronto. 1971.
Behind the Scenes of External Happenings. London, 1947.
The Case for Anthroposophy. Selections from *Von Seelenrätseln* transl. and with Introduction by Owen Barfield. London, 1970.
Christianity as Mystical Fact and the Mysteries of Antiquity. London, 1972.
The Course of My Life. An Autobiography. New York, 1951.
The Driving Force of Spiritual Powers in World History. Toronto, 1972.
Earthly and Cosmic Man. London, 1948.
Goethe's Conception of the World. London, 1928.
Goethe as a Founder of a New Science of Aesthetics. London, 1922.
Knowledge of the Higher Worlds and its Attainment. London, 1972.
Man as Symphony of the Creative Word. London, 1970.
The Mission of the Individual Folk Souls in Relation to Teutonic Mythology. London, 1970.
The Mysteries. A Christmas and Easter poem by Goethe. London, 1946.
Occult Science, an Outline. (Revised translation, 1963.) London, 1969.
The Philosophy of Spiritual Activity and *Truth and Knowledge.* New York, 1963.
The Philosphy of Freedom. (Spiritual Activity.) London, 1964.
Reincarnation and Karma. How Karma Works. New York. 1962.
Reincarnation and Karma and their Significance in Modern Culture. London, 1960.
The Spiritual Guidance of Man. New York, 1970.
The Soul of the People considered in the Light of Spiritual Science. London, 1947.
The Tension between East and West. London, 1963.

Theosophy. An introduction to Supersensible Knowledge of the World and the Destination of Man. London, 1970.

The Threefold Social Order. New York, 1966.

The Twelve Senses and the Seven Life Processes in Man. (Dornach, 1916.) ' The Golden Blade ', 1975.

World History in the Light of Anthroposophy. London, 1950.

Stephens, H. Morse. 'Portugal'. *Story of the Nations*. 1908.

Stoian, Ioan. *Der Grammatiker Timotheus Cipariu*. Jahresbericht des Instituet fuer rumaenische Sprache, No. 12. 1906.

Sucher, Willi C. *Das Drama des Universums*. Interpretation der Beziehungen zwischen Kosmos, Erde und Mensch. Stuttgart, 1960. The Drama of the Universe. Larkfield, 1968.

Isis–Sophia. Umriss einer geisteswissenschaftlichen Kosmologie. 1950. *Isis–Sophia*. Outline of a New Star Wisdom. Larkfield, 1952.

Suess, E. (and others). *Bau und Bild Österreichs*. Wien, Leipzig, 1903.

The Face of the Earth. Oxford, 1904.

Swainson, W. P. 'Jacob Boehme.' in *Three Famous Mystics*. London, 1939.

Tauler, J. *The Following of Christ*. Translated by J. R. Morell. London, 1918.

Todd, James H. (Translator and editor.) *Book of Hymns of the Ancient Church of Ireland*. Dublin. 1855.

Tolstoi, L. N. *Anna Karenina*. World Classics, 1933.

War and Peace. 3 vols. World Classics, 1933.

Tommaso d'Aquino, P. P. *Miscellanea storico-artistica*. P. Innocenzo Taurisano. Roma, 1924.

Topelius, Z. *Aus dem Norden*. Eine Sammlung finnischer Dichtungen. Transl. H. Paul. Helsingfors, 1877.

Trentowski, B. F. *Grundlage der Universellen Philosophie*. Carlsruhe, Frieburg, 1837.

Les Très Riches Heures . . . *The New Testament*, with 21 illustrations from *Les Très Riches Heures du Duc de Berry*. London, 1958.

Les Trés Riches Heures de Duc de Berry. Text by Jean Longnon and Millard Meiss. Thames and Hudson, 1973.

Trevelyan, G. M. *Garibaldi and the Thousand*. London, 1909.

Tschudi, Aegidius. *Chronicon Helveticum*. Basel, 1734–36.

Vogelweide, Walther von der. *I Saw the World*. Sixty poems set in English verse by J. G. Colvin. London, 1938.

Voltaire, F. M. A. de. *Selected Works*. Transl. by J. McCabe. 1935.

Watts, Henry E. 'Spain'. *Story of the Nations*, 1894.

Wertheim Aymès, P. *The Pictoral Language of Hieronymus Bosch*. In preparation. New Knowledge Books. (For 1975).

White, Newport J. D. (Translator.) *Saint Patrick: His Writings and Life*. S.P.C.K., 1930.

Whitman, Sydney. 'Austria'. *Story of the Nations*. 1899.

Wincklemann, J. J. *The History of Ancient Art among the Greeks*. Transl. by G. H. Lodge. London, 1850.

The Wreath of Virtues. Cf. *Sternkalendar*, 1969–70. Dornach.

Wren, Christopher. *Bicentenary Memorial Volume*. Ed. by Rudolf Dircks. Royal Institute of British Architects, 1923.

Zedler, J. H. *Grosser vollstaendiges Universal Lexicon aller Wissenschaften und kuenste.* 1735.

Zernov, Nicolas. *Three Russian Prophets.* S.C.M. Press, 1944.

    St. Sergius, Builder of Russia. London, 1939.

Zeylmans van Emmichoven, F. W. *The Reality in Which We Live.* New Knowledge Books. 1964.

Index

236